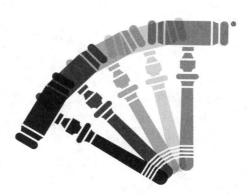

Casenote® Legal Briefs

ADMINISTRATIVE LAW

Keyed to Courses Using

Breyer, Stewart, Sunstein, Vermeule, and Herz's
Administrative Law and Regulatory Policy
Seventh Edition

Copyright © 2011 CCH Incorporated. All Rights Reserved.
www.wolterskluwerlb.com

Published by Wolters Kluwer Law & Business in New York.

Wolters Kluwer Law & Business serves customers worldwide with CCH, Aspen Publishers, and Kluwer Law International products.

No part of this publication may be reproduced or transmitted in any form or by any means, electronic or mechanical, including photocopy, recording, or any information storage and retrieval system, without permission in writing from the publisher. For information about permissions or to request permission online, visit us at *wolterskluwerlb.com* or a written request may be faxed to our permissions department at 212-771-0803.

To contact Customer Service, e-mail customer.service@wolterskluwer.com, call 1-800-234-1660, fax 1-800-901-9075, or mail correspondence to:

Wolters Kluwer Law & Business
Attn: Order Department
P.O. Box 990
Frederick, MD 21705

Printed in the United States of America.

1 2 3 4 5 6 7 8 9 0

ISBN 978-0-7355-9912-3

SUSTAINABLE FORESTRY INITIATIVE
Certified Chain of Custody
Promoting Sustainable Forestry
www.sfiprogram.org
SFI-00756

About Wolters Kluwer Law & Business

Wolters Kluwer Law & Business is a leading global provider of intelligent information and digital solutions for legal and business professionals in key specialty areas, and respected educational resources for professors and law students. Wolters Kluwer Law & Business connects legal and business professionals as well as those in the education market with timely, specialized authoritative content and information-enabled solutions to support success through productivity, accuracy and mobility.

Serving customers worldwide, Wolters Kluwer Law & Business products include those under the Aspen Publishers, CCH, Kluwer Law International, Loislaw, Best Case, ftwilliam.com and MediRegs family of products.

CCH products have been a trusted resource since 1913, and are highly regarded resources for legal, securities, antitrust and trade regulation, government contracting, banking, pension, payroll, employment and labor, and healthcare reimbursement and compliance professionals.

Aspen Publishers products provide essential information to attorneys, business professionals and law students. Written by preeminent authorities, the product line offers analytical and practical information in a range of specialty practice areas from securities law and intellectual property to mergers and acquisitions and pension/benefits. Aspen's trusted legal education resources provide professors and students with high-quality, up-to-date and effective resources for successful instruction and study in all areas of the law.

Kluwer Law International products provide the global business community with reliable international legal information in English. Legal practitioners, corporate counsel and business executives around the world rely on Kluwer Law journals, looseleafs, books, and electronic products for comprehensive information in many areas of international legal practice.

Loislaw is a comprehensive online legal research product providing legal content to law firm practitioners of various specializations. Loislaw provides attorneys with the ability to quickly and efficiently find the necessary legal information they need, when and where they need it, by facilitating access to primary law as well as state-specific law, records, forms and treatises.

Best Case Solutions is the leading bankruptcy software product to the bankruptcy industry. It provides software and workflow tools to flawlessly streamline petition preparation and the electronic filing process, while timely incorporating ever-changing court requirements.

ftwilliam.com offers employee benefits professionals the highest quality plan documents (retirement, welfare and non-qualified) and government forms (5500/PBGC, 1099 and IRS) software at highly competitive prices.

MediRegs products provide integrated health care compliance content and software solutions for professionals in healthcare, higher education and life sciences, including professionals in accounting, law and consulting.

Wolters Kluwer Law & Business, a division of Wolters Kluwer, is headquartered in New York. Wolters Kluwer is a market-leading global information services company focused on professionals.

Format for the Casenote® Legal Brief

Nature of Case: This section identifies the form of action (e.g., breach of contract, negligence, battery), the type of proceeding (e.g., demurrer, appeal from trial court's jury instructions), or the relief sought (e.g., damages, injunction, criminal sanctions).

Fact Summary: This is included to refresh your memory and can be used as a quick reminder of the facts.

Rule of Law: Summarizes the general principle of law that the case illustrates. It may be used for instant recall of the court's holding and for classroom discussion or home review.

Facts: This section contains all relevant facts of the case, including the contentions of the parties and the lower court holdings. It is written in a logical order to give the student a clear understanding of the case. The plaintiff and defendant are identified by their proper names throughout and are always labeled with a (P) or (D).

Palsgraf v. Long Island R.R. Co.

Injured bystander (P) v. Railroad company (D)

N.Y. Ct. App., 248 N.Y. 339, 162 N.E. 99 (1928).

Party ID: Quick identification of the relationship between the parties.

NATURE OF CASE: Appeal from judgment affirming verdict for plaintiff seeking damages for personal injury.

FACT SUMMARY: Helen Palsgraf (P) was injured on R.R.'s (D) train platform when R.R.'s (D) guard helped a passenger aboard a moving train, causing his package to fall on the tracks. The package contained fireworks which exploded, creating a shock that tipped a scale onto Palsgraf (P).

🏛 RULE OF LAW
The risk reasonably to be perceived defines the duty to be obeyed.

FACTS: Helen Palsgraf (P) purchased a ticket to Rockaway Beach from R.R. (D) and was waiting on the train platform. As she waited, two men ran to catch a train that was pulling out from the platform. The first man jumped aboard, but the second man, who appeared as if he might fall, was helped aboard by the guard on the train who had kept the door open so they could jump aboard. A guard on the platform also helped by pushing him onto the train. The man was carrying a package wrapped in newspaper. In the process, the man dropped his package, which fell on the tracks. The package contained fireworks and exploded. The shock of the explosion was apparently of great enough strength to tip over some scales at the other end of the platform, which fell on Palsgraf (P) and injured her. A jury awarded her damages, and R.R. (D) appealed.

ISSUE: Does the risk reasonably to be perceived define the duty to be obeyed?

HOLDING AND DECISION: (Cardozo, C.J.) Yes. The risk reasonably to be perceived defines the duty to be obeyed. If there is no foreseeable hazard to the injured party as the result of a seemingly innocent act, the act does not become a tort because it happened to be a wrong as to another. If the wrong was not willful, the plaintiff must show that the act as to her had such great and apparent possibilities of danger as to entitle her to protection. Negligence in the abstract is not enough upon which to base liability. Negligence is a relative concept, evolving out of the common law doctrine of trespass on the case. To establish liability, the defendant must owe a legal duty of reasonable care to the injured party. A cause of action in tort will lie where harm,

though unintended, could have been averted or avoided by observance of such a duty. The scope of the duty is limited by the range of danger that a reasonable person could foresee. In this case, there was nothing to suggest from the appearance of the parcel or otherwise that the parcel contained fireworks. The guard could not reasonably have had any warning of a threat to Palsgraf (P), and R.R. (D) therefore cannot be held liable. Judgment is reversed in favor of R.R. (D).

DISSENT: (Andrews, J.) The concept that there is no negligence unless R.R. (D) owes a legal duty to take care as to Palsgraf (P) herself is too narrow. Everyone owes to the world at large the duty of refraining from those acts that may unreasonably threaten the safety of others. If the guard's action was negligent as to those nearby, it was also negligent as to those outside what might be termed the "danger zone." For Palsgraf (P) to recover, R.R.'s (D) negligence must have been the proximate cause of her injury, a question of fact for the jury.

Concurrence/Dissent: All concurrences and dissents are briefed whenever they are included by the casebook editor.

▶ ANALYSIS
The majority defined the limit of the defendant's liability in terms of the danger that a reasonable person in defendant's situation would have perceived. The dissent argued that the limitation should not be placed on liability, but rather on damages. Judge Andrews suggested that only injuries that would not have happened but for R.R.'s (D) negligence should be compensable. Both the majority and dissent recognized the policy-driven need to limit liability for negligent acts, seeking, in the words of Judge Andrews, to define a framework "that will be practical and in keeping with the general understanding of mankind." The Restatement (Second) of Torts has accepted Judge Cardozo's view.

Analysis: This last paragraph gives you a broad understanding of where the case "fits in" with other cases in the section of the book and with the entire course. It is a hornbook-style discussion indicating whether the case is a majority or minority opinion and comparing the principal case with other cases in the casebook. It may also provide analysis from restatements, uniform codes, and law review articles. The analysis will prove to be invaluable to classroom discussion.

Quicknotes

FORESEEABILITY A reasonable expectation that change is the probable result of certain acts or omissions.

NEGLIGENCE Conduct falling below the standard of care that a reasonable person would demonstrate under similar conditions.

PROXIMATE CAUSE The natural sequence of events without which an injury would not have been sustained.

Issue: The issue is a concise question that brings out the essence of the opinion as it relates to the section of the casebook in which the case appears. Both substantive and procedural issues are included if relevant to the decision.

Holding and Decision: This section offers a clear and in-depth discussion of the rule of the case and the court's rationale. It is written in easy-to-understand language and answers the issue presented by applying the law to the facts of the case. When relevant, it includes a thorough discussion of the exceptions to the case as listed by the court, any major cites to the other cases on point, and the names of the judges who wrote the decisions.

Quicknotes: Conveniently defines legal terms found in the case and summarizes the nature of any statutes, codes, or rules referred to in the text.

Wolters Kluwer Law & Business is proud to offer *Casenote® Legal Briefs*—continuing thirty years of publishing America's best-selling legal briefs.

Casenote® Legal Briefs are designed to help you save time when briefing assigned cases. Organized under convenient headings, they show you how to abstract the basic facts and holdings from the text of the actual opinions handed down by the courts. Used as part of a rigorous study regimen, they can help you spend more time analyzing and critiquing points of law than on copying bits and pieces of judicial opinions into your notebook or outline.

Casenote® Legal Briefs should never be used as a substitute for assigned casebook readings. They work best when read as a follow-up to reviewing the underlying opinions themselves. Students who try to avoid reading and digesting the judicial opinions in their casebooks or online sources will end up shortchanging themselves in the long run. The ability to absorb, critique, and restate the dynamic and complex elements of case law decisions is crucial to your success in law school and beyond. It cannot be developed vicariously.

Casenote® Legal Briefs represents but one of the many offerings in Legal Education's Study Aid Timeline, which includes:

- *Casenote® Legal Briefs*
- *Emanuel Law Outlines*
- *Examples & Explanations* Series
- *Introduction to Law* Series
- Emanuel *Law in a Flash* Flash Cards
- Emanuel *CrunchTime* Series

Each of these series is designed to provide you with easy-to-understand explanations of complex points of law. Each volume offers guidance on the principles of legal analysis and, consulted regularly, will hone your ability to spot relevant issues. We have titles that will help you prepare for class, prepare for your exams, and enhance your general comprehension of the law along the way.

To find out more about Wolters Kluwer Law & Business' study aid publications, visit us online at *www.wolterskluwerlb.com* or email us at *legaledu@wolterskluwer.com*. We'll be happy to assist you.

Get this Casenote® Legal Brief as an AspenLaw Studydesk eBook today!

By returning this form to Wolters Kluwer Law & Business, you will receive a complimentary eBook download of this Casenote® Legal Brief and AspenLaw Studydesk productivity software.* Learn more about AspenLaw Studydesk today at *www.wolterskluwerlb.com*.

Name	Phone ( )
Address	Apt. No.
City	State	ZIP Code
Law School	Graduation Date Month _____ Year _____

Cut out the UPC found on the lower left corner of the back cover of this book. Staple the UPC inside this box. Only the original UPC from the book cover will be accepted. (No photocopies or store stickers are allowed.)

Attach UPC inside this box.

Email (Print legibly or you may not get access!)
Title of this book (course subject)
ISBN of this book (10- or 13-digit number on the UPC)
Used with which casebook (provide author's name)

Mail the completed form to:

Wolters Kluwer Law & Business
Legal Education Division
130 Turner Street, Bldg 3, 4th Floor
Waltham, MA 02453-8901

* Upon receipt of this completed form, you will be emailed a code for the digital download of this book in AspenLaw Studydesk eBook format and a free copy of the software application, which is required to read the eBook.

For a full list of eBook study aids available for AspenLaw Studydesk software and other resources that will help you with your law school studies, visit *www.wolterskluwerlb.com*.

Make a photocopy of this form and your UPC for your records.

For detailed information on the use of the information you provide on this form, please see the PRIVACY POLICY at *www.wolterskluwerlb.com*.

How to Brief a Case

A. Decide on a Format and Stick to It

Structure is essential to a good brief. It enables you to arrange systematically the related parts that are scattered throughout most cases, thus making manageable and understandable what might otherwise seem to be an endless and unfathomable sea of information. There are, of course, an unlimited number of formats that can be utilized. However, it is best to find one that suits your needs and stick to it. Consistency breeds both efficiency and the security that when called upon you will know where to look in your brief for the information you are asked to give.

Any format, as long as it presents the essential elements of a case in an organized fashion, can be used. Experience, however, has led *Casenote* ® *Legal Briefs* to develop and utilize the following format because of its logical flow and universal applicability.

NATURE OF CASE: This is a brief statement of the legal character and procedural status of the case (e.g., "Appeal of a burglary conviction").

There are many different alternatives open to a litigant dissatisfied with a court ruling. The key to determining which one has been used is to discover *who is asking this court for what.*

This first entry in the brief should be kept as *short as possible.* Use the court's terminology if you understand it. But since jurisdictions vary as to the titles of pleadings, the best entry is the one that addresses who wants what in this proceeding, not the one that sounds most like the court's language.

RULE OF LAW: A statement of the general principle of law that the case illustrates (e.g., "An acceptance that varies any term of the offer is considered a rejection and counteroffer").

Determining the rule of law of a case is a procedure similar to determining the issue of the case. Avoid being fooled by red herrings; there may be a few rules of law mentioned in the case excerpt, but usually only one is *the* rule with which the casebook editor is concerned. The techniques used to locate the issue, described below, may also be utilized to find the rule of law. Generally, your best guide is simply the chapter heading. It is a clue to the point the casebook editor seeks to make and should be kept in mind when reading every case in the respective section.

FACTS: A synopsis of only the essential facts of the case, i.e., those bearing upon or leading up to the issue.

The facts entry should be a short statement of the events and transactions that led one party to initiate legal proceedings against another in the first place. While some cases conveniently state the salient facts at the beginning of the decision, in other instances they will have to be culled from hiding places throughout the text, even from concurring and dissenting opinions. Some of the "facts" will often be in dispute and should be so noted. Conflicting evidence may be briefly pointed up. "Hard" facts must be included. Both must be *relevant* in order to be listed in the facts entry. It is impossible to tell what is relevant until the entire case is read, as the ultimate determination of the rights and liabilities of the parties may turn on something buried deep in the opinion.

Generally, the facts entry should not be longer than three to five *short* sentences.

It is often helpful to identify the role played by a party in a given context. For example, in a construction contract case the identification of a party as the "contractor" or "builder" alleviates the need to tell that that party was the one who was supposed to have built the house.

It is always helpful, and a good general practice, to identify the "plaintiff" and the "defendant." This may seem elementary and uncomplicated, but, especially in view of the creative editing practiced by some casebook editors, it is sometimes a difficult or even impossible task. Bear in mind that the *party presently* seeking something from this court may not be the plaintiff, and that sometimes only the cross-claim of a defendant is treated in the excerpt. Confusing or misaligning the parties can ruin your analysis and understanding of the case.

ISSUE: A statement of the general legal question answered by or illustrated in the case. For clarity, the issue is best put in the form of a question capable of a "yes" or "no" answer. In reality, the issue is simply the Rule of Law put in the form of a question (e.g., "May an offer be accepted by performance?").

The major problem presented in discerning what is *the* issue in the case is that an opinion usually purports to raise and answer several questions. However, except for rare cases, only one such question is really the issue in the case. Collateral issues not necessary to the resolution of the matter in controversy are handled by the court by language known as *"obiter dictum"* or merely *"dictum."* While dicta may be included later in the brief, they have no place under the issue heading.

To find the issue, ask *who wants what* and then go on to ask *why did that party succeed or fail in getting it.* Once this is determined, the "why" should be turned into a question.

The complexity of the issues in the cases will vary, but in all cases a single-sentence question should sum up the issue. *In a few cases,* there will be two, or even more rarely, three issues of equal importance to the resolution of the case. Each should be expressed in a single-sentence question.

Since many issues are resolved by a court in coming to a final disposition of a case, the casebook editor will reproduce the portion of the opinion containing the issue or issues most relevant to the area of law under scrutiny. A noted law professor gave this advice: "Close the book; look at the title on the cover." Chances are, if it is Property, you need not concern yourself with whether, for example, the federal government's treatment of the plaintiff's land really raises a federal question sufficient to support jurisdiction on this ground in federal court.

The same rule applies to chapter headings designating sub-areas within the subjects. They tip you off as to what the text is designed to teach. The cases are arranged in a casebook to show a progression or development of the law, so that the preceding cases may also help.

It is also most important to remember to *read the notes and questions* at the end of a case to determine what the editors wanted you to have gleaned from it.

HOLDING AND DECISION: This section should succinctly explain the rationale of the court in arriving at its decision. In capsulizing the "reasoning" of the court, it should always include an application of the general rule or rules of law to the specific facts of the case. Hidden justifications come to light in this entry: the reasons for the state of the law, the public policies, the biases and prejudices, those considerations that influence the justices' thinking and, ultimately, the outcome of the case. At the end, there should be a short indication of the disposition or procedural resolution of the case (e.g., "Decision of the trial court for Mr. Smith (P) reversed").

The foregoing format is designed to help you "digest" the reams of case material with which you will be faced in your law school career. Once mastered by practice, it will place at your fingertips the information the authors of your casebooks have sought to impart to you in case-by-case illustration and analysis.

B. Be as Economical as Possible in Briefing Cases

Once armed with a format that encourages succinctness, it is as important to be economical with regard to the time spent on the actual reading of the case as it is to be economical in the writing of the brief itself. This does not mean "skimming" a case. Rather, it means reading the case with an "eye" trained to recognize into which "section" of your brief a particular passage or line fits and having a system for quickly and precisely marking the case so that the passages fitting any one particular part of

the brief can be easily identified and brought together in a concise and accurate manner when the brief is actually written.

It is of no use to simply repeat everything in the opinion of the court; record only enough information to trigger your recollection of what the court said. Nevertheless, an accurate statement of the "law of the case," i.e., the legal principle applied to the facts, is absolutely essential to class preparation and to learning the law under the case method.

To that end, it is important to develop a "shorthand" that you can use to make marginal notations. These notations will tell you at a glance in which section of the brief you will be placing that particular passage or portion of the opinion.

Some students prefer to underline all the salient portions of the opinion (with a pencil or colored underliner marker), making marginal notations as they go along. Others prefer the color-coded method of underlining, utilizing different colors of markers to underline the salient portions of the case, each separate color being used to represent a different section of the brief. For example, blue underlining could be used for passages relating to the rule of law, yellow for those relating to the issue, and green for those relating to the holding and decision, etc. While it has its advocates, the color-coded method can be confusing and time-consuming (all that time spent on changing colored markers). Furthermore, it can interfere with the continuity and concentration many students deem essential to the reading of a case for maximum comprehension. In the end, however, it is a matter of personal preference and style. Just remember, whatever method you use, underlining must be used sparingly or its value is lost.

If you take the marginal notation route, an efficient and easy method is to go along underlining the key portions of the case and placing in the margin alongside them the following "markers" to indicate where a particular passage or line "belongs" in the brief you will write:

N   (NATURE OF CASE)
RL   (RULE OF LAW)
I   (ISSUE)
HL   (HOLDING AND DECISION, relates to
       the RULE OF LAW behind the decision)
HR   (HOLDING AND DECISION, gives the
       RATIONALE or reasoning behind the
       decision)
HA   (HOLDING AND DECISION, APPLIES
       the general principle(s) of law to the facts
       of the case to arrive at the decision)

Remember that a particular passage may well contain information necessary to more than one part of your brief, in which case you simply note that in the margin. If you are using the color-coded underlining method instead of marginal notation, simply make asterisks or checks in the margin next to the passage in question in the colors that indicate the additional sections of the brief where it might be utilized.

The economy of utilizing "shorthand" in marking cases for briefing can be maintained in the actual brief writing process itself by utilizing "law student shorthand" within the brief. There are many commonly used words and phrases for which abbreviations can be substituted in your briefs (and in your class notes also). You can develop abbreviations that are personal to you and which will save you a lot of time. A reference list of briefing abbreviations can be found on page xii of this book.

C. Use Both the Briefing Process and the Brief as a Learning Tool

Now that you have a format and the tools for briefing cases efficiently, the most important thing is to make the time spent in briefing profitable to you and to make the most advantageous use of the briefs you create. Of course, the briefs are invaluable for classroom reference when you are called upon to explain or analyze a particular

case. However, they are also useful in reviewing for exams. A quick glance at the fact summary should bring the case to mind, and a rereading of the rule of law should enable you to go over the underlying legal concept in your mind, how it was applied in that particular case, and how it might apply in other factual settings.

As to the value to be derived from engaging in the briefing process itself, there is an immediate benefit that arises from being forced to sift through the essential facts and reasoning from the court's opinion and to succinctly express them in your own words in your brief. The process ensures that you understand the case and the point that it illustrates, and that means you will be ready to absorb further analysis and information brought forth in class. It also ensures you will have something to say when called upon in class. The briefing process helps develop a mental agility for getting to the *gist* of a case and for identifying, expounding on, and applying the legal concepts and issues found there. The briefing process is the mental process on which you must rely in taking law school examinations; it is also the mental process upon which a lawyer relies in serving his clients and in making his living.

Abbreviations for Briefs

acceptance	acp	offer	O
affirmed	aff	offeree	OE
answer	ans	offeror	OR
assumption of risk	a/r	ordinance	ord
attorney	atty	pain and suffering	p/s
beyond a reasonable doubt	b/r/d	parol evidence	p/e
bona fide purchaser	BFP	plaintiff	P
breach of contract	br/k	prima facie	p/f
cause of action	c/a	probable cause	p/c
common law	c/l	proximate cause	px/c
Constitution	Con	real property	r/p
constitutional	con	reasonable doubt	r/d
contract	K	reasonable man	r/m
contributory negligence	c/n	rebuttable presumption	rb/p
cross	x	remanded	rem
cross-complaint	x/c	res ipsa loquitur	RIL
cross-examination	x/ex	respondeat superior	r/s
cruel and unusual punishment	c/u/p	Restatement	RS
defendant	D	reversed	rev
dismissed	dis	Rule Against Perpetuities	RAP
double jeopardy	d/j	search and seizure	s/s
due process	d/p	search warrant	s/w
equal protection	e/p	self-defense	s/d
equity	eq	specific performance	s/p
evidence	ev	statute	S
exclude	exc	statute of frauds	S/F
exclusionary rule	exc/r	statute of limitations	S/L
felony	f/n	summary judgment	s/j
freedom of speech	f/s	tenancy at will	t/w
good faith	g/f	tenancy in common	t/c
habeas corpus	h/c	tenant	t
hearsay	hr	third party	TP
husband	H	third party beneficiary	TPB
injunction	inj	transferred intent	TI
in loco parentis	ILP	unconscionable	uncon
inter vivos	I/v	unconstitutional	unconst
joint tenancy	j/t	undue influence	u/e
judgment	judgt	Uniform Commercial Code	UCC
jurisdiction	jur	unilateral	uni
last clear chance	LCC	vendee	VE
long-arm statute	LAS	vendor	VR
majority view	maj	versus	v
meeting of minds	MOM	void for vagueness	VFV
minority view	min	weight of authority	w/a
Miranda rule	Mir/r	weight of the evidence	w/e
Miranda warnings	Mir/w	wife	W
negligence	neg	with	w/
notice	ntc	within	w/i
nuisance	nus	without	w/o
obligation	ob	without prejudice	w/o/p
obscene	obs	wrongful death	wr/d

Table of Cases

The Constitutional Position of the Administrative Agency

Quick Reference Rules of Law

A.L.A. Schechter Poultry Corp. v. United States

Poultry company (D) v. Federal government (P)

295 U.S. 495 (1935).

NATURE OF CASE: Appeal from a conviction of violation of the Live Poultry Code.

FACT SUMMARY: A.L.A Schechter Poultry Corp. (D) appealed its conviction of violation of the Live Poultry Code (the Code) on the grounds that the Code was enacted pursuant to an unconstitutional delegation of the congressional legislative power.

🏛 **RULE OF LAW**
Congress may not transfer to an administrative agency the power to establish the standards of legal obligations between parties under the regulation of the agency.

FACTS: A.L.A Schechter Poultry Corp. Schechter (Schechter) (D), a corporation involved in operating wholesale poultry operations, was indicted for violations of the Live Poultry Code (the Code). This Code was enacted to promote fair competition within the poultry industry. It was promulgated under § 3 of the National Industrial Recovery Act (the Recovery Act) and provided guidelines for minimum wages for employees and maximum hours of employment. The Code was administered by an industry advisory committee selected by trade associations and members of the industry, yet no provision existed in the Recovery Act limiting or defining the scope of the board's authority, except that codes that are developed to promote fair competition had to be approved by the President. Schechter (D) demurred to the indictment, contending the Code was promulgated under an unconstitutional delegation of congressional legislative power. Schechter (D) was subsequently convicted of the charges against it, and appealed to the United States Supreme Court.

ISSUE: May Congress transfer to an administrative agency the power to establish the standards of legal obligations between parties under the regulation of the agency?

HOLDING AND DECISION: (Hughes, C.J.) No. Congress may not transfer to an administrative agency the power to establish the standards of legal obligations between parties under the regulation of the agency. Congress cannot delegate its legislative power to either the President or an administrative agency. It can delegate the power to prescribe rules and regulations in furtherance of a duly enacted statute, yet where the delegation is so wide in scope that it constitutes a delegation of the power to establish the standards governing legal obligations, it is invalid. In this case, the enabling statute, the National Industrial Recovery Act, failed to define the concept of "fair competition." The Act leaves to an industry advisory committee, with the approval of the President, the power to enact laws to cover anything which might tend to preclude fair competition. As a result, the scope of the committee's power is completely without effective bounds and therefore is an unconstitutional delegation of the legislative power. Reversed.

CONCURRENCE: (Cardozo, J.) In the absence of effective limiting and defining standards, a delegation of power to an agency is invalid. The delegation in this case provides no standards and is in effect a license to enact laws for the well-being of the industry affected. This would, if valid, expand presidential power to equal that of Congress. Clearly this is unconstitutional.

▶ *ANALYSIS*

Prior to the *Schechter* case, congressional statutes were commonly upheld by the Court when attacked on delegability grounds. Examples of such statutes included presidential power to determine whether foreign countries had ceased violating the neutral commerce of the United States, and to equalize tariff duties under some circumstances. Earlier in 1935, the Court decided *Panama Refining Co. v. Ryan*, 293 U.S. 388 (1935). In that case the Court struck down a similar code covering the petroleum industry as an unlawful delegation of legislative power.

■■■

Quicknotes

DELEGATION The authorization of one person to act on another's behalf.

ENABLING ACT A statute that confers new powers upon a person or entity.

SEPARATION OF POWERS The system of checks and balances preventing one branch of government from infringing upon exercising the powers of another branch of government.

TARIFF A duty or fee paid when articles are imported into the United States.

■■■

Industrial Union Department, AFL-CIO v. American Petroleum Institute (The *Benzene* Case)

Secretary of Labor (D) v. Petroleum industry (P)

448 U.S. 607 (1980).

NATURE OF CASE: Appeal from a decision invalidating an OSHA regulation.

FACT SUMMARY: American Petroleum Institute (P) challenged the validity of (D) standards limiting maximum worker exposure to benzene, a reported carcinogen, set by the Occupational Safety and Health Administration under the Occupational Safety and Health Act.

RULE OF LAW

The Secretary of Labor must determine, prior to issuance, that an OSHA standard is reasonably necessary and appropriate to remedy a significant risk of material health impairment.

FACTS: The Occupational Safety and Health Act (the Act) (D) promulgated standards lowering the maximum extent of worker exposure to benzene, a reported carcinogen. The Occupational Safety and Health Administration's (OSHA's) (D) stated policy concerning potential carcinogens was that there is presumed to be no safe level of exposure and in the absence of clear proof establishing a safe level, the lowest feasible exposure level is set as the standard. As a result, OSHA (D) set the maximum standard without determining whether the exposure at this level presented a significant health risk. American Petroleum Institute (P) challenged the validity of the standard. The court of appeals held the standard invalid, and OSHA (D) appealed.

ISSUE: Must the Secretary of Labor determine, prior to issuance, that an OSHA standard is reasonably necessary and appropriate to remedy a significant risk of material health impairment?

HOLDING AND DECISION: (Stevens, J.) Yes. The Secretary of Labor must determine, prior to issuance, that an OSHA standard is reasonably necessary and appropriate to remedy a significant risk of material health impairment. The Occupational Health and Safety Act (the Act) does expressly give the Secretary of Labor such a wide scope of discretion as to allow the promulgation of standards without regard to the risk level the standard is designed to address. If OSHA (D) could regulate substances merely upon expert testimony as to their carcinogenic nature, it would have the power to impose enormous compliance costs without any measurable benefit. Further, it would constitute an unconstitutional delegation of legislative power if the Secretary were not limited in approving OSHA regulations by requiring the health risk to be characterized as significant prior to its being regulated. Therefore,

by approving this regulation without such a finding, the Secretary exceeded his statutory power. Affirmed and remanded for further proceedings.

CONCURRENCE: (Powell, J.) Even if OSHA had determined the significance of the health risk from benzene, the Act requires OSHA to conduct a weighing test and to promulgate standards only which serve benefits that substantially outweigh the cost of compliance.

CONCURRENCE: (Rehnquist, J.) The determination whether the regulation of particular harmful substances will result in any benefit must rest with Congress. In this case, the statute allows the Secretary to adopt regulations if he can. It gives the Secretary no guidance on its face as to what level of risk is significant and therefore worthy of regulation, and there is no such guidance in the legislative history. Moreover, a rule of necessity, whereby broad delegations of authority may be made where it would be unreasonable and impracticable to compel Congress to set forth detailed rules regarding a given situation, is inapplicable here. Congress, by using a "feasibility" standard, has avoided making the tough choice between saving lives and industrial resources, and instead has passed that difficult choice to the Secretary (D). As a result, Congress has delegated too much power over what is essentially a legislative function, and, therefore, the Act unconstitutionally delegates the legislative power.

DISSENT: (Marshall, J.) The plurality's conclusion is based on its interpretation of the applicable statute, which defines an occupational safety and health standard as one "which requires conditions . . . reasonably necessary or appropriate to provide safe or healthful employment. . . ." According to the plurality, a standard is not "reasonably necessary or appropriate" unless the Secretary (D) is able to show that it is "at least more likely than not," that the risk he seeks to regulate is "significant." However, there is nothing in the statute's language or legislative history that supports such an interpretation. Here, the Secretary (D) did not rely blindly on some Draconian carcinogen "policy," but found a risk, albeit unquantifiable, that benzene in certain quantities causes various damage to humans, which is tantamount to a finding a "significant" risk. The Secretary (D) then weighed the costs and benefits of regulation; the Court should not, as the plurality has done, substitute its judgment of what is the appropriate balance of costs and benefits in the occupational safety standards area for that of the Secretary (D).

Continued on next page.

▶ *ANALYSIS*

The Court specifically refused to address the argument presented in Justice Powell's concurrence. This argument stated that OSHA was bound to do a cost-benefit analysis of proposed regulations. In *American Textile Manufacturers' Institute v. Donovan*, 452 U.S. 490 (1981), the Court specifically addressed and rejected this as a requirement. In its place, the Court held that OSHA standards be judged on the basis of their technological and economic feasibility.

■▬■

Quicknotes

DELEGATION   The authorization of one person to act on another's behalf.

SEPARATION OF POWERS   The system of checks and balances preventing one branch of government from infringing upon exercising the powers of another branch of government.

■▬■

American Trucking Associations, Inc. v. Environmental Protection Agency

Commercial association (P) v. Federal agency (D)

175 F.3d 1027 (D.C. Cir. 1999).

NATURE OF CASE: Petition for review of the Environmental Protection Agency's air quality standards.

FACT SUMMARY: The Environmental Protection Agency (D) selected standards to evaluate whether the levels of particulate matter and ozone were a danger to the public health and welfare. Petitions for review were filed for each rule.

🏛 RULE OF LAW
The nondelegation doctrine requires that, when the Environmental Protection Agency determines what factors to use in deciding the degree of public health concern associated with different levels of ozone and particulate matter, the factors used must be based on an intelligible principle.

FACTS: The Environmental Protection Agency (EPA) (D) is required by the Clean Air Act (Act) to promulgate and revise national ambient air quality standards for each air pollutant identified by the agency as meeting certain statutory criteria. For each pollutant, the EPA (D) set both a primary standard requisite to protect the public health with an adequate margin of safety and a secondary standard requisite to protect the public welfare. In 1997, the EPA (D) issued final rules revising the standards for particulate matter and ozone. Numerous petitions for review were filed for each rule.

ISSUE: Does the nondelegation doctrine require that, when the EPA determines what factors to use in deciding the degree of public health concern associated with different levels of ozone and particulate matter, the factors used must be based on an intelligible principle?

HOLDING AND DECISION: (Per curiam) Yes. The nondelegation doctrine requires that, when the EPA determines what factors to use in deciding the degree of public health concern associated with different levels of ozone and particulate matter, the factors used must be based on an intelligible principle. The construction of the Act on which the EPA (D) relied in promulgating the air quality standards effects an unconstitutional delegation of legislative power. Although the factors the EPA (D) used in determining the degree of public health concern associated with different levels of ozone and particulate material are reasonable, the EPA (D) appears to have articulated no "intelligible principle" to guide its application of these factors, nor is one apparent from the statute. The EPA (D) regards both ozone and particulate matter as having some adverse health impact at any exposure level above

zero. The Act requires the EPA (D) to set each standard at the level requisite to protect the public health with an adequate margin of safety. For the EPA (D), therefore, to pick any nonzero level, it must explain the degree permitted. The EPA (D), however, lacks a criterion for how much is too much. There is, therefore, no nondelegation problem with the criteria themselves; rather the problem lies in the EPA's (D) selection of a standard of 0.08 ppm of ozone and its implication that "a less stringent standard would allow the relevant pollutant to inflict a greater quantum of harm on the public health and a more stringent standard would result in less harm." The case is remanded to provide the EPA (D) the opportunity to extract on its own a determinate standard, i.e., a generic unit of harm that accounts for population affected, severity, and probability.

▶ ANALYSIS
Instead of striking down the statute, thus requiring that Congress rework it, the court provided the agency an opportunity to fine-tune its application of it. This may have been because the court believed the EPA (D), with all its expertise in this area, would be better equipped to address the issues involved.

■══■

Quicknotes
CLEAN AIR ACT Required certain states to establish a permit program for stationary sources of air pollution.

■══■

Whitman v. American Trucking Associations, Inc.

Federal agency (D) v. Commercial association (P)

531 U.S. 457 (2001).

NATURE OF CASE: Appeal of judgment remanding for reinterpretation of air quality standards.

FACT SUMMARY: This case was remanded to the Environmental Protection Agency (D) to allow the agency to devise more intelligible principles in support of its rules on air quality standards under the Clean Air Act.

🏛 RULE OF LAW
The nondelegation doctrine is not violated by the Clean Air Act's requirement that the Environmental Protection Agency set air quality standards at the level requisite—neither lower nor higher than necessary—to protect the public health while allowing an adequate margin of safety.

FACTS: The Clean Air Act ("CAA" or "the Act") requires the Environmental Protection Agency (EPA) (D) to set air quality standards that protect the public health. The court of appeals found certain standards selected by the EPA (D) under the CAA—but not the statute itself—lacking in intelligible principles. Accordingly, it concluded that the EPA's (D) interpretation violated the nondelegation doctrine, and it remanded the case to the EPA (D), allowing it the opportunity to establish intelligible principles to guide and support its selected standards. The case was appealed to the United States Supreme Court, which granted certiorari.

ISSUE: Is the nondelegation doctrine violated by the Clean Air Act's requirement that the EPA set air quality standards at the level requisite—neither lower nor higher than necessary—to protect the public health while allowing an adequate margin of safety?

HOLDING AND DECISION: (Scalia, J.) No. The nondelegation doctrine is not violated by the Clean Air Act's requirement that the EPA set air quality standards at the level requisite—neither lower nor higher than necessary—to protect the public health while allowing an adequate margin of safety. The EPA's interpretation of the Act doesn't violate the nondelegation doctrine. When Congress confers decision making authority upon agencies, Congress must lay down by legislative act an intelligible principle to which the body authorized to act is directed to conform. An agency cannot cure an unlawful delegation of unlawful power by adopting in its discretion a limiting construction of the statute. In this case, the Act provides sufficient limits on the EPA's (D) discretion. The Act requires that, for a discrete set of pollutants and based on published air quality criteria reflecting the latest scientific knowledge, the EPA (D) must establish uniform national standards at a level requisite to protect public health from the adverse effects of the pollutant in the ambient air. Requisite means sufficient but not more than necessary. The scope of the discretion allowed by the Act is well within the outer limits of the courts' nondelegation precedents. Although Congress must provide substantial guidance on setting air standards that affect the entire national economy, it is too much to demand that a statute provide a determinate criterion for saying how much of the regulated harm is too much. Reversed.

CONCURRENCE: (Thomas, J.) Instead of arguing solely about this Court's standard of an "intelligible principle," the parties should have grounded this case in the text of the Constitution. The text of Article 1, Section 1, states the threshold analysis in simple terms by vesting *all* legislative powers in Congress. In that context, it is possible for legislation to have an intelligible principle, yet still be a delegation of legislative power, which presents interplay of questions that the Court should reconsider in future cases.

CONCURRENCE: (Stevens, J.) The Court can either admit or deny that the delegation of power to the EPA (D) is a transfer of legislative power. In this case, the Court takes the wrong course by pretending that the agency's rulemaking authority is not legislative power. The Court would do better to admit that the power is legislative, while finding further that Congress also limited the agency's exercise of legislative power by stating an intelligible principle. Although the delegation here is of legislative power, it is also nevertheless constitutional.

▶ ANALYSIS

The Supreme Court reversed the appeals court's conclusion and determined that what Congress articulated in the Act was sufficient and that the EPA need not elaborate. This is consistent with the Court's prior opinions. At the time this case was decided, the Court had found "intelligible principle" lacking in only two statutes, one of which gave no guidance for the exercise of discretion and the other of which gave little such guidance. At the time of this case, the Court had almost never felt qualified to second-guess Congress regarding the permissible degree to which policy judgments can be left to those executing or applying the law.

■■■

Continued on next page.

Quicknotes

CLEAN AIR ACT Required certain states to establish a permit program for stationary sources of air pollution.

ENVIRONMENTAL LAW A body of federal law passed in 1970 that protects the environment against public and private actions that harm the ecosystem.

■▬■

Immigration and Naturalization Service v. Chadha

Federal agency (P) v. Deported immigrant (D)

462 U.S. 919 (1983).

NATURE OF CASE: Challenge to constitutionality of resolution procedure for overturning deportation suspension. [The procedural posture of the case is not presented in the casebook extract.]

FACT SUMMARY: Chadha (D) challenged the constitutionality of an Immigration and Nationality Act provision allowing either the House of Representatives or the Senate, acting individually, to overturn the Attorney General's suspension of deportation proceedings by passing a resolution stating in substance that the deportation suspension is not favored.

🏛 RULE OF LAW
Where the action of either House of Congress is legislative in nature, such action is subject to the presentment and bicameral requirements of Article I of the Constitution.

FACTS: Chadha (D), an East Indian born in Kenya, remained in the United States after his visa expired. He was ordered deported, but the Attorney General suspended the deportation. Pursuant to an Immigration and Nationality Act (INA) provision allowing either House of Congress to overturn a deportation suspension by adopting a resolution to that effect, the House of Representatives adopted a resolution overturning Chadha's (D) suspension, and he was ordered deported. There was no public hearing, report, or meaningful statement of reasons on the committee's recommendation favoring the resolution. Chadha (D) challenged the constitutionality of the House of Representatives' action under the INA provision. The United States Supreme Court granted certiorari. [The procedural posture of the case is not presented in the casebook extract.]

ISSUE: Where the action of either House of Congress is legislative in nature, is such action subject to the presentment and bicameral requirements of Article I of the Constitution?

HOLDING AND DECISION: (Burger, C.J.) Yes. Where the action of either House of Congress is legislative in nature, such action is subject to the presentment and bicameral requirements of Article I of the Constitution. The clear and unambiguous dictates of Article I of the Constitution require that, before any legislation is to take effect, it must have been passed with the concurrence of the prescribed majority of both Houses of Congress, and must be presented to the President for approval. Presentment of legislation to the President establishes a salutary check on the legislature, and assures that a "national" perspective is grafted on the legislative process. The bicameral requirement assures that the legislative power will be exercised only after full study and debate in separate settings. The powers delegated to each branch of government are identifiable, and when any branch acts, it presumptively exercises the power delegated to it. The legislative character of the House's action in the present case is apparent, since it is conceded that, absent the INA provision, Chadha's (D) deportation could only have been accomplished by legislation requiring deportation. The House's action does not fall into one of the constitutionally prescribed exceptions to the bicameral requirement, and involves determinations of policy that should only be implemented by adhering to the presentment and bicameral requirements of Article I. The action taken by the House pursuant to the INA provision was in violation of Article I of the Constitution.

CONCURRENCE: (Powell, J.) Congress here has essentially "adjudicated" Chadha's individual case, thereby invading the province that the Constitution reserves for the judiciary.

DISSENT: (White, J.) If possible, this decision should have been decided on the narrower grounds of separation of powers and sounds a death knell for nearly 200 other statutes where Congress has reserved a legislative veto. The decision is inconsistent with the accepted practice of delegating lawmaking power to independent executive agencies and private persons and ignores the fact that the operation of the INA provision at question satisfies the bicameral and presentment requirements of Article I. If Congress may delegate lawmaking power to independent and executive agencies, it is difficult to understand Article I as forbidding Congress from also reserving a check on legislative power for itself. Absent the veto, the agencies receiving delegations of legislative or quasi-legislative power may issue regulations having the force of law without bicameral approval and without the President's signature. It is thus not apparent why the reservation of a veto over the exercise of that legislative power must be subject to a more exacting test. Most importantly, regarding the legislative veto in this case, any departure from the legal status quo—which is what Article I is aimed at—occurs only upon the concurrence of opinion of the House, the Senate, and the President. The President's approval is found in the Attorney General's action in recommending to Congress that the deportation order for a given alien be suspended. The House and the Senate indicate their approval of the executive's action by not passing a resolution of disapproval within the statutory period. Thus, a change in the legal status quo—the

Continued on next page.

deportability of the alien (Chadha (D))—is consummated only with the approval of each of the three relevant actors. The disagreement of any one of the three maintains the alien's pre-existing status: the executive may choose not to recommend suspension; the House and Senate may each veto the recommendation.

▶ ANALYSIS

It is not clear to what extent the "legislative veto" is dead. It is clear, however, that Congress can accomplish many of the legislative veto's objectives through the use of traditional weapons in its legislative and political arsenal. Among others, Congress can tailor statutes more carefully, can provide that an agency's legislative power will expire after a given period of time, and perhaps most importantly, can control an agency's budget. Each of these alternatives has obvious drawbacks and can serve to greatly undermine an agency's effectiveness.

■━━■

Quicknotes

BICAMERALISM The necessity of approval by a majority of both houses of Congress in ratifying legislation or approving other legislative action.

LEGISLATIVE VETO A resolution passed by one or both legislature houses that is intended to block an administrative regulation or action.

PRESENTMENT The act of bringing a congressional decision before the President for his approval or veto.

SEPARATION OF POWERS The system of checks and balances preventing one branch of government from infringing upon exercising the powers of another branch of government.

■━━■

Buckley v. Valeo

Member of Federal Election Commission (P) v. Opposing member (D)

424 U.S. 1 (1976).

NATURE OF CASE: Appeal of challenge to portions of the Federal Election Campaign Act of 1971.

FACT SUMMARY: Members of the Federal Election Commission were to be appointed by a method deviating from Article II, § 2 of the Constitution.

RULE OF LAW
Officers of the United States must be appointed in a manner consistent with Article II, § 2 of the Constitution.

FACTS: The Federal Election Campaign Act of 1971 (the Act) created the Federal Election Campaign Commission (Commission), which was given broad sanctioning and investigative power with respect to elections. The Commission consisted of six voting members appointed by the President Pro Tem of the Senate, the Speaker of the House, and the President, who each selected two members of the Commission. The Secretary of the Senate and the Clerk of the House were nonvoting members. The Act was challenged on constitutional grounds. The court of appeals upheld the section dealing with the Commission.

ISSUE: Must officers of the United States be appointed in a manner consistent with Article II, § 2 of the Constitution?

HOLDING AND DECISION: (Per curiam) Yes. Officers of the United States must be appointed in a manner consistent with Article II, § 2 of the Constitution. The Constitution provides that no member of Congress will be appointed an officer of the United States during his term. This demonstrates that the Framers intended that strict separation be maintained between executive officers and legislative officials. Further, the Constitution mandates that all such executive officials shall be nominated by the President and confirmed by the Senate. The Commission in question exercises important executive functions, and, therefore, its members are officers of the United States. This being the case, they must be appointed per the constitutional requirements of Article II. Reversed.

▶ ANALYSIS

In theory, the Court created a fairly simple standard to follow in this area. Congress may appoint officials who perform purely legislative acts but not officers who perform executive or judicial acts. Of course, the principle is much easier in theory than in practice, and uncertainty will always exist as to which sort of officials do not have to be appointed pursuant to Article II.

■■■

Quicknotes

FEDERAL ELECTION CAMPAIGN ACT Created a commission to investigate and administrate federal elections.

U.S. CONSTITUTION, ARTICLE II, § 2 Provides that the President shall nominate, with the Senate's advice and consent, executive officials.

■■■

Edmond v. United States

Courts-martial defendant (D) v. Federal government (P)

520 U.S. 651 (1997).

NATURE OF CASE: Appeal in courts-martial proceedings reviewed by the Coast Guard Court of Criminal Appeals, the appointment of the judges of which is challenged as unconstitutional. [The procedural posture of this case is not presented in the casebook extract.]

FACT SUMMARY: Courts-martial defendants whose appeal was heard by the Coast Guard Court of Criminal Appeals contended that the appointment of the judges of that court was unconstitutional, arguing that such judges were "principal officers" under the Appointments Clause who should have been appointed with Senate advice and consent, but were not.

RULE OF LAW
Under the Appointments Clause, judges for the Coast Guard Court of Criminal Appeals are "inferior officers" because their work is directed and supervised by others who have been appointed by presidential nomination with the advice and consent of the Senate.

FACTS: The Coast Guard Court of Criminal Appeals hears appeals from the decisions of courts-martial, and its decisions are subject to review by the United States Court of Appeals for the Armed Forces. Its judges may be commissioned officers or civilians. During the times here relevant, the court had two civilian members, both of whom were originally assigned to the court without Senate advice and consent. Defendants in courts-martial cases contended that this method of appointment was unconstitutional, arguing that the judges were "principal officers" under the Appointments Clause who should have been appointed with the Senate's advice and consent. The United States Supreme Court granted certiorari. [The procedural posture of this case is not presented in the casebook extract.]

ISSUE: Under the Appointments Clause, judges for the Coast Guard Court of Criminal Appeals are "inferior officers" because their work is directed and supervised by others who have been appointed by presidential nomination with the advice and consent of the Senate.

HOLDING AND DECISION: (Scalia, J.) Yes. Under the Appointments Clause, judges for the Coast Guard Court of Criminal Appeals are "inferior officers" because their work is directed and supervised by others who have been appointed by presidential nomination with the advice and consent of the Senate. Despite the importance of the responsibilities the judges in question bear, they are "inferior officers" under the Appointments Clause. Generally speaking, "inferior officers" are officers whose work is directed and supervised at some level by others who were appointed by presidential nomination with the Senate's advice and consent. Supervision of the work of Coast Guard Court of Criminal Appeals judges is divided between the Judge Advocate General of the Department of Transportation (who is subordinate to the Secretary of Transportation) and the Court of Appeals for the Armed Forces. Significantly, these judges have no power to render a final decision on behalf of the United States unless permitted to do so by other executive officers, and hence they are "inferior" within the meaning of the Appointments Clause. [The procedural posture of this case is not presented in the casebook extract.]

ANALYSIS

This case stands for the principle that whether one is an "inferior" officer depends on whether he has a superior, and that "inferior officers" are officers whose work is directed and supervised at some level by other officers appointed by the President with the Senate's consent. In particular, the power to remove officers at will and without cause is a powerful tool for control of an inferior, so that if an officer is subject to such control, it is likely such an officer will be characterized as "inferior." As Justice Scalia points out, however, whether an appointee is charged with exercising significant authority on behalf of the United States—such as the judges at issue in this case—does not demarcate the line between principal and inferior officer for Appointments Clause purposes, but rather, the line between officer and non-officer.

Quicknotes

APPOINTMENTS CLAUSE Article II, Section 2, Clause 2 of the United States Constitution conferring power upon the President to appoint ambassadors, public ministers and consuls, judges of the Supreme Court and all other officers of the United States with the advice and consent of the Senate.

INFERIOR OFFICERS Members of the executive branch having less power or authority in relation to others.

Free Enterprise Fund v. Public Company Accounting Oversight Board

Nonprofit organization (P) v. Government agency (D)

130 S. Ct. 3138 (2010).

NATURE OF CASE: Appeal from affirmance of judgment for government agency in action challenging the agency's constitutionality.

FACT SUMMARY: The Free Enterprise Fund (P), a nonprofit organization, contended, inter alia, that the Public Company Accounting Oversight Board (the Board) (D) was unconstitutional in part because its officers were principal officers that could only be appointed by the President with the advice and consent of the Senate, and that even if such officers were considered inferior officers, they still could not be appointed by the Securities and Exchange Commission (SEC) since the SEC is not a department and the SEC Chairman is not a department head.

> ## ⚖ RULE OF LAW
> The Securities and Exchange Commission is an executive department, and the entire Commission, collectively, is that Department's "Head" so that it may appoint inferior officers, such as those serving on the Public Company Accounting Oversight Board.

FACTS: The Public Company Accounting Oversight Board (the Board) (D) was created as part of a series of accounting reforms in the Sarbanes-Oxley Act of 2002 (the Act). The Board (D) is composed of five members appointed by the Securities and Exchange Commission (SEC). It was modeled on private self-regulatory organizations in the securities industry—such as the New York Stock Exchange—that investigate and discipline their own members subject to the SEC's oversight. Unlike these organizations, the Board (D) is a Government-created entity with expansive powers to govern an entire industry. Every accounting firm that audits public companies under the securities laws must register with the Board (D), pay it an annual fee, and comply with its rules and oversight. The Board (D) may inspect registered firms, initiate formal investigations, and issue severe sanctions in its disciplinary proceedings. The Board (D) is "part of the Government" for constitutional purposes, and its members are "Officers of the United States" who "exercis[e] significant authority pursuant to the laws of the United States." While the SEC has oversight of the Board (D), it cannot remove Board (D) members at will, but only "for good cause shown," "in accordance with" specified procedures. The SEC Commissioners, in turn, cannot themselves be removed by the President except for "inefficiency, neglect of duty, or malfeasance in office." The Board (D) inspected an accounting firm, released a report critical of the firm's auditing procedures, and began a formal investigation. The firm and the

Free Enterprise Fund (P), a nonprofit organization of which the firm was a member, sued the Board (D) and its members, seeking, inter alia, a declaratory judgment that the Board (D) is unconstitutional. The district court rejected the challenge, and the court of appeals affirmed. The United States Supreme Court granted certiorari.

ISSUE: Is the Securities and Exchange Commission (SEC) an executive department, and is the entire Commission, collectively, that Department's "Head" so that it may appoint inferior officers, such as those serving on the Public Company Accounting Oversight Board?

HOLDING AND DECISION: (Roberts, C.J.) Yes. The Securities and Exchange Commission (SEC) is an executive department, and the entire Commission, collectively, is that Department's "Head" so that it may appoint inferior officers, such as those serving on the Public Company Accounting Oversight Board. Board (D) members are not "principal" officers but are "inferior" officers. Inferior officers "are officers whose work is directed and supervised at some level" by superiors appointed by the President with the Senate's consent. Because any good-cause restrictions on the Commission's powers to remove Board (D) members are unconstitutional and void, the Commission possesses the power to remove Board (D) members at will, in addition to its other oversight authority. Second, for constitutional purposes, the SEC is a "Department," because it is a freestanding component of the executive branch not subordinate to or contained within any other such component. Third, the several Commissioners, and not the Chairman, are the Commission's "Head." The Commission's powers are generally vested in the Commissioners jointly, not the Chairman alone. The Commissioners do not report to the Chairman, who exercises administrative functions subject to the full Commission's policies. There is no reason why a multimember body may not be the "Hea[d]" of a "Departmen[t]" that it governs. The Appointments Clause necessarily contemplates collective appointments by the "Courts of Law," Art. II, § 2, cl. 2, and each House of Congress appoints its officers collectively, see, e.g., Art. I, § 2, cl. 5. Affirmed in part and reversed in part.

> ▌ *ANALYSIS*
>
> This part of the Court's decision answered the question specifically reserved in *Freytag v. Commissioner,* 501 U.S. 868 (1991), as to whether a "principal agenc[y], such as" the SEC, is a "Departmen[t]." The Court here adopted the reasoning of the concurring Justices in *Freytag,* who would

Continued on next page.

have concluded that the SEC is such a "Departmen[t]" because it is a freestanding component of the executive branch not subordinate to or contained within any other such component. Such a reading is consistent with the common, near-contemporary definition of a "department"; with the early practice of Congress, and with the Court's precedents, which have never invalidated an appointment made by the head of such an establishment.

∎══∎

Quicknotes

GOOD CAUSE Sufficient justification for failure to perform an obligation imposed by law.

INFERIOR OFFICERS Members of the executive branch having less power or authority in relation to others.

INTER ALIA Among other things.

∎══∎

Myers v. United States

Postmaster appointee (P) v. Federal government (D)

272 U.S. 52 (1926).

NATURE OF CASE: Action for back pay for wrongful discharge.

FACT SUMMARY: Myers (P) challenged the President's authority to discharge without Senate consent those appointed by the President subject to the advice and consent of the Senate.

🏛 RULE OF LAW
The power to remove subordinates is inherent in the constitutional power of the President.

FACTS: A federal statute provided that postmasters be appointed by, and might be removed by, the President with the advice and consent of the Senate. Myers (P) was appointed Postmaster for a four-year term, yet was removed from office by President Wilson prior to the expiration of the term. President Wilson made the removal without applying for Senate consent. Myers (P) sued for back pay contending such removal was unlawful. The Government (D) defended on the ground it would be unconstitutional to limit presidential power to remove an executive branch officer by requiring Senate approval.

ISSUE: Is the power to remove subordinates inherent in the constitutional power of the President?

HOLDING AND DECISION: (Taft, C.J.) Yes. The power to remove subordinates is inherent in the constitutional power of the President. The President is given the duty to effectively enforce the laws. To fulfill this duty, it is imperative he enjoy the power to remove subordinates, who when acting are acting for the President and who do not adequately serve his purpose. The President must be allowed free discretion without undue delay to terminate those members of the executive branch who do not have his confidence. This power is essential to allow the President to promulgate uniform policies in execution of his duties. Congress may under the Constitution limit removal power, yet absent specific legislation to that effect, the President's power in this area is unchecked.

▶ ANALYSIS

This case illustrates the broad power of the President over removal of executive branch officers. Congress has on several occasions created independent agencies whose members cannot be unilaterally removed by the President. Examples of these include the Federal Trade Commission and the National Labor Relations Board. The President is given appointment power, yet not removal power.

■==■

Quicknotes

EXECUTIVE BRANCH The branch of government responsible for the administration of the laws.

SEPARATION OF POWERS The system of checks and balances preventing one branch of government from infringing upon exercising the powers of another branch of government.

WRONGFUL DISCHARGE Unlawful termination of an individual's employment.

■==■

Humphrey's Executor v. United States

Executor of estate (P) v. Federal government (D)

295 U.S. 602 (1935).

NATURE OF CASE: Action to recover back pay for wrongful discharge.

FACT SUMMARY: Humphrey (P) contended the President could not remove him as a commissioner of the Federal Trade Commission merely because of a difference in philosophy.

🏛 RULE OF LAW
The President cannot remove officials whose agency functions are quasi-legislative and quasi-judicial in nature, and not merely extensions of the executive branch of government.

FACTS: President Roosevelt felt that his predecessors had appointed commissioners to the Federal Trade Commission whose philosophies were contradictory to the legislative intent in creating that body. As a result, he attempted to remove Humphrey (P) as a commissioner, based on this conflict of philosophy, and not on any wrongdoing on Humphrey's (P) part. Humphrey (P) challenged his removal as unconstitutional as beyond the President's power. The Government (D) defended, contending the President's power to remove administrators could not be constitutionally limited. The court of claims certified Humphrey's (P) suit for back pay to the United States Supreme Court.

ISSUE: Can the President remove administrative officials whose agencies perform quasi-legislative and quasi-judicial functions and are not merely extensions of the executive branch?

HOLDING AND DECISION: (Sutherland, J.) No. The President cannot remove officials whose agency functions are quasi-legislative and quasi-judicial in nature, and not merely extensions of the executive branch of government. Although the President may remove administrators whose functions are merely executive in nature, those whose statutory authority and duty is to act in a legislature or judicial mode cannot be so removed unless by congressional consent. The Federal Trade Commission was created not as a department of the executive branch but as a means of carrying into effect legislative and judicial powers. Thus it is an agency of the legislative and judicial departments of government. Therefore, in order to prevent the executive department from obtaining indirect control over an agency outside its purview, the President is denied removal power except for enumerated reasons in the Federal Trade Commission Act. Therefore Humphrey's (P) removal was invalid.

▶ ANALYSIS

This case specifically clarifies and limits the holding of an earlier case, *Myers v. United States*, 272 U.S. 52 (1926), which held that the President could unilaterally remove an administrator whose function was purely executive in nature. The rationale stated in *Myers* was that the President must be able to command loyalty and confidence from those performing executive functions. The Court in this case limits *Myers* to executive agencies, and states the President's removal power depends upon the character of the office involved.

Quicknotes

EXECUTIVE BRANCH The branch of government responsible for the administration of the laws.

WRONGFUL DISCHARGE Unlawful termination of an individual's employment.

Morrison v. Olson

Special prosecutor (D) v. Government official (P)

487 U.S. 654 (1988).

NATURE OF CASE: Appeal from order quashing subpoenas issued at behest of a special prosecutor.

FACT SUMMARY: The independent counsel provisions of the Ethics in Government Act were challenged as unconstitutional.

🏛 RULE OF LAW
The independent counsel provisions of the Ethics in Government Act are not unconstitutional.

FACTS: In passing the Ethics in Government Act (the Act), Congress created the office of Special Prosecutor to investigate misdeeds by government officials. The Act provided that the Attorney General must investigate allegations and report to a special judicial division, which was enabled to appoint an independent counsel which in turn would have full prosecutorial authority. The independent counsel could be removed only by impeachment or by the Attorney General for good cause. The Act also provided for congressional oversight. Olson (P), under investigation by Prosecutor Morrison (D), filed an action seeking to quash certain grand jury subpoenas issued at the behest of Morrison (D). The district court denied such relief, but the court of appeals reversed, holding the independent counsel portions of the Act unconstitutional. The United States Supreme Court accepted review.

ISSUE: Are the independent counsel provisions of the Ethics in Government Act unconstitutional?

HOLDING AND DECISION: (Rehnquist, C.J.) No. The independent counsel provisions of the Ethics in Government Act are not unconstitutional. Due to the limited scope of the counsel's office, the independent counsel is an inferior officer, not a principal officer that must be appointed by the President. Also, there is no constitutional prohibition on interbranch appointments, so a judicial body appointing an executive officer does not in itself violate the Constitution. This Court is of the opinion that the supervisory powers of the special division are of a ministerial nature and do not trespass on the authority of the executive. Apart from impeachment, it is only the Attorney General who can remove the Special Prosecutor. Finally, this Court is of the opinion that the office of the Special Prosecutor does not violate the principle of separation of powers. While the Prosecutor does report to Congress, he is much more answerable to the Attorney General, who, significantly, retains the power to remove the Prosecutor. The Court believes that this does not unduly interfere with the powers of the President in enforcing the laws. For these reasons, the Court considers the office of the Special Prosecutor to be constitutional. Reversed.

DISSENT: (Scalia, J.) The independent counsel provisions of the Act essentially remove from the President prosecutorial power and place it in the hands of Congress and the Judiciary, which is a clear violation of separation of powers. The Constitution does not place some executive power in the President; it places all such power in the President. Any law altering this balance must fail.

▶ ANALYSIS

The Appointments Clause of Article II mandates appointment of noninferior officers in the President, with consent of the Senate. The Special Prosecutor is not so appointed. The Court looked to the breadth of the Prosecutor's office and decided that although the Prosecutor has wide-ranging powers, the ad hoc nature of the office mandated a conclusion that the office was inferior.

■═■

Quicknotes

ETHICS IN GOVERNMENT ACT Allows for the appointment of special independent counsel to investigate high-ranking government officials.

■═■

Free Enterprise Fund v. Public Company Accounting Oversight Board

Nonprofit organization (P) v. Government agency (D)

130 S. Ct. 3138 (2010).

NATURE OF CASE: Appeal from affirmance of judgment for government agency in action challenging the agency's constitutionality.

FACT SUMMARY: The Free Enterprise Fund (P), a nonprofit organization, contended, inter alia, that the Public Company Accounting Oversight Board (the Board) (D) was unconstitutional insofar as its establishment violated the Constitution's separation of powers requirement by conferring executive power on Board (D) members without subjecting them to presidential control, since Board (D) members were insulated from presidential control by two layers of tenure protection: Board (D) members could only be removed by the Securities and Exchange Commission (SEC) for good cause, and the SEC Commissioners could in turn only be removed by the President for good cause.

RULE OF LAW

The President may not be restricted in his ability to remove a principal officer, who is in turn restricted in his ability to remove an inferior officer, even though that inferior officer determines the policy and enforces the laws of the United States.

FACTS: The Public Company Accounting Oversight Board (the Board) (D) was created as part of a series of accounting reforms in the Sarbanes-Oxley Act of 2002 (the Act). The Board (D) is composed of five members appointed by the Securities and Exchange Commission (SEC). It was modeled on private self-regulatory organizations in the securities industry—such as the New York Stock Exchange—that investigate and discipline their own members subject to the SEC's oversight. Unlike these organizations, the Board (D) is a Government-created entity with expansive powers to govern an entire industry. Every accounting firm that audits public companies under the securities laws must register with the Board (D), pay it an annual fee, and comply with its rules and oversight. The Board (D) may inspect registered firms, initiate formal investigations, and issue severe sanctions in its disciplinary proceedings. The Board (D) is "part of the Government" for constitutional purposes, and its members are "Officers of the United States" who "exercis[e] significant authority pursuant to the laws of the United States." While the SEC has oversight of the Board (D), it cannot remove Board (D) members at will, but only "for good cause shown," "in accordance with" specified procedures. The SEC Commissioners, in turn, cannot themselves be removed by the President except for "inefficiency, neglect of duty, or malfeasance in office." The Board (D) inspected an accounting

firm, released a report critical of the firm's auditing procedures, and began a formal investigation. The firm and the Free Enterprise Fund (P), a nonprofit organization of which the firm was a member, sued the Board (D) and its members, seeking, inter alia, a declaratory judgment that the Board (D) is unconstitutional. The district court rejected the challenge, and the court of appeals affirmed. The United States Supreme Court granted certiorari.

ISSUE: May the President be restricted in his ability to remove a principal officer, who is in turn restricted in his ability to remove an inferior officer, even though that inferior officer determines the policy and enforces the laws of the United States?

HOLDING AND DECISION: (Roberts, C.J.) No. The President may not be restricted in his ability to remove a principal officer, who is in turn restricted in his ability to remove an inferior officer, even though that inferior officer determines the policy and enforces the laws of the United States. The dual for-cause limitations on the removal of Board members contravene the Constitution's separation of powers. In those cases where limited restrictions on the President's removal power were previously upheld, only one level of protected tenure separated the President from an officer exercising executive power. The President—or a subordinate he could remove at will—decided whether the officer's conduct merited removal under the good-cause standard. Here, the Act not only protects Board (D) members from removal except for good cause, but withdraws from the President any decision on whether that good cause exists. That decision is vested in other tenured officers—the SEC Commissioners—who are not subject to the President's direct control. Because the Commission cannot remove a Board (D) member at will, the President cannot hold the Commission fully accountable for the Board's (D) conduct. He can only review the Commissioner's determination of whether the Act's rigorous good-cause standard is met. Thus, if the President disagrees with that determination, he is powerless to intervene, except where that determination is so unreasonable as to constitute "inefficiency, neglect of duty, or malfeasance in office." This arrangement contradicts the vesting of the executive power in the President, who can neither ensure that the laws are faithfully executed, nor be held responsible for a Board (D) member's breach of faith. If this dispersion of responsibility were allowed to stand, Congress could multiply it further by adding still more layers of good-cause tenure. Such diffusion of power carries with it a diffusion

Continued on next page.

of accountability; without a clear and effective chain of command, the public cannot determine where the blame for a pernicious measure should fall. The need for technical expertise in certain areas does not justify an extensive expansion of legislative power. The pressing needs of the day do not justify creating a dual-layer of insulation between the President and the officers he must supervise, lest an extraconstitutional government be sanctioned. Thus, while for-cause limitations in general are constitutional, two layers of for-cause tenure between the President and executive officers are not. Moreover, there is no construction of the Commission's good-cause removal power that is broad enough to avoid invalidation. Nor is the Commission's broad power over Board (D) functions the equivalent of a power to remove Board (D) members. Altering the Board's (D) budget or powers is not a meaningful way to control an inferior officer; the Commission cannot supervise individual Board (D) members if it must destroy the Board (D) in order to fix it. Moreover, the Commission's power over the Board (D) cannot be said to be plenary, as the Board (D) may take significant enforcement actions largely independently of the Commission. The Act is highly unusual in committing substantial executive authority to officers protected by two layers of good-cause removal. Such a conclusion, however, should not be read as impugning the validity of using what is colloquially known as the civil service system within independent agencies. Additionally, the entire Board (D) is not unconstitutional, as the unconstitutional tenure provisions are severable from the remainder of the statute. Affirmed in part and reversed in part.

DISSENT: (Breyer, J.) The Constitution is completely silent with respect to the power of removal from office, so the Court should take a functional approach here, examining how a particular provision, taken in context, is likely to function. Under such an approach, which recognizes the administrative complexity of modern government, it should be recognized that if the President seeks to regulate through impartial adjudication, then insulation of the adjudicator from removal-at-will can help him achieve that goal. To free a technical decisionmaker from the fear of removal without cause can similarly help create legitimacy with respect to that official's regulatory actions by helping to insulate his technical decisions from nontechnical political pressure. Because the Board (D) adjudicates cases and operates in the area of financial regulation, "for cause" provisions are appropriate in protecting the personal independence of Board (D) members. Notwithstanding the majority's assertion to the contrary, even a narrow reading of what constitutes an "inferior" officer will potentially lead to sweeping hundreds, perhaps thousands of high-level government officials within the scope of the majority's holding, putting their job security and their administrative actions and decisions constitutionally at risk. For example, over 1500 administrative law judges (ALJs), who are considered executive officers, would come within the

majority's holding. This potential problem threatens to impair the government's functioning. Finally, the majority simply assumes, without deciding, that the SEC Commissioners themselves are removable only "for cause," as the statute establishing the SEC says nothing about removal. Thus, the majority reads into that statute a "for cause removal" phrase that does not appear in the relevant statute and that Congress probably did not intend to write. And it does so in order to strike down, not to uphold, another statute. This is not a statutory construction that seeks to avoid a constitutional question, but the opposite. It has been suggested that there are at least 13 "independent" agencies without a removal provision in their statutes, so that not only does the majority's opinion fail to define "inferior officer," but it also leaves unanswered which department heads will be deemed by the majority to be subject to for-cause removal notwithstanding statutes containing no such provision. If any agency deemed "independent" will be similarly treated, the scope of the majority's holding is even broader still.

▶ *ANALYSIS*

The majority emphasized that it was not here overruling the Court's decision in *Humphrey's Executor v. United States*, 295 U.S. 602 (1935), which held that Congress "can, under certain circumstances, create independent agencies run by principal officers appointed by the President, whom the President may not remove at will but only for good cause." However, given the majority's expansive view of presidential power, it seems that given the right case, it might indeed overrule *Humphrey's*, at least to the extent of giving the President wide latitude as to what constitutes "cause" for the purposes of removing a federal official.

▪■▪

Quicknotes

GOOD CAUSE Sufficient justification for failure to perform an obligation imposed by law.

INFERIOR OFFICERS Members of the executive branch having less power or authority in relation to others.

INTER ALIA Among other things.

PLENARY Unlimited and open; as broad as a given situation may require.

▪■▪

Bowsher v. Synar

Congress (D) v. Comptroller General (P)

478 U.S. 714 (1986).

NATURE OF CASE: Appeal from order invalidating the Balanced Budget Act.

FACT SUMMARY: Synar (P) contended that the Balanced Budget Act violated separation of powers by providing strict requirements for appointment of an executive branch office.

🏛 RULE OF LAW
Congress cannot retain power to remove executive branch officers except by impeachment.

FACTS: Congress enacted the Balanced Budget Act which invested in the Comptroller General the power to make broad budgetary decisions as a member of the executive branch. The Comptroller was appointed by the President from a list provided by Congress. Removal was obtained by a joint resolution of Congress. Synar (P) sued, contending the statute unconstitutionally violated the separation of powers doctrine. The district court invalidated the statute. The court of appeals affirmed, and the United States Supreme Court granted certiorari.

ISSUE: Can Congress retain power to remove executive branch officers except by impeachment?

HOLDING AND DECISION: (Burger, C.J.) No. Congress cannot retain power to retain control over the removal of executive branch officers except by impeachment. Congressional removal may be accomplished only through impeachment. Any other removal power over executive officers imposes undue power over that branch and is inconsistent with separation of powers. Such would make the executive officer subservient to Congress and, in effect, allow Congress to execute the laws. As a result, the statute was unconstitutional. Affirmed.

CONCURRENCE: (Stevens, J.) The Comptroller has long been considered subservient to Congress.

DISSENT: (White, J.) The application of separation of powers in this manner interferes with the mutual workings of the legislative and executive branches.

DISSENT: (Blackmun, J.) The "removal authority" provision is unconstitutional, and it should be severed from the rest of the statute, which should remain in force because it is constitutional.

▌ ANALYSIS

The Comptroller performs many functions which identify the office more closely with Congress than with the executive branch. The office settles all claims against the government and determines all accounts owed or owing. Despite this, the office was created under the executive branch.

◼︎▬◼︎

Quicknotes

EXECUTIVE BRANCH The branch of government responsible for the administration of the laws.

IMPEACHMENT The discrediting of a witness by offering evidence to show that the witness lacks credibility.

LEGISLATIVE BRANCH The branch of government charged with the promulgation of laws.

SEPARATION OF POWERS The system of checks and balances preventing one branch of government from infringing upon exercising the powers of another branch of government.

◼︎▬◼︎

Crowell v. Benson

Deputy Commissioner (D) v. Employer (P)

285 U.S. 22 (1932).

NATURE OF CASE: Appeal from an order restraining enforcement of an employee's injury award.

FACT SUMMARY: Benson (P) sued to enjoin enforcement of a worker's compensation award made by Crowell (D), a deputy commissioner of the United States Employee's Compensation Commission, contending the enabling Act was unconstitutional in that it vested adjudicatory power in an administrative agency.

RULE OF LAW

Congress may not substitute an administrative agency for constitutional courts for final determination of the existence of facts upon which enforcement of the constitutional rights of a citizen depend.

FACTS: Crowell (D), a deputy commissioner of the United States Employee's Compensation Commission (the Commission), found that Knudsen had been injured while in the employ of Benson (P) and performing a service upon the navigable waters of the United States. These findings of fact were necessary for the case to come under the Commission's jurisdiction under the Longshoremen's and Harbor Workers' Compensation Act (the Act). On the basis of these findings, Crowell (D) made an award to Knudsen. Benson (P) sued to enjoin enforcement of the award on the basis that the Act was unconstitutional in that it vested final adjudicatory power over constitutional rights in an administrative agency rather than a constitutional court. The district court denied Crowell's (D) motion to dismiss and, on an independent finding that Knudsen was not in Benson's (P) employ, restrained enforcement of the award. The court of appeals affirmed, and the United States Supreme Court took jurisdiction.

ISSUE: May Congress substitute an administrative agency for a constitutional court for final determination of the existence of facts upon which enforcement of a citizen's constitutional rights depend?

HOLDING AND DECISION: (Hughes, C.J.) No. Congress may not substitute an administrative agency for a constitutional court for the final determination of the existence of the facts upon which enforcement of the constitutional rights of a citizen depend. The judicial power of the United States is vested in the courts, established under the Constitution. Where, as in this case, a suit is brought to enforce constitutional rights, the judicial power must extend to all questions, both of law and of fact. Therefore, the jurisdictional questions of fact—whether Knudsen was employed by Benson (P), and whether he was performing a service on the navigable waters of the

United States—cannot be, even though purely factual in nature, completely within the power of the Commission to decide. If the Act were so interpreted, it would be invalid. However, the Act in question here allows an independent factual finding by the federal court on review and, therefore, is valid. Affirmed.

DISSENT: (Brandeis, J.) To require a federal court to conduct de novo hearings on findings of fact involving constitutional rights would be duplicative and unnecessary. Congress has the constitutional power to vest in an agency the power to collect and record evidence on factual issues, whether or not such issues are constitutional issues or jurisdictional issues. Further, denial of a right to a de novo trial on such issues is not subversive of the federal judicial power. Courts may take administrative findings as the basis for their decisions. This case should be reversed and remanded.

ANALYSIS

This case makes a distinction between adjudication of public and of private rights. It is argued that determinations of private rights cannot be completely withdrawn from constitutional courts. On the other hand, in *Federal Radio Comm. v. General Electric Co.*, 281 U.S. 464 (1923), the Supreme Court held that some issues of an administrative character, such as final authority to grant a broadcast license, could not be given to the courts for decision. These administrative issues had to be decided by an appropriate agency. Despite this distinction, courts have broadly interpreted their powers and discretion in interpreting enabling statutes.

Quicknotes

DE NOVO The review of a lower court decision by an appellate court, which is hearing the case as if it had not been previously heard and as if no judgment had been rendered.

JUDICIAL BRANCH The branch of government charged with the interpretation and application of the laws.

JURISDICTION The authority of a court to hear and declare judgment in respect to a particular matter.

QUESTION OF LAW An issue regarding the legal significance of a particular act or event, which is usually left to the judge to ascertain.

Note: There are no principal cases in Chapter 3 of the casebook.

CHAPTER 4

The Scope of Judicial Review

Quick Reference Rules of Law

NLRB v. Universal Camera Corp. (I)

Federal agency (P) v. Corporation (D)

179 F.2d 749 (2d Cir. 1950).

NATURE OF CASE: Appeal from an NLRB reinstatement order.

FACT SUMMARY: Universal Camera Corp. (D) contended that the court of appeals should closely scrutinize the National Labor Relations Board's (P) reversal of its examiner's findings of fact.

🏛 RULE OF LAW
A court of appeals is barred from considering the report of an examiner on questions of fact insofar as the report was rejected on review by the National Labor Relations Board.

FACTS: The National Labor Relations Board (NLRB) (P) reversed findings of fact made by its examiner, finding Universal Camera Corp. (Universal) (D) had dismissed a supervisory employee because of his adverse testimony at a representation hearing. Universal (D) defended against the NLRB's (P) petition to enforce its order of reinstatement contending the court of appeals should closely scrutinize the Board's (P) findings as unsupported by substantial evidence when viewed in conjunction with the examiners findings.

ISSUE: Is a court of appeals barred from considering the report of an examiner on questions of fact insofar as the report was rejected on review by the NLRB?

HOLDING AND DECISION: (Hand, C.J.) Yes. A court of appeals is barred from considering the report of an examiner on questions of fact insofar as the report was rejected on review by the NLRB (P). The Taft-Hartley Amendments to the National Labor Relations Act (NLRA) provide that findings shall be conclusive if supported by substantial evidence on the record taken as a whole. Findings of examiners are less immune from challenge by the NLRB (P) than are the findings of special masters from judicial review. As a result it can be concluded that a reviewing court must accept the Board's (P) findings of fact and must disregard findings of the examiner rejected by the Board. Because it is clear that the Board's (P) findings, when considered not in isolation but upon the record taken as a whole, are supported by substantial evidence, the order of reinstatement shall be enforced.

DISSENT: (Swan, J.) The NLRB has ignored evidence given by one side and given undue credence to the evidence of the other so as to render its conclusion arbitrary and contrary to law.

▶ ANALYSIS

This case is the court of appeal's determination of its scope of review of questions and findings of fact. Subsequently, the Supreme Court reversed the holding, stating that examiners' reports could not be ignored by a reviewing court. Subsequently, on remand, the court of appeals vacated its enforcement order.

■═■

Quicknotes

JUDICIAL REVIEW The authority of the courts to review decisions, actions or omissions committed by another agency or branch of government.

QUESTION OF FACT An issue relating to a factual assertion that is disputed at trial and left to the jury to resolve.

■═■

Universal Camera Corp. v. NLRB

Corporation (D) v. Federal agency (P)

340 U.S. 474 (1951).

NATURE OF CASE: Appeal from an order enforcing a reinstatement order.

FACT SUMMARY: The court of appeals held it was precluded from considering evidence in the record of a National Labor Relations Board (NLRB) (P) hearing which contradicted factual findings of the NLRB (P) which were supported by substantial evidence.

🏛 RULE OF LAW
A reviewing court may set aside factual findings of the National Labor Relations Board when such findings are found not to be supported by substantial evidence in the record viewed as a whole.

FACTS: The National Labor Relations Board (NLRB) (P) rejected the findings of its hearing examiner and determined that Universal Camera Corp. (Universal) (D) had discharged an employee in violation of the NLRA. In an action seeking enforcement of the NLRB's (P) order to reinstate the employee, the court of appeals held it was precluded from considering the examiner's report and that it was bound by the NLRB's (P) findings of fact because the findings were supported in the record; and issued an order enforcing the NLRB (P) order.

ISSUE: May a reviewing court set aside factual findings of the NLRB when such findings are found not to be supported by substantial evidence in the record viewed as a whole?

HOLDING AND DECISION: (Frankfurter, J.) Yes. A reviewing court may set aside factual findings of the NLRB when such findings are found not to be supported by substantial evidence in the record viewed as a whole. The report of an examiner is clearly part of the record, as is the complaint and any testimony taken. As a result, it must under the Taft-Hartley Act be considered when a court determines whether the NLRB's (P) factual findings are supported by substantial evidence. Because the Act requires the record be read as a whole, a reviewing court is not required to accept the NLRB (P) findings merely because some evidence exists in the record to support them. The court has a duty to weigh the record evidence, both supportive and contradictory of the NLRB (P) findings, and to determine if the findings are based on substantial evidence. Therefore, the court of appeals erred in holding it was bound by the NLRB (P) findings. Order vacated and case remanded.

▶ *ANALYSIS*

This case resolves an important question concerning the scope of judicial review over agency findings of fact. In *NLRB v. Universal Camera Corp. (I)*, 179 F.2d 749 (2d Cir. 1950), the court of appeals held that the extent of judicial review was to find any evidence in the record in support of the agency findings. This review promotes the argument that agencies are created to lend specialized expertise in areas where such is essential to just administration of law, and because of this expertise, its factual findings should be given great weight. The Court in this case provides that an examiner is also endowed with such expertise and his findings should be given some weight in agency findings.

■■■

Quicknotes

JUDICIAL REVIEW The authority of the courts to review decisions, actions or omissions committed by another agency or branch of government.

QUESTION OF FACT An issue relating to a factual assertion that is disputed at trial and left to the jury to resolve.

■■■

NLRB v. Universal Camera Corp. (II)

Federal agency (P) v. Corporation (D)

190 F.2d 429 (2d Cir. 1951).

NATURE OF CASE: Consideration on remand of a petition for an enforcement order for a NLRB reinstatement order.

FACT SUMMARY: After the National Labor Relations Board (NLRB) (P) rejected factual findings of its examiner and found Universal Camera Corp. (D) had improperly dismissed a supervisory employee for his adverse testimony in a representation hearing, in the enforcement action the court of appeals held itself bound by the NLRB's (P) findings to the exclusion of the examiner's report.

🏛 **RULE OF LAW**
A court of appeals may not completely disregard an examiner's report which has been rejected by the National Labor Relations Board in its findings of fact without inquiring into whether the report was overruled based on a very substantial preponderance in the record.

FACTS: The National Labor Relations Board (NLRB) (P) rejected the factual findings of its examiner and found that Chairman, a supervisory employee, had been discharged by Universal Camera Corp. (Universal) (D) for his testimony adverse to Universal (D) at a representation hearing. The NLRB (P) petitioned the Second Circuit Court of Appeals for an order enforcing its reinstatement order. The court of appeals held itself bound to accept the Board's (P) findings and to disregard those of the examiner. The United States Supreme Court vacated the enforcement order and remanded the case to the court of appeals with instructions to consider the examiner's report in its determination.

ISSUE: May a court of appeals completely disregard an examiner's report which has been rejected by the NLRB (P) in its findings of fact without inquiring into whether the report was overruled based on a very substantial preponderance in the record?

HOLDING AND DECISION: (Hand, J.) No. A court of appeals may not completely disregard an examiner's report which has been rejected by the NLRB in its findings of fact without inquiring into whether the report was overruled based on a very substantial preponderance of evidence in the record. The Taft-Hartley Amendments (the Amendments) require some weight be given to the examiner's findings by the NLRB (P). It is impossible for a court to prescribe the quantum of such weight yet at the least they should not be disregarded unless the substituted findings have a very great preponderance of evidence

supporting them in the record. As no such preponderance is present in this case, the enforcement order is reversed and the complaint dismissed.

CONCURRENCE: (Frank, J.) The Amendments require evaluation of an examiner's findings, yet a reviewing court in such a case plays a different role from its role in reviewing trial court findings. Further, even where the findings are within the Board's (P) special area of expertise, a court cannot try the cases de novo.

▶ **ANALYSIS**

Some commentators articulate the necessity for judicial review of agency fact-finding in terms of ensuring limits on agency power. A free reign to find facts, vests in a body the power to manipulate statutes to such a degree as to effectively rewrite their purpose. Judicial review for substantiality of supporting evidence effectively limits agency administration.

■=■

Quicknotes

JUDICIAL REVIEW The authority of the courts to review decisions, actions or omissions committed by another agency or branch of government.

■=■

Allentown Mack Sales and Service v. National Labor Relations Board

Employer (P) v. Federal agency (D)

522 U.S. 359 (1998).

NATURE OF CASE: Appeal of a finding by the National Labor Relations Board (D) of unfair labor practices.

FACT SUMMARY: Allentown Mack Sales and Service (Allentown) (P) was accused by Local 724 of unfair labor practices. Local 724 filed a charge with the National Labor Relations Board (NLRB) (D), which found Allentown (P) guilty of unfair labor practices because it did not have a good-faith reasonable doubt about the extent of support for Local 724 among Allentown's (P) employees when it conducted a poll of employees. Allentown (P) appealed.

🏛 RULE OF LAW
Basing its actions on statements from a substantial portion of its employees provides a company with reasonable good-faith grounds for doubting the degree of union support; polls taken on that basis are valid.

FACTS: Mack Trucks, Inc. (Mack) employees were represented by Local 724. Mack sold its business, and several of its former managers formed Allentown Mack Sales and Service (Allentown) (P). Allentown (P) hired 32 of the original 45 Mack employees. During the period before and after the sale, many Mack employees made statements to the prospective owners of Allentown (P) suggesting that the incumbent union had lost support among employees. Allentown (P) rejected a request from Local 724 that it be recognized as the employee's collective bargaining representative, claiming a good-faith doubt as to the extent of the employees' support for the Union. Allentown (P) also conducted an independent poll by secret ballot of its hourly employees, using guidelines prescribed by the National Labor Relations Board (NLRB or "the Board") (D). The union lost 19 to 13, and it subsequently filed an unfair-labor practice charge with the NLRB (D). The Board adopted the Administrative Law Judge findings and held Allentown (P) guilty of an unfair labor practice in its conduct of the polling; the court reasoned that Allentown had not demonstrated that it held a reasonable doubt, based on objective considerations regarding Union support among a majority of the bargaining unit employees. The Court of Appeals for the District of Columbia Circuit found in favor of the NLRB (D). Allentown (P) appealed.

ISSUE: Is the NLRB's (D) standard for employer polling rational and consistent with the National Labor Relations Act, and are the Board's factual determinations in this case supported by substantial evidence in the record?

HOLDING AND DECISION: (Scalia, J.) The Board's "reasonable doubt" test for employer polls is facially rational and consistent with the National Labor Relations Act (the Act), but the Board's finding that Allentown (P) lacked such a doubt is not supported by substantial evidence on the record as a whole. A reasonable jury could have found that Allentown (P) had a good-faith reasonable doubt about whether Local 724 enjoyed the continuing support of a majority of employees. The employee statements contribute to a reasonable uncertainty about whether a majority in favor of the union existed. Seven of 32 employees, or 20 percent, made statements expressing nonsupport of the union. In addition, an eighth employee said that he paid $35 but was not represented. Furthermore, one additional employee stated that the entire night shift did not want the union. Another employee told Allentown (P) managers that if a vote were to be taken, the union would lose and that his feeling was that the employees did not want the union. Allentown (P), therefore, had reasonable, good-faith grounds to doubt the union's retention of majority support. Reversed.

CONCURRENCE AND DISSENT: (Rehnquist, C.J.) Concurrence as to everything except that the NLRB (D) standard is rational and consistent with the Act.

CONCURRENCE AND DISSENT: (Breyer, J.) The three additional employee statements shouldn't be taken into consideration because these statements were made when the employees were being interviewed by Allentown (P) managers for possible future employment and are therefore tainted, as it is likely that a job applicant will say whatever he believes the prospective employer wants to hear. In addition, employer statements purporting to represent the views of other employees are to be viewed with suspicion and caution.

▶ ANALYSIS

In this case, the Court decided to be overly inclusive, rather than under-inclusive, in the type of evidence it chose to consider in evaluating the claims.

■==■

Quicknotes

GOOD FAITH An honest intention to abstain from taking advantage of another.

■==■

Zhen Li Iao v. Gonzales

Foreign national (P) v. Attorney General (D)

400 F.3d 530 (7th Cir. 2005).

NATURE OF CASE: Petition to review administrative order to deport an asylum-seeker from the United States.

FACT SUMMARY: A Chinese citizen who practiced Falun Gong fled her home in China and sought asylum in the United States. An administrative judge denied her application for asylum because, he concluded, she did not have a well-founded fear of persecution.

RULE OF LAW
A foreign national who applies for asylum in the United States is entitled to a rational analysis of the evidence that supports the application for asylum.

FACTS: While she still lived in China, Zhen Li Iao (P), a Chinese citizen, began to practice Falun Gong, which seeks spiritual self-perfection through physical exercises. Falun Gong was prohibited by the Chinese government in 1999. Local officials in China tried to persuade Li (P) to stop practicing Falun Gong. Several times the police visited her parents' home where she lived, but she was never there when they arrived. Eventually the police delivered a summons at her parents' home in China ordering her to appear for an interview, but she did not obey the order. She left China, arriving in the United States in 2000. Her testimony on such matters at her asylum hearing was corroborated by letters from China from her mother and the man who had introduced her to Falun Gong in China. She exhibited much less than a strict academic expertise on several features of Falun Gong, but she was quite familiar with the exercises that are the heart of Falun Gong practice. After a hearing, the immigration judge ordered that Li (P) be deported from the United States because, in his assessment of the evidence, she did not face a reasonable fear of being persecuted if she returned to China. Li (P) petitioned for review of that order.

ISSUE: Is a foreign national who applies for asylum in the United States entitled to a rational analysis of the evidence that supports the application for asylum?

HOLDING AND DECISION: (Posner, J.) Yes. A foreign national who applies for asylum in the United States is entitled to a rational analysis of the evidence that supports the application for asylum. In this case, Li (P) did not receive the rational analysis to which she was entitled. The immigration judge incorrectly decided that Li (P) had not been persecuted in China—but Li (P) herself never claimed to have been persecuted, and the issue thus was not before the immigration judge. Further, the immigration judge simply misread the record when he discredited Li's (P) evidence based on her brother's failure to attest that Li (P) was a follower of Falun Gong: her brother is not a follower of Falun Gong, and his silence thus deserves no particular weight. The immigration judge also wrongly attributed too much weight to Li's (P) lack of academic expertise about Falun Gong, to inconsistencies in her testimony that are readily attributable to the vagueness inherent in the process of translations between Chinese and English, and to Li's (P) alleged failure to testify that she "hid" from the Chinese police (another alleged problem readily explained by the translation process). The immigration judge's order therefore is not truly reasoned and, accordingly, Li (P) did not receive the administrative process to which she is entitled. Petition for review granted, deportation order vacated, case remanded.

ANALYSIS

At a minimum, Judge Posner's opinion in *Zhen Li Iao*—which was a unanimous decision by the three-judge panel—skirts a very fine line between appropriate appellate review and simply reweighing the evidence to reach different findings of fact than those determined by the trier of fact who personally heard the testimony and was in the presumptively best position to assess credibility and related intangible fact-issues. Typically, it is the trier of fact who should decide whether "the inconsistencies were trivial." At the same time, the manifestly wrong findings and conclusions by the immigration judge here (on Li's (P) lack of persecution in China, on her brother's supposed failure to vouch for her practice of Falun Gong) substantially undercut the immigration judge's own credibility. But despite Judge Posner's disavowal of deciding the merits of Li's (P) application ("We do not decide that Li is entitled to asylum"), how much room does the immigration service actually have now to deny Li's (P) application?

Quicknotes

ASYLUM A place of protection or refuge.

JUDICIAL REVIEW The authority of the courts to review decisions, actions or omissions committed by another agency or branch of government.

Smyth v. Ames

Railroad (P) v. State legislature (D)

169 U.S. 466 (1898).

NATURE OF CASE: Appeal of a decision holding a rate order unconstitutional.

FACT SUMMARY: The Nebraska legislature set a maximum rate on railroads operating within the state which precluded the railroads from recovering their operating expenses.

🏛 RULE OF LAW
The fixing of rates must be based on the fair value of the property being used by a corporation for the public convenience to ensure the corporation receives just compensation for its services.

FACTS: Certain railroads operating in Nebraska challenged the constitutionality of a maximum rate set by the Nebraska legislature. The rate was 29.5 percent less than previously allowed and did not cover the railroads' operating expenses, not to mention providing any profit. The lower court held the rate was an unconstitutional deprivation of property without due process of law. The United States Supreme Court took jurisdiction.

ISSUE: Must the fixing of rates be based on the fair value of the property being used by a corporation for the public convenience in order to ensure the corporation receives just compensation for its services?

HOLDING AND DECISION: (Harlan, J.) Yes. The fixing of rates must be based on the fair value of the property being used by a corporation for the public convenience to ensure the corporation receives just compensation for its services. In fixing rates, a legislature must ensure just compensation to the company subject to the rates. A failure to do so constitutes a deprivation of property without due process of law. Such rates must be based on the fair value of the property being used by the company for the public convenience. This value must take into account the original cost of construction, the earning capacity of the property, the sum required to meet operating expenses and other factors relevant under the circumstances. In this case the rate set was too low to even cover operating expenses. Therefore, it was not just and reasonable and cannot be upheld. Affirmed.

▶ ANALYSIS

This case illustrates the high profile position assumed by courts in attempting to oversee administrative rate setting in the first half of the century. As years went by, this active role became less and less evident and today some commentators have argued that courts have simply abandoned any efforts to control ratemaking.

■■■

Quicknotes

TAKING A governmental action that substantially deprives an owner of the use and enjoyment of his or her property, requiring compensation.

UNCONSTITUTIONAL DUE PROCESS A violation of the constitutional mandate requiring the courts to protect and enforce individuals' rights and liberties consistent with prevailing principles of fairness and justice and prohibiting the federal and state governments from such activities that deprive its citizens of a life, liberty or property interest.

■■■

FPC v. Hope Natural Gas Co.

Regulatory agency (P) v. Gas company (D)

320 U.S. 591 (1944).

NATURE OF CASE: [The nature of case is not stated in the casebook excerpt.]

FACT SUMMARY: [The facts are not stated in the casebook excerpt.]

🏛 RULE OF LAW
A rate order that is not unjust or unreasonable in effect is not subject to judicial review even if the method used to set the rate contains some infirmities.

FACTS: [The facts are not stated in the casebook excerpt.]

ISSUE: Is a rate order that is not unjust or unreasonable in effect subject to judicial review even if the method used to set the rate contains some infirmities?

HOLDING AND DECISION: (Douglas, J.) No. A rate order that is not unjust or unreasonable in effect is not subject to judicial review even if the method used to set the rate contains some infirmities. Under the National Gas Act, the rate order issued by the Federal Power Commission (FPC) is to be judged for fairness and reasonableness in result not necessarily on the reasonableness of the method employed in setting the rate. Merely because the value of the property is reduced does not render the rate order invalid. Only where the order is found to be unjust and unreasonable taken as a whole in its effect will it be invalid.

▌ ANALYSIS

This case illustrates the constitutional requirements of ratemaking orders under the Natural Gas Act. This requirement demands no particular formula be observed, only that the effect or result of the order be just and reasonable. It is observed that in formulating this approach the Court stated that the congressional power to regulate commodities in interstate commerce is at least as great under the Fifth Amendment as is that of the states under the Fourteenth Amendment to regulate interstate commerce.

■══■

Quicknotes

COMMERCE CLAUSE Article 1, section 8, clause 3 of the United States Constitution, granting Congress the power to regulate commerce with foreign countries and between the states.

FIFTH AMENDMENT Provides that no person shall be compelled to serve as a witness against himself, or be subject to trial for the same offense twice, or be deprived of life, liberty, or property without due process of law.

FOURTEENTH AMENDMENT Declares that no state shall make or enforce any law which shall abridge the privileges and immunities of citizens of the United States.

JUDICIAL REVIEW The authority of the courts to review decisions, actions or omissions committed by another agency or branch of government.

■══■

United States v. Fifty-Three Eclectus Parrots

Federal government (P) v. Parrot breeder (D)

685 F.2d 1131 (9th Cir. 1982).

NATURE OF CASE: Appeal from summary judgment ordering forfeiture.

FACT SUMMARY: Allen (D) appealed from a summary judgment ordering the forfeiture of 53 eclectus parrots to Customs (P).

🏛 RULE OF LAW
Under 19 U.S.C. § 1527 (1976), the definition of "wild bird" extends to any foreign bird whose species is normally found in a wild state if the country of origin protects the species.

FACTS: Allen (D) was in the business of raising and trading birds. He bought eclectus parrots that had originated in Indonesia from a dealer in Singapore and imported them. Neither Allen (D) nor Customs (P) was aware of Indonesian law prohibiting the export of eclectus parrots. Pursuant to 19 U.S.C. § 1527 (1976), which provided that if the laws of any country prohibited the exportation of any wild bird, any such bird imported in violation of such laws would be subject to seizure and forfeiture, Customs (P) sought the seizure and forfeiture of the parrots. From a summary judgment in favor of Customs (P), Allen (D) appealed.

ISSUE: Under 19 U.S.C. § 1527 (1976), does the definition of "wild bird" extend to any foreign bird whose species is normally found in a wild state if the country of origin protects the species?

HOLDING AND DECISION: (Canby, J.) Yes. Under 19 U.S.C. § 1527 (1976), the definition of "wild bird" extends to any foreign bird whose species is normally found in a wild state if the country of origin protects the species. This is Customs' (P) construction of the statute. [The court first ruled that Allen (D) could still be liable under the statute for an innocent mistake, and rejected his argument that Customs (P) had a duty to inform Allen (D) of Indonesian law.] Allen (D) contended that under § 1527, his parrots were not wild, since there had been some success in breeding them in captivity, and the parrots in question showed signs of having been so bred. Customs' (P) construction of the statute is the better one, since the inquiry is directed at the species, and any contrary interpretation would create significant enforcement problems. Indonesian law clearly protects the parrots, and Allen (D) made no showing that the species is no longer found in a wild state. There was no genuine issue of material fact, and Customs (P) was entitled to summary judgment. Affirmed.

▶ ANALYSIS

Even though Allen (D) raised questions of fact as to the specific birds imported, the court in the present case adopted Customs' (P) definition as a matter of law. Since that definition was species-directed, Allen's (D) considerations were effectively nullified. The court may have in the present case deferred to Customs' (P) interpretation, given its increased familiarity with the operating realities of customs enforcement.

Quicknotes

QUESTION OF FACT An issue relating to a factual assertion that is disputed at trial and left to the jury to resolve.

MATERIAL FACT A fact without the existence of which a contract would not have been entered.

FORFEITURE The loss of a right or interest as a penalty for failing to fulfill an obligation.

SUMMARY JUDGMENT Judgment rendered by a court in response to a motion by one of the parties, claiming that the lack of a question of material fact in respect to an issue warrants disposition of the issue without consideration by the jury.

NLRB v. Hearst Publications

Federal agency (P) v. News publisher (D)

322 U.S. 111 (1944).

NATURE OF CASE: Appeal of an NLRB bargaining order.

FACT SUMMARY: The National Labor Relations Board (P) found that newsboys selling Hearst Publications (Hearst) (D) newspapers were employees under the National Labor Relations Act and therefore Hearst (D) was ordered to engage in collective bargaining with their representative.

⚖ RULE OF LAW
A reviewing court must accept an agency's application of a broad statutory term if such application is supported in the record and has a reasonable basis in law.

FACTS: Several Hearst Publications (Hearst) (D) newspapers were distributed in Los Angeles through vendors, called newsboys. The price at which the newsboys bought the papers from Hearst (D) and the price they could charge the public were set by Hearst (D). The location, conditions, and hours within which the papers could be sold were determined either expressly or implicitly by Hearst (D). The newsboys organized to bargain collectively, claiming they were "employees" under the National Labor Relations Act (NLRA). Hearst (D) refused to bargain, contending the newsboys were independent contractors and therefore not protected by the NLRA. The National Labor Relations Board (NLRB) (P) concluded the newsboys were employees and ordered Hearst (D) to bargain. The court of appeals made an independent evaluation of the record and found the newsboys were independent contractors. The NLRB (P) appealed, and the United States Supreme Court granted certiorari.

ISSUE: Must a reviewing court accept an agency's application of a broad statutory term if such application is supported in the record and has a reasonable basis in law?

HOLDING AND DECISION: (Rutledge, J.) Yes. A reviewing court must accept an agency's application of a broad statutory term if such application is supported in the record and has a reasonable basis in the law. Congress has vested the duty of administering the NLRA in the NLRB (P). The NLRB's (P) experience in dealing with labor matters makes it a logical choice to determine the application of broad statutory terms within the context of national labor policy. Therefore, the NLRB's (P) application of the term "employee" within the present context must be upheld if supported in the record and if reasonably based in law. The measure of control over the newsboy's activities exercised by Hearst (D) is sufficient evidence for the NLRB

(P) to conclude the existence of an employer-employee relationship under recognized legal principles. Therefore, the court of appeals improperly substituted its own application of the term. Reversed.

▶ ANALYSIS

In *Gary v. Powell*, 314 U.S. 402 (1941), the Court laid the foundation for *Hearst*. It held that where a term's definition is delegated to an agency, the development of the definition will be upheld in respect of the delegation. After the *Hearst* decision, Congress amended the NLRA to exclude persons having a common-law independent contractor status. In *Hearst*, the court of appeals holding of independent contractor status was based on common-law interpretations, while the NLRB's determination of employee status was a modification of the common-law idea of independent contractor status as equivalent to employee status under the NLRA.

***

Quicknotes

DELEGATION The authorization of one person to act on another's behalf.

INDEPENDENT CONTRACTOR A party undertaking a particular assignment for another who retains control over the manner in which it is executed.

QUESTION OF FACT An issue relating to a factual assertion that is disputed at trial and left to the jury to resolve.

QUESTION OF LAW An issue regarding the legal significance of a particular act or event, which is usually left to the judge to ascertain.

***

Skidmore v. Swift & Co.

Employees (P) v. Employer (D)

323 U.S. 134 (1944).

NATURE OF CASE: Suit to recover overtime wages allegedly due.

FACT SUMMARY: Skidmore (P) and other employees (P) of Swift & Co. (D) sued to recover overtime pay for time spent waiting for fires to occur.

🏛 RULE OF LAW

In resolving a controversy which no agency has been authorized to adjudicate, the courts may consider the reports and opinions of an administrator whose duty it is to seek injunctive relief from violations of the laws involved in the controversy.

FACTS: Skidmore (P) and six other employees (P) of Swift & Co. (D) sued to recover overtime pay for time spent on company (D) premises waiting to respond to fire alarms. The only duties imposed upon the employees (P) were those of remaining within hearing distance of the alarms and responding to alarms and actual fires. The employees (P) were permitted to occupy reasonably comfortable quarters which included recreational facilities, and were allowed to engage in any activities, including eating and sleeping. They (P) received no pay for the time spent waiting and listening, but were compensated for each occasion on which they (P) actually responded to a fire or an alarm. By their suit, they (P) sought compensation for time spent waiting as well. The company (D) argued that the hours thus spent did not constitute "working time" within the meaning of the Fair Labor Standards Act. The lower court denied the employees' (P) claim, relying upon an administrative bulletin which expressed the opinion that time spent waiting did not constitute time worked.

ISSUE: May courts, in determining controversies not committed to the jurisdiction of any agency, take account of reports, recommendations and opinions of administrators?

HOLDING AND DECISION: (Jackson, J.) Yes. In determining controversies such as the present one, which no agency has been given the authority to resolve, the court may take account of opinions and recommendations of administrators. Congress has, in fact, appointed a special Administrator whose duty it is to inform of matters pertaining to industries subject to the Fair Labor Standards Act (the Act). The Administrator is also empowered to bring injunctive relief against violators of the Act. He possesses considerable knowledge and expertise, much of which is reflected in the interpretive bulletins and informal rulings which he issues. His expressions, while not binding on the court, are entitled to an amount of respect commensurate with their thoughtfulness, thoroughness, and internal consistency. In the present case, the court below seems to have accorded proper weight to the opinions of the Administrator that all on-the-job time is compensable except those periods spent eating and sleeping. However, that court's interpretations were colored by its mistaken legal conclusion that waiting time will never be "working time." The case must, therefore, be remanded for reconsideration of the evidence and the Administrator's opinions, this time viewed in light of the conclusion that time spent waiting may also be determined to be "working time." Reversed.

▶ *ANALYSIS*

Skidmore v. Swift & Co. is significant for its expression of the proposition that courts may rely upon interpretive rules promulgated by agencies. Rules of this type do not have the force of law, and the courts are, in fact, free to ignore them. However, interpretive rules typically are accorded some deference, and are more likely to be relied upon when the problems with which the court must grapple are uncomfortably complex. In evaluating the authority of interpretive rules, courts are likely to be influenced by (1) the formality and public participation involved in their promulgation, (2) the sophistication and expertise of the agency involved, (3) the consistency with which the interpretive rules have been maintained, (4) whether Congress has reenacted the applicable enabling statute with knowledge of the interpretive rules promulgated pursuant to it, and (5) the period of time which elapsed between passage of the enabling statute and the adoption of the interpretive rules. Note that the *Skidmore* court expressly adverted to several of these factors.

■━■

Quicknotes

INJUNCTIVE RELIEF A court order issued as a remedy, requiring a person to do, or prohibiting that person from doing, a specific act.

JURISDICTION The authority of a court to hear and declare judgment in respect to a particular matter.

RULEMAKING The promulgation of a rule by an administrative agency, acting within the scope of its power pursuant to statute, enacting a rule governing a particular activity.

■━■

Chevron U.S.A., Inc. v. Natural Resources Defense Council

Petroleum company (D) v. Environmental concern (P)

467 U.S. 837 (1984).

NATURE OF CASE: Appeal from order interpreting a statute.

FACT SUMMARY: The court of appeals held that the Environmental Protection Agency could not impose its own definition of stationary source in interpreting pollution standards under the Clean Air Act.

🏛 RULE OF LAW
In the absence of clear congressional intent, courts must accept the reasonable interpretations of administrative statutes given by the agency it governs.

FACTS: Congress amended the Clean Air Act, which required states to develop air pollution plans requiring permits for construction and operation of stationary sources of pollution. No definition of stationary sources appeared in the statute, yet the Environmental Protection Agency (EPA) interpreted the term as allowing states to consider an entire plant a stationary source, even if it contained different kinds of pollution emitting sources. This allowed the development of individual sources in a plant without triggering the amendments. The Natural Resources Defense Council (P) contended that Chevron U.S.A., Inc. (D) violated the statute. The EPA, applying its definition, rejected the complaint. The district court affirmed, yet the court of appeals held that the EPA could not use this definition. Chevron (D) appealed.

ISSUE: Must courts use the reasonable interpretation of a statute given by an agency in the absence of clear congressional intent?

HOLDING AND DECISION: (Stevens, J.) Yes. In the absence of clear congressional intent, courts must accept the reasonable interpretation of administrative statutes given by the agency. Courts may not fashion their own interpretation of the statute which encroaches upon the rulemaking power of the agency. The agency promulgates enacting regulations based upon its expertise in the area. These regulations arise out of an interpretation of the statute. Unless the regulations are arbitrary, capricious, or manifestly contrary to the statute, they must be upheld. In this case, the regulations were proper, and the interpretation must be upheld. Reversed.

▶ ANALYSIS

Chevron has become one of the most-cited cases of all time. At its heart is the following logic: legislation is enacted after congressional hearings are held; testimony from experts is considered in drafting the legislation; administrative agencies charged with the enforcement of the legislation play a large part in the prelegislation process; thus, their expertise in interpreting the statute is necessary where Congress fails to specify its intent.

■■■

Quicknotes

CONGRESSIONAL INTENT Congress's motivation or rationale for promulgating a statute.

RULEMAKING The promulgation of a rule by an administrative agency, acting within the scope of its power pursuant to statute, enacting a rule governing a particular activity.

■■■

United States v. Mead Corporation

Federal government (P) v. Importer (D)

533 U.S. 218 (2001).

NATURE OF CASE: Appeal in a tariff assessment action.

FACT SUMMARY: Mead Corporation (P) was assessed a tariff on its day planners, and it protested to Customs. Customs issued a ruling letter explaining why Mead (P) was assessed a tariff.

🏛 RULE OF LAW
Classification rulings, which do not require deference under *Chevron*, are eligible to claim respect according to their persuasiveness under *Skidmore*.

FACTS: Mead Corporation (D) imports "day planners." The tariff schedule in regard to day planners is regulated by the Harmonized Tariff Schedule of the U.S. (the Schedule), which subjects day planners to a tariff of 4.0 percent. Until 1993, when Customs issued a Headquarters ruling letter classifying Mead's day planners as "Diaries . . . bound," day planners had been duty-free. In response to Mead's protest of the reclassification, Custom's Headquarters issued a new letter, never published, and discussed the two definitions of diary from the dictionary; it concluded that the definition reflects commercial usage. As for the definition of "bound," Custom's Headquarters concluded that "bound" meant "reinforcements or fittings of metal, plastics, etc." In the Schedule, Congress had conferred upon Customs the power to issue regulations to establish procedures for the issuance of binding rulings prior to the entry of the merchandise concerned and to disseminate information necessary to secure uniformity. A ruling letter represents the official position of the Customs Service with respect to a particular transaction or issue described therein. Since ruling letters respond to transactions of the moment, they are not subject to notice and comment before being issued, and although they may be published, they need only be made available for public inspection. In addition, the ruling has no bearing on nonparties to the transaction at issue. Forty-six different Customs offices issue 10,000 to 15,000 ruling letters per year. The court of appeals ruled that Customs ruling letters do not fall within *Chevron*.

ISSUE: Are classification rulings, which do not require deference under *Chevron*, eligible to claim respect according to their persuasiveness under *Skidmore*?

HOLDING AND DECISION: (Souter, J.) Yes. Classification rulings, which do not require deference under *Chevron*, 467 U.S. 837 (1984), are eligible to claim respect according to their persuasiveness under *Skidmore*, 323 U.S. 134 (1944). A tariff classification has no claim to judicial deference under *Chevron* because there is no indication that Congress intended such a ruling to carry the force of law; under *Skidmore*, however, the ruling is eligible to claim respect according to its persuasiveness. On the face of the statute, there is no Congressional intent to give Custom's classification rulings the force of law. In addition, there is in the agency's practice no indication that Customs ever set out with a lawmaking pretense in mind when it undertook to make such classifications. Moreover, the amendments to the statute don't reveal any new congressional objective of treating classification decisions generally as rulemaking with force of law. Furthermore, the authorization for classification rulings, and Custom's practice in making them, present a case far removed not only from the notice-and-comment process but from any other circumstances reasonably suggesting that Congress ever thought of classification rulings as deserving the deference claimed for them here. The Custom ruling at issue here fails to qualify for deference under *Chevron*, although the possibility that it deserves some deference under *Skidmore* means the case is to be vacated and remanded. Remanded.

DISSENT: (Scalia, J.) Established jurisprudence states that a reasonable agency application of an ambiguous statutory provision should be sustained, because Congress gives the agency discretion as to how to resolve the ambiguity, so long as it represents the agency's authoritative interpretation. In this case, therefore, deference should be given to the interpretation the Customs Service has given to the statute it is charged with enforcing, and the judgment of the court of appeals should be reversed. The majority opinion states that this ambiguity, however, is to be resolved by the courts and not the agencies; therefore, the practical effect of the majority's rule is confusion, an increase in informal rulemaking, and the exclusion of large portions of statutory law. The weight it gives to *Skidmore*, which is a statement of the obvious—"A judge should take into account the well-considered views of expert observers"—will lead to uncertainty.

▶ ANALYSIS

This case demonstrates that the majority of the Court didn't want to take an all-or-nothing approach in deferring to administrative agencies but preferred to support a variety of forms for such deference.

■■■

Quicknotes

RULEMAKING The promulgation of a rule governing a particular activity by an administrative agency, acting within the scope of its power pursuant to statute.

■■■

Gonzales v. Oregon

U.S. Attorney General (D) v. State (P)

546 U.S. 243 (2006).

NATURE OF CASE: Appeal in action challenging the U.S. Attorney General's (D) Interpretive Rule that made illegal under federal law the prescription of drugs for physician-assisted suicide, which was lawful under state law. [The procedural posture of the case is not presented in the casebook excerpt.]

FACT SUMMARY: Oregon (P) challenged the U.S. Attorney General's (D) Interpretive Rule that made illegal under federal law the prescription of drugs for physician-assisted suicide, which was lawful under Oregon law, asserting that he was not authorized to make a rule declaring illegitimate a medical standard for care and treatment of patients that was specifically authorized under state law.

🏛 RULE OF LAW
The Controlled Substances Act does not allow the Attorney General to prohibit doctors from prescribing regulated drugs for use in physician-assisted suicide under state law permitting the procedure.

FACTS: The Oregon Death With Dignity Act (ODWDA) exempts from civil or criminal liability state-licensed physicians who, in compliance with ODWDA's specific safeguards, dispense or prescribe a lethal dose of drugs upon the request of a terminally ill patient. The Attorney General (D) issued an Interpretive Rule to address the implementation and enforcement of the Controlled Substances Act (CSA) or (Act) with respect to ODWDA, declaring that using controlled substances to assist suicide is not a legitimate medical practice and that dispensing or prescribing them for this purpose is unlawful under the CSA. The Act, which was enacted with the main objectives of combating drug abuse and controlling legitimate and illegitimate traffic in controlled substances, criminalizes, inter alia, the unauthorized distribution and dispensation of substances classified in any of its five schedules. The Attorney General (D) may add, remove, or reschedule substances only after making particular findings, and on scientific and medical matters, he must accept the findings of the Secretary of Health and Human Services (Secretary). These proceedings must be on the record after an opportunity for comment. The dispute here involves controlled substances listed in Schedule II, which are generally available only by written prescription. A 1971 regulation promulgated by the Attorney General (D) requires that such prescriptions be used "for a legitimate medical purpose by an individual practitioner acting in the usual course of his professional practice." To prevent diversion of controlled substances, the CSA regulates the activity of

physicians, who must register in accordance with rules and regulations promulgated by the Attorney General (D). He may deny, suspend, or revoke a registration that would be "inconsistent with the public interest." In determining consistency with the public interest, he must consider five factors, including the State's recommendation, compliance with state, federal, and local law regarding controlled substances, and "public health and safety." The CSA explicitly contemplates a role for the States in regulating controlled substances. Oregon (P) challenged the Interpretive Rule as exceeding the Attorney General's (D) authority. The United States Supreme Court granted certiorari. [The procedural posture of the case is not presented in the casebook excerpt.]

ISSUE: Does the Controlled Substances Act allow the Attorney General to prohibit doctors from prescribing regulated drugs for use in physician-assisted suicide under state law permitting the procedure?

HOLDING AND DECISION: (Kennedy, J.) No. The Controlled Substances Act does not allow the Attorney General to prohibit doctors from prescribing regulated drugs for use in physician-assisted suicide under state law permitting the procedure. The Interpretive Rule is also not entitled to *Chevron* deference (*Chevron U.S.A., Inc. v. Natural Resources Defense Council*, 467 U.S. 837 (1984)). The statutory phrase "legitimate medical purpose" is ambiguous in the relevant sense. However, *Chevron* deference is not accorded merely because the statute is ambiguous and an administrative official is involved. A rule must be promulgated pursuant to authority Congress has delegated to the official. The specific respects in which the Attorney General (D) is authorized to make rules under the CSA show that he is not authorized to make a rule declaring illegitimate a medical standard for patient care and treatment specifically authorized under state law. Congress delegated to the Attorney General (D) only the authority to promulgate rules relating to "registration" and "control" of the dispensing of controlled substances, and "for the efficient execution of his functions." Control means "to add a . . . substance . . . to a schedule," following specified procedures. Because the Interpretive Rule does not concern scheduling of substances and was not issued under the required procedures, it cannot fall under the Attorney General's (D) control authority. Even if "control" were understood to signify something other than its statutory definition, it could not support the Interpretive Rule. Nor can the Interpretive Rule be justified under the CSA's registration provisions. It does not undertake the Act's

Continued on next page.

five-factor analysis for determining when registration is "inconsistent with the public interest," and it deals with much more than registration. It purports to declare that using controlled substances for physician-assisted suicide is a crime, an authority going well beyond the Attorney General's (D) statutory power to register or deregister physicians. It would be anomalous for Congress to have painstakingly described the Attorney General's (D) limited authority to deregister a single physician or schedule a single drug, but to have given him, just by implication, authority to declare an entire class of activity outside the course of professional practice and therefore a criminal violation of the CSA. The claim that the Attorney General's (D) decision is a legal, not medical, one does not suffice, for the Interpretive Rule places extensive reliance on medical judgments and views of the medical community in concluding that assisted suicide is not a legitimate medical purpose. This confirms that the authority claimed by the Attorney General (D) is both beyond his expertise and incongruous with the statutory purposes and design. The idea that Congress gave him such broad and unusual authority through an implicit delegation is not sustainable. For these reasons, the Interpretive Rule was not promulgated pursuant to the Attorney General's authority, and, therefore, its interpretation of "legitimate medical purpose" does not receive *Chevron* deference. Instead, it receives deference only in accordance with *Skidmore v. Swift & Co.,* 323 U.S. 134 (1944), under which the Court follows an agency's rule only to the extent it is persuasive. However, even under *Skidmore,* the Attorney General's (D) opinion is unpersuasive, especially in light of his lack of expertise in this area and the apparent absence of any consultation with anyone outside the Department of Justice who might aid in a reasoned judgment. The CSA and this Court's case law amply support the conclusion that Congress regulates medical practice insofar as it bars doctors from using their prescription-writing powers as a means to engage in illicit drug dealing and trafficking as conventionally understood. Beyond this, the Act manifests no intent to regulate the practice of medicine generally, which is understandable given federalism's structure and limitations. In the face of the CSA's silence on the practice of medicine generally and its recognition of state regulation of the medical profession, it is difficult to defend the Attorney General's (D) declaration that the statute impliedly criminalizes physician-assisted suicide. This difficulty is compounded by the CSA's consistent delegation of medical judgments to the Secretary and its otherwise careful allocation of powers for enforcing the limited objects of the CSA. Ultimately, the text and structure of the Act do not manifest Congress's intent that a single Executive officer has the power to effect a radical shift of authority from the States to the Federal Government to define general standards of medical practice in every locality. [The procedural posture of the case is not presented in the casebook excerpt.]

DISSENT: (Scalia, J.) The Interpretive Rule is entitled to *Chevron* deference. The Attorney General's (D)

interpretation of "legitimate medical purpose" is not only a valid interpretation of the Act, it is also the most natural reading thereof. This interpretation definitively establishes that a doctor's order authorizing the dispensation of a Schedule II substance for the purpose of assisting a suicide is not a "prescription" within the Act's meaning. From this, the Interpretive Rule's other conclusions follow, namely that it is illegal to prescribe such substances for such a purpose and that a physician who does so is acting counter to the public interest, thus subjecting that physician's registration to possible suspension or revocation. Even if no deference at all were due, the Interpretive Rule would nevertheless be entitled to be upheld, since the overwhelming weight of authority supports the notion that assisted suicide is not a "legitimate medical purpose;" "legitimate medicine" has simply not evolved so far. Moreover, even if the main purpose of the CSA is to curtail addiction and recreational drug abuse, there is no reason to believe that is its only purpose and that it does not sweep broadly enough to encompass the type of regulation provided for in the Interpretive Rule. Finally, the Attorney General's (D) power to issue regulations against questionable uses of controlled substances in no way alters "the fundamental details" of the CSA, and, therefore does not contravene precedent holding that Congress does not alter the fundamental details of a regulatory scheme in vague terms or ancillary provisions.

▶ *ANALYSIS*

Justice Thomas pointed out that the majority's conclusions that the CSA was merely concerned with fighting "drug abuse" and only insofar as that abuse led to "addiction or abnormal effects on the nervous system" was entirely inconsistent with the Court's broad conclusions, a few months earlier in *Gonzales v. Raich,* 545 U.S. 1 (2005), about the scope of the CSA as it pertained to the medicinal use of controlled substances such as medical marijuana. In *Raich,* the Court ruled that Congress may criminalize the production and use of home-grown marijuana even where states approve its use for medicinal purposes. This stark contrast illustrates how congressional intent, as perceived by the Court, may be fictitious and vary from case to case.

■═■

Quicknotes

CONTROLLED SUBSTANCE A drug whose medical distribution is regulated by the federal government; certain classifications are unlawful.

DEFERENCE Consideration of the decision or judgment of another.

INTERPRETIVE RULE A rule issued by an administrative agency for the purpose of explaining or interpreting a statute.

■═■

Long Island Care at Home, Ltd. v. Coke

Former employer (D) v. Former "companionship services" employee (P)

551 U.S. 158 (2007).

NATURE OF CASE: Appeal from reversal of Department of Labor regulation promulgated under the Fair Labor Standards Act in action for minimum wages and overtime wages. [The complete procedural posture of this case is not presented in the casebook excerpt.]

FACT SUMMARY: Coke (P) brought suit against her former employer, Long Island Care at Home, Ltd. (Long Island Care) (D), seeking minimum wages and overtime wages that she claimed were owed to her under the Fair Labor Standards Act (FLSA) for work she performed as a "companionship services" employee. The parties agreed that the FLSA required payment of those wages only if the Department of Labor's (DOL) "companionship services" exemption, contained in a DOL Interpretation (also referred to as a "third-party regulation"), did not apply to workers paid by third-party agencies such as Long Island Care (D), but only applied to workers hired directly by those to whom they provided the services or by their households. Coke (P) contended that the DOL's interpretation was not entitled to deference; that it fell outside the scope of Congress's delegation; that it was inconsistent with another, legally governing regulation; that was is an "interpretive" regulation not warranting judicial deference; and that it was improperly promulgated.

RULE OF LAW

An agency regulation is entitled to *Chevron* deference, where the regulation fills a statutory gap, the agency focuses fully and directly upon the issue and uses full notice-and-comment procedures, and the resulting rule falls within the statutory grant of authority and is reasonable.

FACTS: The Fair Labor Standards Amendments of 1974 exempted from the minimum wage and maximum hours rules of the Fair Labor Standards Act of 1938 (FLSA) persons "employed in domestic service employment to provide companionship services for individuals . . . unable to care for themselves." Under a Labor Department (DOL) regulation labeled an "Interpretation" (also referred to as a "third-party regulation"), the exemption included those "companionship" workers "employed by an . . . agency other than the family or household using their services." However, the DOL's "General Regulations" also defined the statutory term "domestic service employment" as "services of a household nature performed by an employee in or about a private home . . . of the person by whom he or she is employed." Coke (P), a "companionship services" provider to the elderly and infirm, sued her former employer, Long Island Care at Home, Ltd. (Long Island Care)

(D) seeking minimum and overtime wages allegedly owed her. The parties assumed the FLSA required payment of those wages only if its "companionship services" exemption did not apply to workers paid by third-party agencies such as Long Island Care (D). Coke (P) contended that the DOL's interpretation was not entitled to deference; that it fell outside the scope of Congress' delegation; that it was inconsistent with another, legally governing regulation; that was is an "interpretive" regulation not warranting judicial deference; and that it was improperly promulgated. The court of appeals agreed with Coke (P) and held that the interpretation was unenforceable. The United States Supreme Court granted certiorari.

ISSUE: Is an agency regulation entitled to *Chevron* deference, where the regulation fills a statutory gap, the agency focuses fully and directly upon the issue and uses full notice-and-comment procedures, and the resulting rule falls within the statutory grant of authority and is reasonable?

HOLDING AND DECISION: (Breyer, J.) Yes. An agency regulation is entitled to *Chevron* deference where the regulation fills a statutory gap, the agency focuses fully and directly upon the issue and uses full notice-and-comment procedures, and the resulting rule falls within the statutory grant of authority and is reasonable. An agency's power to administer a congressionally created program necessarily requires the making of rules to fill any "gap" left, implicitly or explicitly, by Congress. When an agency fills such a gap reasonably, and in accordance with other applicable (e.g., procedural) requirements, the result is legally binding. On its face, the DOL's interpretation seems to fill a statutory gap, and, therefore, on its face is entitled to *Chevron* deference, *Chevron U.S.A., Inc. v. Natural Resources Defense Council*, 467 U.S. 837 (1984). Coke's (P) various contentions asserting legal deficiencies with the interpretation must be rejected. First, the FLSA explicitly leaves gaps as to the scope and definition of its "domestic service employment" and "companionship services" terms, and empowers the DOL to fill these gaps through regulations. Whether to include workers paid by third parties is one of the details left to the DOL to work out. Although the pre-1974 FLSA already covered some third-party-paid companionship workers, e.g., those employed by large private enterprises, it did not then cover others, e.g., those employed directly by the aged person's family or by many smaller private agencies. Thus, whether, or how, the statutory definition should

Continued on next page.

apply to such workers raises a set of complex questions. For example, should the FLSA cover all of them, some of them, or none of them? How should the need for a simple, uniform application of the exemption be weighed against the fact that some (but not all) of the workers were previously covered? Given the DOL's expertise, satisfactory answers to the foregoing questions may well turn upon its thorough knowledge of the area and ability to consult at length with affected parties. It is therefore reasonable to infer that Congress intended its broad grant of definitional authority to the DOL to include the authority to answer such questions. Second, notwithstanding the apparent conflict between DOL's interpretation and the General Regulations, there is no reason to doubt the DOL's assertion that it intended its interpretation to represent its position. Third, the third-party regulation was not merely an interpretative regulation, meant not to fill a statutory "gap," but simply to describe the DOL's view of what the FLSA meant, and therefore not entitled to *Chevron* deference. For one thing, the regulation directly governs the conduct of members of the public, "affecting individual rights and obligations." When promulgating the regulation and when considering amending it, the DOL always employed full public notice-and-comment procedures, which under the Administrative Procedure Act (APA) need not be used when producing an "interpretive" rule, and, for the past 30 years, according to the Advisory Memorandum (and not disputed by respondent), the DOL has treated the regulation as a legally binding exercise of its rulemaking authority. For another thing, the DOL may have placed the third-party regulation in a subpart (Subpart B), entitled "Interpretations," rather than in a subpart (Subpart A), "General Regulations," because Subpart B contains matters of detail, interpreting and applying Subpart A's more general definitions. Indeed, Subpart B's other regulations—involving, for example, employer "credit[s]" against minimum wages for provision of "food," "lodging," and "dry cleaning"—strongly indicates that such details, not a direct interpretation of the statute's language, are at issue. Finally, the Court assumes Congress meant and expected courts to treat a regulation as within a delegation of "gap-filling" authority where, as here, the rule sets forth important individual rights and duties, the agency focuses fully and directly upon the issue and uses full notice-and-comment procedures, and the resulting rule falls within the statutory grant of authority and is reasonable. [The procedural result of this case is not presented in the casebook excerpt.]

▌ *ANALYSIS*

The unanimous Court also disagreed with Coke's (P) claim that the DOL's 1974 notice-and-comment proceedings were legally "defective" because the DOL's notice and explanation were inadequate. Initially, the DOL's proposed regulation would have placed outside the exemption (and hence left subject to FLSA wage and hour rules) individuals employed by the large enterprise third-party employers (such as Long Island Care (D)) covered before 1974. Coke (P) asserted that DOL's explanation for its departure from this proposed rule was deficient. However, the Court found that since that was simply a proposal, its presence meant that the DOL was considering the matter and might later choose to keep the proposal or to withdraw it, so it was reasonably foreseeable when the DOL finally withdrew it, resulting in a determination exempting all third-party-employed companionship workers from the FLSA. The Court also determined there was no significant legal problem with the DOL's explanation that its final interpretation was more consistent with FLSA language, as no one seemed to have objected to this explanation at the time, and it still remained a reasonable, albeit brief, explanation.

■■■

Quicknotes

DEFERENCE Consideration of the decision or judgment of another.

FAIR LABOR STANDARDS ACT Enacted in 1938, the statute establishes a minimum wage applicable to all employees of covered employers and provides for mandatory overtime payment for covered employees who work more than 40 hours a week. Executive, administrative and professional employees paid on a salary basis are exempt from the statute.

INTERPRETATION The determination of the meaning of a statute.

■■■

Babbitt v. Sweet Home Chapter of Communities for a Great Oregon

Secretary of the Interior (D) v. Community group (P)

515 U.S. 687 (1995).

NATURE OF CASE: Review of judgment upholding a regulation promulgated by the U.S. Secretary of the Interior defining certain terms contained within the Endangered Species Act.

FACT SUMMARY: The Secretary of the Interior (D) promulgated a regulation that interpreted the term "takings" within the Endangered Species Act (ESA) to prohibit "significant habitat modification or degradation where it actually kills or injures wildlife," compelling landowners to cease activities that detrimentally affected the habitat of the spotted owl and the red-cockaded woodpecker.

🏛 **RULE OF LAW**
The word "harm" as it appears in the definition of the term "take" contained in the Endangered Species Act includes significant habitat modification or degradation where it actually kills or injures wildlife by significantly impairing essential behavioral patterns, including breeding, feeding, or sheltering.

FACTS: The Secretary of the Interior (D) promulgated a regulation that interpreted the term "takings" within the Endangered Species Act to prohibit "significant habitat modification or degradation where it actually kills or injures wildlife." Under this language, landowners, logging companies, and other businesses were compelled to cease activities that detrimentally affected the habitat of the spotted owl and red-cockaded woodpecker. Sweet Home Chapter of Communities for a Great Oregon (P) brought an action alleging that application of the "harm" regulation to the red-cockaded woodpecker, an endangered species, and the northern spotted owl, a threatened species, had injured them economically. The lower courts agreed, and Interior Secretary Babbitt petitioned for review by the United States Supreme Court.

ISSUE: Does the word "harm" as it appears in the definition of the term "take" contained in the Endangered Species Act include significant habitat modification or degradation where it actually kills or injures wildlife by significantly impairing essential behavioral patterns, including breeding, feeding, or sheltering?

HOLDING AND DECISION: (Stevens, J.) Yes. the word "harm" as it appears in the definition of the term "take" contained in the Endangered Species Act (ESA) includes significant habitat modification or degradation where it actually kills or injures wildlife by significantly impairing essential behavioral patterns, including breeding, feeding, or sheltering. The dictionary definition of the term

"harm" is "to cause hurt or damage to injure." In the context of the ESA, that definition naturally encompasses habitat modification that results in actual injury or death to members of an endangered or threatened species. The Secretary's definition of "harm" is a permissible construction of the ESA. Reversed.

CONCURRENCE: (O'Connor, J.) This regulation is appropriately limited to actual, possibly foreseeable harm rather than hypothetical harm.

DISSENT: (Scalia, J.) To define "harm" as an act or omission that however remotely "actually kills or injures" a population of wildlife through habitat modification is to choose a meaning that makes nonsense of the word that "harm" defines (i.e., "take"). It should take the strongest evidence to lead to the conclusion that Congress has defined a term in a manner repugnant to its ordinary and traditional sense. That ordinary and traditional meaning does not include an omission or indirect act, but rather requires an affirmative act that is immediate and intentional. The Act's penalty provisions support such an interpretation, since when combined with the regulation, they make routine habit-modifying activities subject to strict liability, no matter how remotely connected to an animal's injury in a chain of causality—a result that no legislature could reasonably thought to have intended. Further, while the majority indicates that the regulation should be read to include a foreseeability and proximate-cause limitation, such a reading is foreclosed by the language of the regulation itself, which requires "actual" injury or death to an animal. In sum, only action directed at living animals constitutes a "take."

▎ *ANALYSIS*

Section 9 (a)(1) of the ESA provides the following protection for endangered species: "Except as provided in sections 1535(g)(2) and 1539 of this title, with respect to any endangered species of fish or wildlife listed pursuant to section 1533 of this title it is unlawful for any person subject to the jurisdiction of the United States . . . (B) take any such species within the United States or the territorial sea of the United States." The ESA defines the term "take" to mean to harass, harm, pursue, hunt, shoot, wound, kill, trap, capture, or collect.

■■■

Continued on next page.

Quicknotes

PROXIMATE CAUSE The natural sequence of events without which an injury would not have been sustained.

RULEMAKING The promulgation of a rule by an administrative agency, acting within the scope of its power pursuant to statute, enacting a rule governing a particular activity.

■▬■

MCI Telecommunications Corp. v. American Telephone & Telegraph Co.

Long distance carrier (P) v. Long distance carrier (D)

512 U.S. 218 (1994).

NATURE OF CASE: Review of judgment upholding Federal Communications Commission interpretation of the 1934 Communications Act.

FACT SUMMARY: Under language of the 1934 Communications Act, which allow for Commission modifications, the Federal Communications Commission (FCC) provided that only American Telephone & Telegraph Co., the dominant long-distance carrier, was required to file tariffs for services and rates with the FCC.

RULE OF LAW
Alterations to the 1934 Communications Act that would result in a fundamental revision of the statute are not considered "modifications" under the language of the Act.

FACTS: The 1934 Communications Act (the Act) requires long-distance telephone carriers to file tariffs for services and rates with the Federal Communications Commission (FCC). Carriers may charge customers only in accordance with filed tariffs. Under language in the Act that allows for Commission modifications, the FCC by rule provided that only the historically dominant long-distance carrier American Telephone & Telegraph Co. (ATT) (D) was required to file tariffs. Other new long-distance carriers, such as MCI Telecommunications Corp. (MCI) (P), were not required to file tariffs. ATT (D) challenged the FCC interpretation and ruling before the United States Supreme Court.

ISSUE: Should alterations to the 1934 Communications Act that would result in a fundamental revision of the statute be considered "modifications" under the language of the Act?

HOLDING AND DECISION: (Scalia, J.) No. Alterations to the 1934 Communications Act that would result in a fundamental revision of the statute should not be considered "modifications" under the language of the Act. In this case, the FCC has effected a fundamental revision of the statute, changing it from a scheme of rate regulation in long-distance common-carrier communications to a scheme of rate regulation only where effective competition does not exist. Reversed.

DISSENT: (Stevens, J.) Even if the sole possible meaning of "modify" were to make "minor" changes, further elaboration is needed to show why the detariffing policy should fail. The FCC came to its present policy through a series of rulings that gradually relaxed the filing requirements for nondominant carriers.

▶ ANALYSIS

This case turns largely on assorted dictionary definitions of the term "modification." Before looking to legislative intent or policy, Justice Scalia refers to *The Random House Dictionary of the English Language*, *Webster's Third New International Dictionary*, the *Oxford English Dictionary* and *Black's Law Dictionary* to assist him in his linguistic interpretation.

■■■

Quicknotes

TARIFF Duty or tax imposed on articles imported into the United States.

■■■

Food and Drug Administration v. Brown & Williamson Tobacco Corporation

Federal agency (P) v. Tobacco company (D)

529 U.S. 120 (2000).

NATURE OF CASE: Appeal of dismissal for lack of jurisdiction of an agency in a regulatory action.

FACT SUMMARY: The Food and Drug Administration (FDA) (P) began to regulate tobacco products based on the authority given to it by the Food, Drug, and Cosmetic Act (the Act). Brown & Williamson Tobacco Corporation (D) asserted that the FDA (P) did not have jurisdiction to regulate.

🏛 RULE OF LAW
The Food and Drug Administration (FDA) does not have the authority to regulate tobacco products because Congress has, by foreclosing a ban on tobacco and through six separate pieces of legislation, expressly precluded such jurisdiction.

FACTS: In 1996, the Food and Drug Administration (FDA) (P) asserted jurisdiction to regulate tobacco products, after having stated since it was founded that it didn't have such authority. It concluded that nicotine is a "drug" within the meaning of the Act and that cigarettes and smokeless tobacco are "combination products" that deliver nicotine to the body. The Act grants the FDA (P) the authority to regulate "drugs," "devices," and "combination products" (combinations of a drug, device, or biological product). Under the Act, the FDA (P) may require that a device be restricted to sale, distribution, or use or upon such other conditions as the FDA (P) may prescribe in such regulation because of its potential for harmful effect or the collateral measures necessary to its use; the FDA (P) determines that there cannot otherwise be reasonable assurance of its safety and effectiveness. The FDA (P) issued regulations restricting the sale and distribution of cigarettes and smokeless tobacco to protect children and adolescents. The Court of Appeals for the Fourth Circuit concluded that the FDA (P) did not have the jurisdiction. The FDA (P) appealed.

ISSUE: Is the FDA's (P) assertion of jurisdiction impermissible?

HOLDING AND DECISION: (O'Connor, J.) Yes. The FDA's (P) assertion of jurisdiction is impermissible because Congress has clearly precluded the FDA (P) from asserting jurisdiction to regulate tobacco products. Moreover, the authority the FDA (P) has given itself is inconsistent with the intent that Congress has expressed in the Act's overall regulatory scheme and in the tobacco-specific legislation that it has enacted. The FDA's (P) misbranding and device classification provisions make it evident that, were the FDA (P) to regulate cigarettes and smokeless tobacco, the Act would require the FDA (P) to ban them; Congress, however, has foreclosed the removal of tobacco products from the market by directly addressing the problem of tobacco and health through legislation on six occasions. One of the Act's core objectives is to ensure that any product regulated by the FDA (P) is safe and effective for its intended use. The Act requires the FDA (P) to prevent the marketing of any drug or device where the potential for inflicting death or physical injury is not offset by the possibly therapeutic benefit. Given the FDA's (P) conclusions concerning the health consequences of tobacco use, there are no directions that could adequately protect consumers. Thus, were tobacco products within the FDA's (P) jurisdiction, the Act would deem them misbranded devices, because they are dangerous to health when used in the manner and with the frequency suggested by the label and because tobacco product labels bear no adequate directions for tobacco use such that users can be protected. In addition, the FDA's (P) judgment that leaving tobacco products on the market more effectively achieves public health goals than would a ban (which could be dangerous, due to the high level of addiction among users), is no substitute for the specific safety determinations required by the Act's various operative provisions: that the product itself be safe, and that its therapeutic benefits outweigh its risk of harm. Furthermore, since 1965, Congress has enacted six separate pieces of legislation addressing the problem of tobacco use and human health. Those statutes address labeling, advertisements, addictiveness, and prohibitions against selling tobacco to minors. In addition, Congress considered and rejected bills that would have given the FDA jurisdiction, and it preempted any other regulation of cigarette labeling and advertising. Affirmed.

DISSENT: (Breyer, J.) Cigarettes come within the FDA's (P) statutory authority because tobacco products fall within the scope of the statutory definition; the statute's basic purpose, the protection of public health, also supports the inclusion of cigarettes within its scope. The statutes enacted by Congress do not bar FDA jurisdiction, and the FDA can change its policy.

Continued on next page.

▶ *ANALYSIS*

Pertaining to the regulation of the same issue, the Court here gives preference to actions by Congress over those of an agency.

■═■

Quicknotes

FOOD AND DRUG ADMINISTRATION A federal agency responsible for establishing safety and quality standards for foods, drugs, and cosmetics.

FOOD, DRUG AND COSMETIC ACT Federal law regulating the transportation of food, drugs and cosmetics and interstate commerce.

REGULATORY POWER Power granting authority pursuant to statute to a government agency or body to govern a particular area.

■═■

Massachusetts v. Environmental Protection Agency

State member of coalition (P) v. Government agency (D)

549 U.S. 497 (2007).

NATURE OF CASE: Appeal from affirmance of denial of rulemaking petition by agency.

FACT SUMMARY: A coalition of state and local governments and private organizations (P) petitioned the Environmental Protection Agency (EPA) (D) to regulate greenhouse gas emissions from new motor vehicles pursuant to the Clean Air Act. The EPA (D) rejected the petition, contending, among other things, that it lacked statutory authority over greenhouse gas emissions, in part based on Congress's historical response to this type of pollutant and to the problem of global warming.

🏛 RULE OF LAW
An agency has authority to regulate under a statute where the statute is unambiguous and the political history of the area to be regulated does not evince Congress's intent that the agency abstain from regulating.

FACTS: A coalition of state and local governments and private organizations (collectively "coalition") (P) petitioned the Environmental Protection Agency (EPA) (D) to regulate four greenhouse gases (GHGs), including carbon dioxide emissions from new motor vehicles pursuant to the Clean Air Act (CAA), § 202(a)(1). That section provides that the administrator of the EPA "shall by regulation prescribe . . . standards applicable to the emission of any air pollutant from any class . . . of new motor vehicles . . . which in [the EPA administrator's] judgment causes, or contributes to, air pollution . . . reasonably . . . anticipated to endanger public health or welfare." The act defines "air pollutant" to include "any air pollution agent . . . , including any physical, chemical . . . substance . . . emitted into . . . the ambient air." The rulemaking petition argued that EPA's own statements indicated that the statutory standard had been met—that in the administrator's judgment, GHG emissions from new motor vehicles did cause air pollution reasonably anticipated to endanger public health or welfare—and that therefore the administrator had a duty to promulgate standards limiting those emissions. After requesting and receiving public comments on the issues raised in the rulemaking petition, the EPA (D) denied the petition. In reaching its decision, the EPA (D) concluded that—contrary to the opinions of some of its former general counsels—the CAA did not authorize it to issue regulations to address global climate change, and, even if the EPA (D) did have the authority to set greenhouse gas emissions standards, it would decline to do so because such regulation would conflict with other administration priorities and would be unwise. Not only was there not an unequivocal causal connection between increased GHGs resulting from human activity and increased earth temperatures, but also numerous cues indicated that Congress did not intend for EPA (D) to regulate in this area. EPA (D) accordingly believed given the residual uncertainty, regulation would be unwise. Moreover, it explained that any regulation it could effect would be a piecemeal approach that would undercut the President's comprehensive approach. In reaching its conclusion that it lacked statutory authority to set greenhouse gas emissions standards, the EPA (D) contended, among other things, that Congress' history in dealing with such emissions and the political history of global warming meant that Congress did not intend for the EPA (D) to regulate in this area. Specifically, the EPA (D) observed that Congress was well aware of the global climate change issue when it last comprehensively amended the CAA in 1990, yet it declined to adopt a proposed amendment establishing binding emissions limitations. Congress instead chose to authorize further investigation into climate change. The EPA (D) further reasoned that Congress's GHGs counseled against reading the general authorization of the Act to confer regulatory authority over greenhouse gases. The EPA (D) relied on the Supreme Court's decision in *FDA v. Brown & Williamson Tobacco Corp.*, 529 U.S. 120 (2000), where, relying on tobacco's unique political history, the Court invalidated the Food and Drug Administration's reliance on its general authority to regulate drugs as a basis for asserting jurisdiction over an industry constituting a significant portion of the American economy. Similarly, the EPA (D) reasoned that climate change had its own political history: Congress designed the original Clean Air Act to address local air pollutants rather than a substance that is fairly consistent in its concentration throughout the world's atmosphere; declined in 1990 to enact proposed amendments to force the EPA (D) to set emission standards for motor vehicles; and addressed global climate change in other legislation. Because of this political history, and because imposing emission limitations on greenhouse gases would have even greater economic and political repercussions than regulating tobacco, the EPA (D) was persuaded that it lacked the power to do so. Thus, the EPA (D) concluded that climate change was so important that unless Congress spoke with exacting specificity, it could not have meant the EPA (D) to address it. EPA (D) also reasoned that since a significant method of reducing GHG emissions from cars would be to increase fuel efficiency, and since Congress had already given

Continued on next page.

authority of such efforts to the Department of Transportation, Congress had not intended for the EPA (D) to regulate in this area. The EPA (D) also observed that even if it did conclude that GHGs were dangerous to human health, it would not, under the CAA, be required to regulate GHGs, but instead could take a discretionary approach that took into account various policy considerations. The coalition (P) challenged the EPA's (D) order denying the petition in the court of appeals, which ruled against the coalition (P). In so doing, the court of appeals panel concluded that the EPA (D) had wide discretion in this area, especially in light of the scientific uncertainties involved and the implications unilateral U.S. regulation of vehicle emissions might have on international regulatory efforts, and that, in any event, the petitioners lacked standing to sue because they had failed to allege any particularized injury. The United States Supreme Court granted certiorari.

ISSUE: Does an agency have authority to regulate under a statute where the statute is unambiguous and the political history of the area to be regulated does not evince Congress's intent that the agency abstain from regulating?

HOLDING AND DECISION: (Stevens, J.) Yes. An agency has authority to regulate under a statute where the statute is unambiguous and the political history of the area to be regulated does not evince Congress's intent that the agency abstain from regulating. When the CAA was first enacted, the study of climate change was just starting. Then, over the years, Congress enacted the National Climate Program Act, which required the President to establish a program to "assist the Nation and the world to understand and respond to natural and man-induced climate processes and their implications." The National Research Council unequivocally tied global climate change to increased carbon dioxide. In 1987, Congress enacted the Global Climate Protection Act and directed the EPA (D) to propose to Congress a "coordinated national policy on global climate change." The U.S. also participated in nonbinding international treaties for the purpose of reducing GHGs. First, it must be noted that judicial review in this area is highly deferential and extremely limited. Although an agency's refusal to initiate enforcement proceedings is not ordinarily subject to judicial review, there are key differences between nonenforcement and denials of rulemaking petitions that are, as in the present circumstances, expressly authorized. The statutory text forecloses the EPA's (D) position. Because greenhouse gases fit well within the Act's capacious definition of "air pollutant," the EPA (D) has statutory authority to regulate emission of such gases from new motor vehicles. That definition—which includes "any air pollution agent . . . , including any physical, chemical, . . . substance . . . emitted into . . . the ambient air . . ."—embraces all airborne compounds of whatever stripe. "Welfare" is also defined broadly and includes impacts on weather and climate. The EPA's (D) reliance on postenactment congressional actions and

deliberations it views as tantamount to a command to refrain from regulating greenhouse gas emissions is unavailing. Even if postenactment legislative history could shed light on the meaning of an otherwise-unambiguous statute, the EPA (D) identifies nothing suggesting that Congress meant to curtail the EPA's (D) power to treat greenhouse gases as air pollutants. It is not difficult to reconcile Congress's various efforts to promote interagency collaboration and research to better understand climate change with the EPA's (D) pre-existing mandate to regulate "any air pollutant" that may endanger the public welfare. Thus, *FDA v. Brown & Williamson Tobacco Corp.* is distinguished. First, in *Brown & Williamson* the Court thought it unlikely that Congress meant to ban tobacco products. Here, in contrast, EPA (D) jurisdiction would lead to no such extreme measures, since the EPA (D) would only regulate emissions. Second, in *Brown & Williamson* there was an unbroken series of congressional enactments that made sense only if adopted "against the backdrop of the FDA's consistent and repeated statements that it lacked authority under the Food, Drug and Cosmetic Act (FDCA) to regulate tobacco." No such enactments are involved here, and there has been no congressional action that conflicts in any way with the EPA's (D) regulation of greenhouse gases from new motor vehicles. While the statute conditions EPA (D) action on its formation of a "judgment," that judgment must relate to whether an air pollutant "cause[s], or contribute[s] to, air pollution which may reasonably be anticipated to endanger public health or welfare." Under the Act's clear terms, EPA (D) can avoid promulgating regulations only if it determines that greenhouse gases do not contribute to climate change or if it provides some reasonable explanation as to why it cannot or will not exercise its discretion to determine whether they do. It has refused to do so, offering instead a laundry list of reasons not to regulate, including the existence of voluntary executive branch programs providing a response to global warming and impairment of the President's ability to negotiate with developing nations to reduce emissions. These policy judgments have nothing to do with whether greenhouse gas emissions contribute to climate change and do not amount to a reasoned justification for declining to form a scientific judgment. Nor can the EPA (D) avoid its statutory obligation by noting the uncertainty surrounding various features of climate change and concluding that it would therefore be better not to regulate at this time. If the scientific uncertainty is so profound that it precludes the EPA (D) from making a reasoned judgment, it must say so. The statutory question is whether sufficient information exists for it to make an endangerment finding. Instead, the EPA (D) rejected the rulemaking petition based on impermissible considerations. Its action was therefore arbitrary, capricious, or otherwise not in accordance with law. On remand, the EPA (D) must ground its reasons for action or inaction in the statute. Reversed and remanded.

Continued on next page.

DISSENT: (Scalia, J.) Without support in the statute or precedent, the majority narrows what is a reasonable justification for not regulating to the situation where the EPA (D) finds scientific uncertainty is too profound. The majority thus rejects as acceptable other perfectly valid reasons for not regulating. Under the CAA, when the EPA (D) makes a judgment that a pollutant must be regulated, that judgment must relate to whether the pollutant is one that will "cause, or contribute to, air pollution which may reasonably be anticipated to endanger public health or welfare." But the statute says nothing at all about the reasons for which the EPA (D) may defer making a judgment, i.e., the permissible reasons for deciding not to grapple with the issue at the present time. Thus, the various "policy" rationales that the majority criticizes are not "divorced from the statutory text," except in the sense that the statutory text is silent. The reasons the EPA (D) gave are considerations executive agencies regularly take into account when deciding whether to consider entering a new field. Accordingly, there is no basis in law for the majority's imposed limitation. Moreover, even under the majority's erroneous limitation, the EPA's (D) stated reason passes muster, since by saying that there is not an unambiguous connection between greenhouse gasses and global warming, the EPA (D) is essentially saying that "scientific uncertainty is too profound."

The majority also errs in determining that the Act's "capacious" definition of "air pollutant" includes vehicle emissions. While it is correct that vehicle emissions are physical substances emitted into the air, the definition requires that such emissions be "air pollution agent[s] or combination of such agents." The majority ignores this part of the definition. The EPA (D), on the other hand, urges that "[A] substance does not meet the CAA definition of 'air pollutant' simply because it is a 'physical, chemical, . . . substance or matter which is emitted into or otherwise enters the ambient air.' It must also be an 'air pollution agent.'" The majority fails to defer to the EPA's (D) interpretation, notwithstanding that *Chevron*, 467 U.S. 837 (1984), requires such deference. Applying the EPA's (D) interpretation of the definition of "air pollutant," the next issue becomes whether greenhouse gases are "agent[s]" of "air pollution." If so, the statute would authorize regulation; if not, the EPA (D) would lack authority to regulate. Under this approach, the EPA (D) had to determine if the concentration of greenhouse gases, asserted as responsible for "global climate change," qualifies as "air pollution." The EPA (D) determined that high concentrations of greenhouse gasses in the upper atmosphere is not what is typically considered "air pollution," which occurs at lower atmospheric levels. Such an interpretation is reasonable and in line with dictionary definitions of the term—and, under *Chevron*, the majority should have deferred to this interpretation, regardless of its own views on global warming.

ANALYSIS

In *Brown & Williamson,* the Court emphasized a canon of construction that statutes should not be construed to give agencies authority over questions of great "economic and political" significance unless Congress has spoken clearly (known as the "major questions" canon). Arguably, the Court in the *Massachusetts* decision abandoned this canon by failing to defer to the EPA (D) and forcing Congress to more clearly authorize greenhouse gas regulation if it wanted the EPA (D) to act in this area. In any event, after this decision, the EPA (D) and Department of Transportation jointly crafted an auto policy that sets the first-ever greenhouse gas standards and strictest fuel efficiency standards for cars and light-duty trucks. This policy was made possible because the EPA (D) eventually made the endangerment determination that was the subject of the *Massachusetts v. EPA* case.

■■■

Quicknotes

RULEMAKING The promulgation of a rule governing a particular activity by an administrative agency, acting within the scope of its power pursuant to statute.

■■■

Entergy Corp. v. Riverkeeper, Inc.

Powerplant operator (D) v. Environmental group (P)

129 S. Ct. 1498 (2009).

NATURE OF CASE: Appeal from reversal of Environmental Protection Agency regulations.

FACT SUMMARY: Environmental groups (P) and various States (P) contended that Environmental Protection Agency (EPA) regulations that set national performance standards for powerplants' (D) cooling water intake structures were impermissible because, they argued, the Clean Water Act, under which the regulations were promulgated, prohibited the EPA from conducting a cost-benefit analysis in setting the national performance standards and in providing for cost-benefit variances from those standards.

RULE OF LAW

Under the Clean Water Act, the Environmental Protection Agency (EPA) may permissibly rely on cost-benefit analysis in setting national performance standards for powerplant cooling water intake structures, and in providing for cost-benefit variances from those standards.

FACTS: Various powerplants (D) have "cooling water intake structures" that threaten the environment by squashing against intake screens ("impingement") or suctioning into the cooling system ("entrainment") aquatic organisms from the water sources tapped to cool the plants. Thus, the facilities are subject to regulation under the Clean Water Act (the Act), which mandates that "[a]ny standard established pursuant to section 1311 . . . or section 1316 . . . and applicable to a point source shall require that the location, design, construction, and capacity of cooling water intake structures reflect the best technology available for minimizing adverse environmental impact." 33 U.S.C. § 1326(b). The Environmental Protection Agency (EPA) promulgated Phase II national performance standards, requiring facilities to reduce impingement mortality for aquatic organisms by 80 to 95 percent and requiring a subset of facilities to reduce entrainment of such organisms by 60 to 90 percent. However, the EPA expressly declined to mandate closed-cycle cooling systems, which would affect even greater reductions, in part because the cost of implementing closed-cycle systems would impose far greater compliance costs and achieve only small performance gains. Environmental groups (P) and various States (P) challenged the Phase II regulations, contending that the Act's requirement that the "best technology available for minimizing adverse environmental impacts," be used precluded an interpretation of the statute that would permit the EPA to use a cost-benefit analysis in setting the national performance standards and in providing for cost-benefit variances from those standards as part of the Phase

II regulations. The court of appeals concluded that cost-benefit analysis is impermissible under § 1326(b) in setting national performance standards. The United States Supreme Court granted certiorari.

ISSUE: Under the Clean Water Act, may the EPA permissibly rely on cost-benefit analysis in setting national performance standards for powerplant cooling water intake structures, and in providing for cost-benefit variances from those standards?

HOLDING AND DECISION: (Scalia, J.) Yes. Under the Clean Water Act, the EPA may permissibly rely on cost-benefit analysis in setting national performance standards for powerplant cooling water intake structures, and in providing for cost-benefit variances from those standards. The EPA's view that § 1326(b)'s "best technology available for minimizing adverse environmental impact" standard permits consideration of the technology's costs and of the relationship between those costs and the environmental benefits produced governs if it is a reasonable interpretation of the statute—not necessarily the only possible interpretation, nor even the interpretation deemed most reasonable by the courts. The court of appeals took "best technology" to mean the technology that achieves the greatest reduction in adverse environmental impacts at a reasonable cost to the industry, but it may also describe the technology that most efficiently produces a good, even if it produces a lesser quantity of that good than other available technologies. This reading is not precluded by the phrase "for minimizing adverse environmental impact." Minimizing admits of degree and is not necessarily used to refer exclusively to the "greatest possible reduction." Other Act provisions show that when Congress wished to mandate the greatest feasible reduction in water pollution, it used plain language, e.g., "elimination of discharges of all pollutants." Thus, § 1326(b)'s use of the less ambitious goal of "minimizing adverse environmental impact" suggests that the EPA has some discretion to determine the extent of reduction warranted under the circumstances, plausibly involving a consideration of the benefits derived from reductions and the costs of achieving them. Considering § 1326(b)'s text, and comparing it with the text and statutory factors applicable to parallel Clean Water Act provisions, prompts the conclusion that it was well within the bounds of reasonable interpretation for the EPA to conclude that cost-benefit analysis is not categorically forbidden. In the Phase II rules, the EPA sought only to avoid extreme disparities between costs and benefits, limiting

Continued on next page.

variances from Phase II's "national performance standards" to circumstances where the costs are "significantly greater than the benefits" of compliance. In defining "national performance standards" the EPA assumed the application of technologies whose benefits approach those estimated for closed-cycle cooling systems at a fraction of the cost. The EPA's interpretation is a reasonable, and, therefore, legitimate exercise of discretion, and there is no statutory basis for limiting the comparison of costs and benefits to situations where the benefits are de minimis rather than significantly disproportionate. Reversed and remanded.

CONCURRENCE AND DISSENT: (Breyer, J.) The legislative and drafting history shows that the statute did not intend to prohibit cost-benefit analyses, but did mean to restrict such comparisons. Because every real choice requires a weighing of advantages against disadvantages, which often can be quantified by cost, a total prohibition on cost-benefit comparisons would not only be difficult to enforce, but could also lead to irrational results. The EPA's reading of the statute seems to permit it to describe environmental benefits in non-monetized terms and to evaluate both costs and benefits in accordance with its expert judgment and scientific knowledge, and it can thereby avoid lengthy formal cost-benefit proceedings and futile attempts at comprehensive monetization; take account of Congress's technology-forcing objectives; and still prevent results that are absurd or unreasonable in light of extreme disparities between costs and benefits. Because this is a reasonable interpretation of the statute, it is permitted under *Chevron*, 467 U.S. 837 (1984).

DISSENT: (Stevens, J.) The plain text of Section 316(b) of the Act (§ 1326(b)) requires that unless costs are so high that the best technology is not "available," they are outweighed by the benefits of minimizing adverse environmental impact. The Act neither expressly nor implicitly authorizes the EPA to use cost-benefit analysis when setting regulatory standards, but a fair interpretation of it leads to the conclusion that the use of cost-benefit analysis is prohibited. Under such an analysis, the costs and benefits of a regulation are monetized, balanced, and the cheaper route chosen. However, in the environmental context in which a regulation's financial costs are often more obvious and easier to quantify than its environmental benefits, cost-benefit analysis often, if not always, yields a result that does not maximize environmental protection. Because benefits can be more accurately monetized in some industries than in others, Congress typically decides whether it is appropriate for an agency to use cost-benefit analysis in crafting regulations and then clearly indicates its intent that an agency engage in cost-benefit analysis. Thus, a provision's silence as to such analysis should not be treated as an implicit source of cost-benefit authority, particularly when such authority is elsewhere expressly granted and it has the potential to fundamentally alter an agency's approach to regulation. Under the Clean Water Act's structure and intent, the "best technology available," or "BTA" standard,

provides a clear directive that EPA must require industry to adopt the best technology possible to minimize the adverse environmental impacts of water intake structures. Contrary to the majority's interpretation that the statute's silence as to how EPA should implement BTA gives EPA wide discretion, the statute's history and structure make plain that Congress did not intend to give EPA the authority to engage in cost-benefit comparisons in this area.

▶ *ANALYSIS*

The holding in this case, as well as Justice Stevens' dissent, suggest that if Congress intends that an agency not engage in cost-benefit analysis, it should explicitly say so in regulatory statutes, lest a statute's silence as to such analysis be treated as an implicit source of cost-benefit authority. The majority in this case seems to hold that, other things being equal, courts should read silences or ambiguities in the language of regulatory statutes as permitting, not forbidding, this type of regulation.

■=■

Quicknotes

DE MINIMIS Insignificant; trivial; not of sufficient significance to require legal action.

REGULATORY POWER Power granting authority pursuant to statute to a government agency or body to govern a particular area.

■=■

Ohio v. Department of Interior

State (P) v. Federal agency (D)

880 F.2d 432 (D.C. Cir. 1989).

NATURE OF CASE: Petition for review of agency regulations.

FACT SUMMARY: Ohio (P) and various environmental groups sought judicial review of the Department of the Interior's (D) natural resource assessment regulations.

🏛 RULE OF LAW
Restoration cost is an adequate measure of recovery in natural resource damage cases.

FACTS: The Department of the Interior (DOI) (D) promulgated a regulation that damages for despoilment of natural resources shall be the lesser of restoration or replacement costs; or diminution of use values. State and environmental groups (P) alleged that this rule contradicted Congress's preference for restoration in such cases by permitting replacement or diminution damages where those costs are lower than the costs of restoration. The DOI's (D) emphasis on market value in determining use values was also alleged to be unreasonable. Finally, the contingent valuation process which the DOI (D) included in its assessment methodology was alleged not to be the best available procedure. The court of appeals granted review.

ISSUE: Is restoration cost an adequate measure of recovery in natural resource damage cases?

HOLDING AND DECISION: (Wald, J.) Yes. Restoration cost is an adequate measure of recovery in natural resource damage cases. Congress has established a distinct preference for restoration cost as the measure of recovery in natural resource damage cases, and DOI's (D) "lesser-of" rule contradicts the language and purpose of Comprehensive Environmental Response, Compensation and Liability Act (CERCLA). By mandating the use of all damages to restore the injured resources, Congress underscored in § 107(f)(1) its paramount restorative purpose for imposing damages. DOI (D) justifies its "lesser of" rule as being economically efficient, and under this economic efficiency view, making restoration cost the measure of damages would be a waste of money whenever restoration would cost more than the use value of the resource. The fatal flaw of this approach, however, is that it assumes that natural resources are fungible goods, just like any other, and that the value to society generated by a particular resource can be accurately measured in every case—assumptions Congress rejected. Congress's refusal to view use value and restoration cost as having equal presumptive legitimacy merely recognizes that natural resources have

value that is not readily measured by traditional means. DOI (D) therefore erred by establishing a strong presumption in favor of market price and appraisal methodologies. Petition for review granted as to this issue.

(Mikva, J.) DOI's (D) emphasis on market value is an unreasonable interpretation of the statute that cannot stand under *Chevron*, 467 U.S. 837 (1984). While market value can be one factor of value, it cannot be the exclusive measure. The problem cannot be solved by permitting nonmarket technologies to be used when the market for the resource is not "reasonably competitive" since there are many resources whose components may be traded in "reasonably competitive markets," but whose total use values are not fully reflected in the prices they command in those markets. The statute does not evince any congressional intent to limit use value to market price. To the contrary, CERCLA requires that damage assessment fully account for all aspects of loss. The hierarchy of use values is an erroneous construction of CERCLA because the statute expressly requires use value to be considered among other factors; furthermore, DOI (D) has failed to justify excluding option value and existence value from the class of recognized use values. Petition for review granted as to this issue.

DOI's (D) use of a 10% discount rate to discount future year costs and benefits in determining damages and making restoration decisions is, however, acceptable. Regulation upheld as to this issue.

(Robinson, J.) Moreover, DOI (D) correctly concluded that contingent valuation (CV) is a "best available procedure" because DOI's (D) use of the CV methodology is both reasonable and consistent with congressional intent. CV methodology enables, through a series of interview questions, ascertainment of individually-expressed values for different levels of quality of resources, and dollar values of individuals' changes in well-being. Any overstatements of value resulting from the CV methodology not only do not merit judicial invalidation of the methodology, but they are also easily corrected simply by asking better questions of interviewees. Regulation upheld as to this issue.

▶ ANALYSIS

The court in this case applied the second step in the test from *Chevron v. Natural Resources Defense Council*, 467 U.S. 837 (1984). This case established a two-part test for judicial review of agency interpretation of law. Step one deals with how to tell if a statute is ambiguous. In step two,

Continued on next page.

agency interpretations of ambiguous provisions are to be upheld if they are permissible or reasonable.

■≡■

Quicknotes

AMBIGUITY Language that is capable of more than one interpretation.

MEASURE OF DAMAGES Monetary compensation that may be awarded by the court to a party who has sustained injury or loss to his or her person, property or rights due to another party's unlawful act, omission or negligence.

REPLACEMENT VALUE The monetary amount necessary in order to replace property or improvements.

RULES PROMULGATION The promulgation of a rule by an administrative agency, acting within the scope of its power pursuant to statute, enacting a rule governing a particular activity.

■≡■

National Cable and Telecommunications Association v. Brand X Internet Services

Cable industry association (D) v. Internet service provider (P)

545 U.S. 967 (2005).

NATURE OF CASE: Appeal from judgment vacating a Federal Communications Commission (FCC) ruling.

FACT SUMMARY: The court of appeals vacated the Federal Communications Commission's ruling that cable modem internet service is an "information service" rather than a "telecommunications service," and therefore not subject to regulation under the Communications Act, on the stare decisis grounds that a prior court of appeals' decision had held that such service is "telecommunications service."

🏛 RULE OF LAW
A court's prior judicial construction of a statute trumps an agency construction otherwise entitled to *Chevron* deference only if the prior court decision holds that its construction follows from the unambiguous terms of the statute and thus leaves no room for agency discretion.

FACTS: The Communications Act (the Act) provides that "information service" is not subject to regulation under the Act, whereas "telecommunications service" is. After public hearings, the Federal Communications Commission (FCC) ruled that cable modem internet service provided by cable companies is an "information service" rather than a "telecommunications service," and therefore not subject to regulation under the Communications Act. The court of appeals vacated this ruling. Rather than analyzing the issue under the deferential *Chevron* framework, *Chevron U.S.A., Inc. v. Natural Resources Defense Council*, 467 U.S. 837 (1984), the court of appeals, applying principles of stare decisis, relied on the purported precedential effect of that court's decision in an earlier case, *AT&T Corp. v. Portland*, 216 F.3d 871 (9th Cir. 2000), in which the court had held that cable modem service was a "telecommunications service." In *Portland*, the court was not reviewing an administrative proceeding, and the FCC was not a party to the case. The United States Supreme Court granted certiorari.

ISSUE: Does a court's prior judicial construction of a statute trump an agency construction otherwise entitled to *Chevron* deference only if the prior court decision holds that its construction follows from the unambiguous terms of the statute and thus leaves no room for agency discretion?

HOLDING AND DECISION: (Thomas, J.) Yes. A court's prior judicial construction of a statute trumps an

agency construction otherwise entitled to *Chevron* deference only if the prior court decision holds that its construction follows from the unambiguous terms of the statute and thus leaves no room for agency discretion. Here, the court of appeals should have applied *Chevron*'s framework, instead of following the contrary construction it adopted in *Portland*. This principle follows from *Chevron* itself, as *Chevron* established a presumption that Congress, when it left ambiguity in a statute meant for implementation by an agency, understood that the ambiguity would be resolved, in the first instance, by the agency, rather than by the courts. Contrary to this principle, allowing a judicial precedent to foreclose an agency from interpreting an ambiguous statute, as the court of appeals assumed it could, would allow a court's interpretation to override an agency's. A contrary rule would mean that whether an agency's interpretation of an ambiguous statute is entitled to *Chevron* deference would turn on the order in which the interpretations issue: If the court's construction came first, its construction would prevail, whereas if the agency's came first, the agency's construction would command *Chevron* deference. However, whether Congress has delegated to an agency the authority to interpret a statute does not depend on the order in which the judicial and administrative constructions occur. Such a rule would also prevent agencies from revising unwise judicial constructions of ambiguous statutes. Moreover, the dissent's objection that allowing an agency to override what a court believes to be the best interpretation of a statute makes "judicial decisions subject to reversal by executive officers" is mistaken: because under *Chevron* a court's opinion as to the best reading of an ambiguous statute an agency is charged with administering is not authoritative, the agency's decision to construe that statute differently from a court does not say that the court's holding was legally wrong; instead, the agency may, consistent with the court's holding, choose a different construction, since the agency remains the authoritative interpreter (within the limits of reason) of such statutes and the court's holding remains binding law and is not "reversed." Here, *Portland* did not hold that the Communications Act unambiguously required treating cable internet providers as telecommunications carriers, but merely held that this was only the best construction of the statutory section at issue in that case. Also, the court in that case did not reach the conclusion that the Act was unambiguous. For these reasons, the court of appeals erred in this case in applying *Portland*, rather than deferring to the FCC under *Chevron*,

Continued on next page.

under which the FCC's ruling must be upheld on the merits. Reversed.

DISSENT: (Scalia, J.) The majority's rule means that now judicial decisions are subject to reversal by executive officers. A hypothetical example of this result is where this Court rules that agency action is unlawful (under a best interpretation standard), and the agency promptly conducts a rulemaking, adopting a rule that comports with its earlier position—in effect disagreeing with the Supreme Court concerning the best interpretation of the statute. According to the majority's rule, the agency is thereupon free to take the action that the Supreme Court found unlawful. The rule therefore gives rise to an unconstitutional situation under Article III. Moreover, it raises numerous questions and uncertainties for the lower courts. For example, will courts now have to expressly state—presumably in dicta—whether their holding is a "best" interpretation rather than an "only permissible" interpretation, or vice versa? Presumably, too, the majority rule will affect hundreds of past court decisions that were silent as to this distinction, rendering them agency-reversible. How much extra work will it entail for each court confronted with an agency-administered statute to determine whether it has reached, not only the right ("best") result, but "the only permissible" result? Is the standard for "unambiguous" under the majority's new agency-reversal rule the same as the standard for "unambiguous" under step one of *Chevron*? (If so, of course, every case that reaches step two of *Chevron* will be agency-reversible.) Does the "unambiguous" dictum produce stare decisis effect even when a court is affirming, rather than reversing, agency action—so that in the future the agency must adhere to that affirmed interpretation? If so, does the victorious agency have the right to appeal a court of appeals judgment in its favor, on the ground that the text in question is in fact not (as the court of appeals held) unambiguous, so the agency should be able to change its view in the future? These and other issues will now bedevil the lower courts. Instead, the rule should remain what it has been: When a court interprets a statute without *Chevron* deference to agency views, its interpretation (whether or not asserted to rest upon an unambiguous text) is the law.

▶ *ANALYSIS*

Not only did the Court in this case issue its stare decisis ruling, it also seemingly resolved the issue of whether agency inconsistency is a basis for declining to analyze the agency's interpretation under the *Chevron* framework. The Court held that such inconsistency or flip-flopping, does not reduce or undermine *Chevron* deference. Instead, the Court indicated that unexplained inconsistency is, at most, a reason for holding an interpretation to be an arbitrary and capricious change from agency practice under the Administrative Procedure Act. The Court reasoned that if the agency adequately explains the reasons for a reversal of policy, change is not invalidating, since the whole point of *Chevron* is to leave the discretion provided by the ambiguities of a statute with the implementing agency, and since agencies must consider varying interpretations and the wisdom of their policies on a continuing basis, for example, in response to changed factual circumstances, or a change in administrations.

■≡■

Quicknotes

ADMINISTRATIVE PROCEDURE ACT (AP) Enacted in 1946 to govern practices and proceedings before federal administrative agencies.

STARE DECISIS Doctrine whereby courts follow legal precedent unless there is good cause for departure.

■≡■

Citizens to Preserve Overton Park, Inc. v. Volpe

Citizens and conservation organizations (P) v. Secretary of Transportation (D)

401 U.S. 402 (1971).

NATURE OF CASE: Appeal from affirmance of summary judgment for government agency's secretary in action to stay construction of a highway.

FACT SUMMARY: Citizens and conservation organizations (P) contended that a reviewing court must conduct either a de novo review or a review for the substantiality of the evidence of Secretary of Transportation Volpe's (D) decision that no feasible and prudent alternative existed to building a highway through Overton Park.

RULE OF LAW
In reviewing agency actions under the general review requirements of § 706 of the Administrative Procedure Act, a court must: (1) determine whether the action is within the scope of statutory authority; (2) determine whether the action was arbitrary, capricious, an abuse of discretion, or otherwise contrary to law; and (3) determine whether the agency followed procedural requirements.

FACTS: Federal statutes prohibit the authorization of federal funds to build highways through public parks if a feasible and prudent alternative route existed. Secretary of Transportation Volpe (D) approved authorization of federal funds for a highway to be built through Overton Park, a public municipal park. Citizens and conservation organizations (collectively "Citizens") (P) contended that the authorization was invalid in that the Secretary (D) was bound statutorily to make formal findings and state his reasons for an independent decision, which he had not done. The district court granted summary judgment to the Secretary's (D), but only on the basis of litigation affidavits and the court of appeals affirmed. The United States Supreme Court heard oral argument, granted a stay of the construction, and treated the stay as a petition for certiorari, which the Supreme Court granted.

ISSUE: In reviewing agency actions under the general review requirements of § 706 of the Administrative Procedure Act, must a court: (1) determine whether the action is within the scope of statutory authority; (2) determine whether the action was arbitrary, capricious, an abuse of discretion, or otherwise contrary to law; and (3) determine whether the agency followed procedural requirements?

HOLDING AND DECISION: (Marshall, J.) Yes. In reviewing agency actions under the general review requirements of § 706 of the Administrative Procedure Act, a court must: (1) determine whether the action is within the scope of statutory authority; (2) determine

whether the action was arbitrary, capricious, an abuse of discretion, or otherwise contrary to law; and (3) determine whether the agency followed procedural requirements. Although the Secretary (D) was not required to make formal findings, the lower courts' review, based entirely on litigation affidavits, was insufficient. As a threshold matter, Citizens (P) were entitled to judicial review because such review was not proscribed by Congress, and because the Secretary's (D) decision did not come within the exception for agency action "committed to agency discretion." Instead, the statutes at issue provided clear directives for agency action that the Secretary (D) had to follow, and, contrary to his arguments, he did not have broad leeway in this regard. Having established that judicial review was available, the key issue becomes what the appropriate standard of that judicial review should be. Citizens (P) argue that either the substantial evidence standard must apply or that there should be de novo review of the Secretary's (D) action to determine if it was "unwarranted," but neither of these standards is applicable. The substantial evidence standard is used only in rulemaking procedure reviewed under the Administrative Procedure Act (APA) or for public adjudicatory hearings. Here, the Secretary's (D) action clearly was not "rule-making" and there was no adjudicatory hearing involved; the only hearing, required at the local level, was quasi-legislative and nonrulemaking in nature. Further, de novo review is only used in review of adjudicative actions where the agency's finding procedures are inadequate. Therefore, de novo review is not warranted. Even though these standards of review are inapplicable, the reviewing courts must nevertheless engage in a substantial inquiry, as mandated by the general requirements of § 706 of the APA. The courts must first inquire whether the Secretary (D) acted within the scope of his authority. Here, that scope was of a quite limited range. Then the court must determine whether the Secretary's (D) actual choice was "arbitrary, capricious, an abuse of discretion, or otherwise not in accordance with law." To make this determination, the court must assess whether the Secretary (D) considered all the relevant facts and whether he made an error of judgment—but must be careful not to substitute its judgment for that of the Secretary (D). Finally, the court must determine whether the Secretary (D) committed any procedural errors. While the absence of formal findings hampers such review, such findings were not required. However, the case must be remanded for a more in-depth, probing inquiry that is not based on post-hoc litigation affidavits. Instead, the reviewing court must base

Continued on next page.

its decision on whatever facts are available, testimony from agency officials, and other relevant sources that will serve to explain the Secretary's (D) position. Reversed and remanded.

▶ ANALYSIS

On remand the district court engaged in a thorough, in-depth review of the Secretary's decision and concluded he had not given adequate consideration to alternative routes. This illustrates the scope of judicial power to review a matter within an agency's discretion. A court cannot merely rubber stamp such a determination. It must engage in an adequate review of the action.

■===■

Quicknotes

AGENCY DISCRETION The authority conferred upon a public agency by law to act reasonably in accordance with its own judgment under certain circumstances.

JUDICIAL REVIEW The authority of the courts to review decisions, actions or omissions committed by another agency or branch of government.

RULEMAKING The promulgation of a rule by an administrative agency, acting within the scope of its power pursuant to statute, enacting a rule governing a particular activity.

■===■

Motor Vehicle Manufacturers' Association v. State Farm Mutual Automobile Insurance Co.

Trade association (P) v. Insurance company (D)

463 U.S. 29 (1983).

NATURE OF CASE: Appeal from decision finding agency action arbitrary and capricious.

FACT SUMMARY: The National Highway Traffic Safety Administration (NHTSA) appealed from a decision of the court of appeals finding that the revocation of the requirement that new motor vehicles produced after September 1982 be equipped with passive restraints to protect occupants in the event of a collision was arbitrary and capricious.

🏛 RULE OF LAW
When an agency modifies or rescinds a previously promulgated rule, it is required to supply a satisfactory, rational analysis supporting its decision.

FACTS: Standard 208 was a rule promulgated by the Department of Transportation dealing with motor vehicle occupant safety, and since originally issued in 1967, had been subject to constant rescission, modification, and amendment. In 1969, the standard first formally proposed to include a passive restraint requirement. Between 1976 and 1980, a mandatory passive restraint requirement was issued. The two systems that would satisfy the standard would be an air bag system or a passive seat belt system, with the choice of system being left up to the manufacturer. It was assumed that manufacturers would install approximately 60 percent airbags and 40 percent passive belts. By 1981, 99 percent of the cars produced were being equipped with passive belts, belts which were designed in a way that they could be detached easily and permanently. In 1981, even though studies, surveys, and other empirical evidence indicated that the use rate associated with the passive belts was more than double that associated with manual belts, the NHTSA (D) concluded that the safety benefits associated with the standard's implementation did not justify the costs of implementing the standard. In that same year, the NHTSA (D), without considering the possible use of air bags, rescinded the passive restraint requirement. From a court of appeals decision finding the revocation of the passive restraint requirement arbitrary and capricious, the NHTSA (D) appealed.

ISSUE: When an agency rescinds or modifies a previously promulgated rule, is it required to supply a satisfactory, rational analysis supporting its decision?

HOLDING AND DECISION: (White, J.) Yes. When an agency rescinds or modifies a previously promulgated rule, it is required to supply a satisfactory, rational analysis supporting its decision. A change or rescission is akin to the promulgation of the rule itself, and is subject to the same arbitrary and capricious standard. The agency may be required to more fully justify its decision than if the agency had not acted in the first instance. The agency must show a rational connection between the facts found and the decision rendered. If an agency relies on improper factors, fails to consider important aspects of the problem, or renders a decision that runs contrary to the evidence, its decision may be considered arbitrary and capricious. The National Traffic and Motor Vehicle Safety Act of 1966 (the Act) mandates the achievement of traffic safety. Given the conceded effectiveness of air bags, the logical response to the manufacturers' actions would have been to require air bags. Not only was this not done, it appears that the NHTSA (D) did not even consider it. A rational rescission decision cannot be made without the consideration of technologically feasible alternatives of proven value. Further, the empirical evidence runs counter to the agency's determination that the safety aspects associated with the use of passive belts could not be determined. The empirical evidence indicates that there is a doubling of use over the use of manual belts, and the safety benefits associated with the increased use of safety belts is unquestioned. Finally, the NHTSA (D) has failed to articulate a basis for not requiring non-detachable passive belts. By failing to consider feasible, logical alternatives and dismissing the safety benefits associated with passive restraints in light of the evidence, the NHTSA (D) has failed to present an adequate basis or explanation for rescinding the mandatory passive restraint requirement. Vacated and remanded.

CONCURRENCE AND DISSENT: (Rehnquist, J.) The agency's decision was not arbitrary and capricious for discounting the safety benefits of automatic seat belts. The election of a new President seems to have prompted the agency's changed view of automatic seat belts, and such a change of administration is itself a reasonable basis for changing course. An agency may set its priorities in accordance with its governing administration's philosophy, so long as the agency acts within the limits laid down by Congress.

▌ANALYSIS

Standard-setting by the NHTSA (D) has proved most troublesome. Initial promulgation of standards was in large part mere adoption of already existing standards. The promulgation of new standards is associated with a whole

Continued on next page.

host of problems, including the problem of obtaining accurate information and the problem of enforcement, and the problems that may be encountered in negotiating such standards with industry and other interest groups.

■══■

Quicknotes

EMPIRICAL EVIDENCE Evidence based on observation or experimentation.

RULEMAKING The promulgation of a rule by an administrative agency, acting within the scope of its power pursuant to statute, enacting a rule governing a particular activity.

■══■

Federal Communications Commission v. Fox Television Stations, Inc.

Federal agency (P) v. Broadcasting company (D)

129 S. Ct. 1800 (2009).

NATURE OF CASE: Appeal from reversal of federal agency's order.

FACT SUMMARY: Fox Television Stations, Inc. (D) contended that the Federal Communications Commission's (P) abrupt change in policy regarding the broadcasting of indecent language was unsupported by adequate justification.

🏛 **RULE OF LAW**
The Administrative Procedure Act does not require an agency's change in policy to be justified by reasons more substantial than those required to adopt a policy in the first instance.

FACTS: Federal law bans the broadcasting of "any . . . indecent . . . language," 18 U.S.C. § 1464, which includes references to sexual or excretory activity or organs. The Federal Communications Commission ("Commission" or "FCC") (P) for a long time interpreted this to prohibit "language that describes, in terms patently offensive as measured by contemporary community standards for the broadcast medium, sexual or excretory activities or organs, at times of the day when there is a reasonable risk that children may be in the audience." The Commission (P) distinguished between literal and nonliteral uses of offensive language. (A literal use is a use of the word to describe a sexual or excretory activity or organ. A nonliteral use of a word does not refer to the sexual or excretory activity or organ.) In 1987, the Commission (P) determined that a single literal use may, depending on the context, result in a finding of indecency. With regard to nonliteral uses, the Commission (P) had determined that "deliberate and re-petitive use . . . is a requisite to a finding of indecency." Then, in 2004, the Commission's (P) *Golden Globes Order* repudiated this standard and declared for the first time that an expletive (nonliteral) use of sexual or excretory words could be actionably indecent, even when the word is used only once. The Commission (P) brought proceedings against Fox Television Stations, Inc. (Fox) (D) after a series of highly publicized occurrences of offensive language on live television broadcasts. On judicial review of orders penalizing Fox (D) for violating the prohibition on inde-cent broadcasting, but without imposing sanctions, Fox (D) argued that the Commission (P) had not provided adequate justification for its admitted change in policy. The court of appeals reversed the Commission (P), and the United States Supreme Court granted certiorari.

ISSUE: Does the Administrative Procedure Act require an agency's change in policy to be justified by reasons more

substantial than those required to adopt a policy in the first instance?

HOLDING AND DECISION: (Scalia, J.) No. The Administrative Procedure Act (APA) does not require an agency's change in policy to be justified by reasons more substantial than those required to adopt a policy in the first instance. Nowhere does the APA itself require a heightened standard of review of an agency's policy changes, nor does precedent contain such a rule. Although an agency must ordinarily display awareness that it is changing position, and may sometimes need to account for prior factfinding or certain reliance interests created by a prior policy, it need not demonstrate to a court's satisfaction that the reasons for the new policy are better than the reasons for the old one. It suffices that the new policy is permissible under the statute, that there are good reasons for it, and that the agency believes it to be better, which the conscious change adequately indicates. Under these standards, the Commission's (P) new policy and its order finding the broadcasts at issue actionably indecent were neither arbi-trary nor capricious. First, the Commission (P) forthrightly acknowledged that its recent actions had broken new ground, taking account of inconsistent prior Commission (P) and staff actions, and explicitly disavowing them as no longer good law. The agency's reasons for expanding its enforcement activity, moreover, were entirely rational. It was rational for the Commission (P) to conclude that even when used as an expletive, the "F-Word's" power to insult and offend derives from its sexual meaning, so that the decision to look at the patent offensiveness of even isolated uses of sexual and excretory words fits with a context-based approach. It was also rational for the Commission (P) to conclude that because its prior safe-harbor-for-single-words approach would likely lead to more widespread use, and, in light of technological advances reducing the costs of bleeping offending words, it was rational for the agency to step away from its old regime. The Commission's (P) decision not to impose sanctions also precludes any argument that it was arbitrarily punishing parties without notice of their actions' potential consequences. In addition, none of the court of appeals' grounds for finding the Commission's (P) action arbitrary and capricious is valid. First, the Commission (P) did not need empirical evidence proving that fleeting expletives constitute harmful "first blows" to children; it suffices to know that children mimic behavior they observe. Second, the court of appeals' finding that fidelity to the Commission's (P) "first blow"

Continued on next page.

theory would require a categorical ban on all broadcasts of expletives is not responsive to the actual policy under review since the Commission (P) has always evaluated the patent offensiveness of words and statements in relation to the context in which they were broadcast. The Commission's (P) decision to retain some discretion in less egregious cases does not invalidate its regulation of the broadcasts under review. Third, the Commission's (P) prediction that a per se exemption for fleeting expletives would lead to their increased use merits deference and makes entire sense. As to the dissents' arguments, independent agencies are not, contrary to the dissent, insulated from political oversight but are only insulated from presidential control, and thus there is no need for enhanced judicial review when they render major decisions. While the dissent is correct in pointing out that independent agencies in fact are more like agents of Congress, it does not follow from this observation that independent agencies must explain their decisions in detail. Instead, if the agencies are truly congressional agents, it should follow that it suffices that the agencies are acting at the behest of Congress, and no greater explanation for a change in agency policy is needed. Regardless, it is not current law that rulemaking by independent regulatory agencies is subject to heightened scrutiny. Finally, the dissents' concern for small broadcasters who may not have screening equipment is misplaced. Leaving aside the issue of whether small broadcasters run a heightened risk of punishment for use of fleeting expletives, the Commission's (P) order made clear that it would address each case on its own particular facts and circumstances, so it is not possible to know how it would treat a broadcaster that does not have screening equipment—although its treatment of Fox (D) in this case suggests that the Commission (P) would consider the burden of punishing broadcasters for failing to purchase equipment they cannot afford. In sum, the Commission (P) did not need to address small local broadcasters in detail, and its failure to do so is not an omission that renders its decision inadequate. Reversed and remanded.

DISSENT: (Stevens, J.) Independent agencies such as the FCC (P) are better viewed as Congress's agents, rather than as executive agencies. When the FCC (P) changes its policies—which it is permitted to do—it must follow its congressional mandate. Broadcasters have a substantial interest in regulatory stability, and here the FCC's (P) shifting and impermissibly vague indecency policy only imperils these broadcasters and muddles the regulatory landscape. It therefore makes eminent sense to require the Commission (P) to justify why its prior policy is no longer sound before allowing it to change course. The FCC's (P) congressional charter, the APA, and the rule of law all favor stability over administrative whim.

DISSENT: (Breyer, J.) The Commission (P) failed to adequately explain why it changed its policy position. Whatever explanation it did provide lacked any significant justification for a change of policy. Therefore, its change

was arbitrary and capricious. When an agency seeks to change its own rules, it must focus on the fact of change and explain the basis for that change. To explain a change requires more than setting forth reasons why the new policy is a good one. It also requires the agency to answer the question: "Why did you change?" The rational answer to which typically requires a more complete explanation than would prove satisfactory were change itself not at issue. However, requiring the agency to explain the rationality of its decision to effect a change is not the same as requiring it to provide a justification that is better than the reasons for the old policy. The APA nowhere grants agencies the freedom to change major policies on the basis of nothing more than political considerations or even personal whim. Here, the Commission's (P) explanations fall short in explaining why its policy change was justified and rest upon three considerations previously known to the agency. The Commission (P) also left out of its explanations factors that were critically important to its earlier policy (including local broadcasting considerations). The FCC (P) failed to consider the requirement that an agency at least minimally "consider . . . important aspect[s] of the problem." It said next to nothing about the relation between the change it made to its prior "fleeting expletive" policy and the First-Amendment-related need to avoid "censorship," though previously the Commission (P) had emphasized the need to avoid treading too close to the constitutional line. The Commission (P) also failed to assess the impact of its new policy on local broadcasters. This "aspect of the problem" is particularly important because the FCC (P) explicitly took account of potential broadcasting impact and because the concept of localism has been a cornerstone of broadcast regulation for decades. According to local and public service broadcasters, the FCC's (P) new policy will potentially impose great burdens on them, especially given that they are unable to afford bleeping technology. Had the FCC (P) used traditional administrative notice-and-comment procedures, these failures would clearly require a court to vacate the resulting agency decision; there is no reason to not reach a similar conclusion notwithstanding that notice-and-comment procedures were not used here, given that the policy is important, the significance of the issues is clear, and the agency's failures are nearly complete. With one exception, it provided no empirical or other information explaining why the three offered considerations, which did not justify its new policy before, justified it now, and even its discussion of the one exception (technological advances in bleeping/delay systems), which failed to take account of local broadcast coverage, was seriously incomplete. Essentially, the Commission's (P) answer to the question, "Why change?" is, "We like the new policy better." This kind of answer, while perfectly satisfactory were it given by an elected official, when given by an agency, in respect to a major change of an important policy where much more might be said, is insufficient, and renders the decision arbitrary and capricious, and an abuse of discretion.

▶ *ANALYSIS*

Because it is conceivable that the Commission's (P) orders could cause some broadcasters to avoid certain language that is beyond the Commission's (P) reach under the Constitution, Fox (D) asked the Court to rule on the constitutionality of the Commission's changed policy. However, the Court sidestepped this constitutional issue, remarking that any chilled references to excretory and sexual material "surely lie at the periphery of First Amendment concern," and indicating that it would instead await a lower court ruling on the issue that it could review, as per its customary procedure. On remand, the Second Circuit held the FCC's (P) new policy was impermissibly vague and unconstitutional under the First Amendment.

■═■

Quicknotes

ADMINISTRATIVE PROCEDURE ACT (AP) Enacted in 1946 to govern practices and proceedings before federal administrative agencies.

ARBITRARY AND CAPRICIOUS STANDARD Standard imposed in reviewing the decision of an agency or court when the decision may have been made in disregard of the facts or law.

■═■

Common-Law Requirements

Quick Reference Rules of Law

Boyce Motor Lines, Inc. v. United States

Common carrier (D) v. Federal government (P)

342 U.S. 337 (1952).

NATURE OF CASE: Appeal from a reversal of a decision holding an agency regulation impermissively vague.

FACT SUMMARY: Boyce Motor Lines, Inc. (D) contended that criminal charges in an indictment against it should have been dismissed because the Interstate Commerce Commission regulation on which the charges were based was impermissibly vague.

🏛 RULE OF LAW
An agency's regulation criminalizing conduct will be upheld where it provides a reasonable degree of certainty as to what constitutes criminal conduct, requires criminal intent, and has been carefully crafted on the basis of extensive study and public comment.

FACTS: Boyce Motor Lines, inc. (Boyce) (D) was charged with violating an Interstate Commerce Commission (ICC) regulation which prohibited the transport of dangerous commodities through congested thoroughfares. The regulation stated such activity shall be avoided "so far as practicable, and where feasible, by prearrangement of routes." The regulation was promulgated under a statute which directed that anyone knowingly violating the regulation be subject to fine or imprisonment or both. The district court dismissed those counts based on the regulation, holding the language impermissibly vague. The court of appeals reversed, and the United States Supreme Court granted certiorari.

ISSUE: Will an agency's regulation criminalizing conduct be upheld where it provides a reasonable degree of certainty as to what constitutes criminal conduct, requires criminal intent, and has been carefully crafted on the basis of extensive study and public comment?

HOLDING AND DECISION: (Clark, J.) Yes. An agency's regulation criminalizing conduct will be upheld where it provides a reasonable degree of certainty as to what constitutes criminal conduct, requires criminal intent, and has been carefully crafted on the basis of extensive study and public comment. Although a criminal statute must be sufficiently clear to inform citizens how to avoid its penalties, an agency in promulgating rules administering such statutes must be allowed to fulfill the statutory intent. No more than a reasonable degree of certainty can be demanded. Because the statute at bar requires specific intent to commit the violation, those subject to the regulation are put on adequate notice of its proscriptions, so that it is not unfair to prosecute them when they act with the requisite criminal intent. Whether Boyce (D) acted with such intent is a question that should be presented to a jury, and the indictment should be reinstated. Affirmed.

DISSENT: (Jackson, J.) Where the federal crime-making power is delegated to an agency such as the ICC, the exercise of that power must be rendered with a high degree of precision. The regulation here gives no standard by which "practicability" is to be judged; instead it leaves all routes equally open and all equally closed. There is no standard, either for a carrier or for a jury, to apply. Therefore, the regulation fails for vagueness.

▶ *ANALYSIS*

A legislature, as in this case, may allow an agency to establish regulations and provide that the violation thereof carry a criminal penalty. However, agencies themselves cannot impose criminal sanctions for violation of their regulations. Only a legislature may establish criminal sanctions.

■■■

Quicknotes

SPECIFIC INTENT The intent to commit a specific unlawful act which is a required element for criminal liability for certain crimes.

VAGUENESS AND OVERBREADTH Characteristics of a statute that make it difficult to identify the limits of the conduct being regulated.

■■■

Forsyth County, Georgia v. The Movement

County (D) v. Citizens' group (P)

505 U.S. 123 (1992).

NATURE OF CASE: Appeal from temporary restraining order and permanent injunction granted in favor of plaintiff on the grounds of facial invalidity of a county ordinance.

FACT SUMMARY: When The Movement (P) proposed to demonstrate in Forsyth County (the County) (D) in opposition to the federal holiday honoring the birthday of Martin Luther King, Jr., the County (D) imposed a $100 fee to cover the cost of maintaining public order, but instead of paying the fee, The Movement (P) sought injunctive relief and alleged that the ordinance was unconstitutional because it granted too much discretion to the government official setting the fee.

RULE OF LAW
A law subjecting the exercise of First Amendment freedoms to the prior restraint of a license must contain narrow, objective, and definite standards to guide the licensing authority.

FACTS: Forsyth County (County) (D) had enacted an ordinance requiring the payment of a fee in order for parade permits to be issued, to pay for the extra cost in maintaining public order. When The Movement (P) proposed to demonstrate in Forsyth County (the County) (D) in opposition to the federal holiday honoring the birthday of Martin Luther King, Jr., the County (D) imposed a $100 fee, but instead of paying the fee, The Movement (P) sought injunctive relief and alleged that the ordinance was unconstitutional because it granted too much discretion to the government official setting the fee. The fee did not include any calculation for expenses incurred by law enforcement authorities, but was capped at $1,000. The Movement (P) alleged that the ordinance was facially invalid because it offended the First and Fourteenth Amendments because it did not include standards by which the administrator had to calculate the amount of the fee charged. When the ordinance was struck down, Forsyth County (D) appealed, and the United States Supreme Court granted certiorari.

ISSUE: Must a law subjecting the exercise of First Amendment freedoms to the prior restraint of a license contain narrow, objective, and definite standards to guide the licensing authority?

HOLDING AND DECISION: (Blackmun, J.) Yes. A law subjecting the exercise of First Amendment freedoms to the prior restraint of a license must contain narrow, objective, and definite standards to guide the licensing authority. The administrator in this case was not required to rely on any objective factors when deciding how much to charge for police protection or administrative time. The law did not prevent the government official from encouraging some views and discouraging others by arbitrarily setting the fee amount. As construed here, the ordinance often required that the fee be based on the content of the speech. Moreover, the $1,000 cap on the fee cannot save it from being a content-based prior restriction, since the level of the fee is irrelevant. Affirmed.

DISSENT: (Rehnquist, J.) The case should be remanded so that a record of the way in which the ordinance was actually administered may be created.

ANALYSIS

The Court in this case found that the fee could be varied according to the content of the views expressed. Only viewpoint neutral time, place, and manner restrictions are allowed in such circumstances. The overbreadth doctrine was found to apply since application for a parade permit created a risk of suppression of ideas.

Quicknotes

FIRST AMENDMENT Prohibits Congress from enacting any law respecting an establishment of religion, prohibiting the free exercise of religion, abridging freedom of speech or the press, the right of peaceful assembly and the right to petition for a redress of grievances.

FOURTEENTH AMENDMENT No state shall deny to any person within its jurisdiction the equal protection of the laws.

OVERBREADTH That quality or characteristic of a statute, regulation, or order which reaches beyond the problem it was meant to solve causing it to sweep within it activity it cannot legitimately reach.

PRIOR RESTRAINT A restriction imposed on speech imposed prior to its communication.

SEC v. Chenery Corp. (I)

Federal agency (D) v. Company (P)

318 U.S. 80 (1943).

NATURE OF CASE: Appeal from an SEC reorganization approval order.

FACT SUMMARY: The Securities and Exchange Commission (D), purporting to base its determination on existing judge-made rules of equity, refused to approve a reorganization plan which would have allowed the Chenerys (P) to gain control of the newly organized company by dealing in the stock of the old company and obtaining preferred stock convertible into the common stock of the new corporation.

🏛 RULE OF LAW
The failure of an agency to state the basis upon which its determinations are made renders any such determinations invalid.

FACTS: The Public Utility Holding Company Act required Federal Water Service Corp. (Federal) to reorganize. The Chenerys (P), who were officers, directors, and controlling shareholders of Federal, unsuccessfully attempted to persuade the Securities and Exchange Commission ("SEC" or "Commission") (D) to authorize the conversion of the Class B common stock they owned into the common stock of the reorganized company. Subsequently, the Chenerys (P) purchased preferred stock authorized by the SEC (D) to be convertible into common stock of the reorganized company. This purchase was not made on inside information and was not fraudulent in any way. The SEC (D), however, refused to allow the Chenerys (P) to convert the stock and issued an order authorizing an alternative reorganization plan, which precluded the Chenerys (P) from gaining a controlling number of shares. The SEC (D), in issuing its order, failed to enumerate the grounds on which it rejected the original plan, except that, based on its idea of judicially imposed rules of equity, it concluded that, as a matter of fair dealing, managers and directors and other corporate fiduciaries cannot trade in the securities of the corporation while its reorganization plans are before the Commission (D). The Chenerys (P) appealed the order, the court of appeals reversed, and the United States Supreme Court granted certiorari.

ISSUE: Does the failure of an agency to state the basis upon which its determinations are made render any such determinations invalid?

HOLDING AND DECISION: (Frankfurter, J.) Yes. The failure of an agency to state the basis upon which its determinations are made renders any such determinations invalid. Although matters subject to administrative discretion are not to be overturned absent abuse, where an agency fails to base its determinations on its discretion, it must state the basis upon which the determination is made. In this case, the SEC (D) specifically stated its determination was based on judicial rules of equity. However, established rules of equity do not preclude corporate directors and managers from dealing in the stock of the corporation under the circumstances of this case. Therefore, absent a clear statement by the SEC (D) as to what specific basis underlay its rejection of the original plan, its order is invalid. Remanded.

DISSENT: (Black, J.) The majority does not question the SEC's (D) power to reject the original plan under the agency's statutory authority. Instead, the majority mistakenly concludes that the SEC's (D) decision was not entirely based on the Commission's (D) own experience. Contrary to the majority's conclusion, the Commission (D) made clear its findings, and, in light of those findings, determined that the proposed plan of reorganization would be unfair and inequitable. Moreover, it made its conclusion based on its members' experience. Although the agency did not burden its order with miniscule factual considerations, the omission merely saved the Commission (D) much unnecessary effort. The Court's requirement of more detailed findings will not profitably improve agencies' orders (here, for example, it will just require the Commission (D) to reformulate its findings and use more words) and indeed will only pave the way for courts to intrude into matters that are properly reserved for policy-making bodies. The SEC's (D) decision in this case was clearly a valid exercise of its power.

DECISION ON REMAND: (Federal Water Service Corp., 18 S.E.C. 231 (1945)): Proof that a corporation's managers intentionally purchased the company's stock at bargain prices during a corporate reorganization would, of course, invalidate the proposed reorganization. The same result applies, however, even without proof of an intentional breach of management's fiduciary responsibilities. Even without intentional wrongdoing, in such cases management would pit its interests against those of its stockholders; even in such circumstances, it is the incentive to misuse management's power that must be eliminated in order to protect the public. In our interpretation, the statute permits us to make such a determination, even in the absence of affirmative evidence of actual misconduct. Admittedly, promulgating a general rule proscribing such conduct as what occurred here might prove beneficial and feasible. At the same time, the agency has a duty to decide the merits of the reorganization plan now, even in the

Continued on next page.

absence of a general rule. The request for reorganization in this case is therefore denied.

▶ *ANALYSIS*

This case illustrates that even though an agency may make discretionary determinations, it must either base the determinations on its special expertise or specifically enumerate the basis for its decision. When an agency departs from its past rule of decision, or relies on judicial decisions, such must be fully explained to ensure adequate review.

■▬■

Quicknotes

AGENCY DISCRETION The authority conferred upon a public agency by law to act reasonably in accordance with its own judgment under certain circumstances.

CONVERTIBLE STOCK Stock that may be converted into common stock or some other type of security pursuant to its terms.

RULEMAKING The promulgation of a rule by an administrative agency, acting within the scope of its power pursuant to statute, enacting a rule governing a particular activity.

■▬■

SEC v. Chenery Corp. (II)

Federal agency (D) v. Company (P)

332 U.S. 194 (1947).

NATURE OF CASE: Appeal from a denial of a motion to amend a reorganization plan.

FACT SUMMARY: The Chenerys (P) contended that the Securities and Exchange Commission's (SEC's) (D) failure to promulgate a general rule prohibiting their trading in the stock of their controlled corporation during the pendency of its reorganization precluded the SEC (D) from reinstating its order to that effect after it was vacated and remanded.

🏛 RULE OF LAW
An agency, within its discretion, may issue ad hoc orders to cover specific situations and need not promulgate general rules in every case.

FACTS: The Securities and Exchange Commission's (SEC's) (D) order prohibiting the Chenerys (P) from converting preferred stock, purchased while a reorganization plan for their controlled corporation was pending, into common stock of the reorganized corporation was invalidated by the United States Supreme Court. The invalidation was premised on the SEC's (D) failure to specifically enumerate the judicial decisions it purportedly relied upon. Since prevailing law was contrary to the SEC (D) interpretation, the order was invalidated. On remand, the SEC (D) enumerated that the basis for its decision was its experience in reorganizations and issued the order under its discretionary power. The Chenerys (P) claimed that the only valid action by the SEC (D) would be by a general rule with prospective effect and that the order was invalid. The court of appeals set aside the SEC's (D) denial of the Chenerys' (P) motion to amend, and the United States Supreme Court granted certiorari.

ISSUE: May an agency issue ad hoc orders covering specific situations rather than promulgating general rules with purely prospective effect?

HOLDING AND DECISION: (Murphy, J.) Yes. When acting within its statutorily authorized scope of discretion, an agency may issue ad hoc orders covering specific situations. It need not issue general orders which only carry prospective effect. In this case, the original order was invalidated because the grounds stated for its basis were inconsistent with established law. The order, now supported by a clear articulation of the SEC's (D) reasons, and based on the SEC's (D) discretionary power, is valid. Because the SEC (D) clearly and thoroughly specified the bases for its decision, the order is valid and the SEC (D) need not have promulgated a general rule. The retroactive effect of the order is not fatal to its validity as such effect must be weighed against the interruption of the statutory design presented in the absence of such order. Accordingly, absent any abuse of discretion, the order is valid. Reversed.

DISSENT: (Jackson, J.) The order upheld in this case is the same order struck down previously; the same result is reached by the SEC's (D) order only via a different rationale. This is based more on the changing composition of the court than on sound legal principles. There remains no law or regulation consistent with the result of the Commission's (D) order, which works a forfeiture of private property based on no law, and, therefore, the order should not be upheld.

▶ ANALYSIS

After the *Chenery* litigation was concluded, the SEC seemed to retrench. In *Cities Service Co.,* 26 S.E.C. 678 (1947), it approved a plan allowing management to profit from trading in shares of its corporation during reorganization. The SEC stated that the *Chenery* litigation was limited to its peculiar facts.

■=■

Quicknotes

AGENCY DISCRETION The authority conferred upon a public agency by law to act reasonably in accordance with its own judgment under certain circumstances.

AD HOC For a specific purpose.

RULEMAKING The promulgation of a rule by an administrative agency, acting within the scope of its power pursuant to statute, enacting a rule governing a particular activity.

■=■

Arizona Grocery Co. v. Atchison, Topeka & Santa Fe Railway

Grocery company (P) v. Railroad (D)

284 U.S. 370 (1932).

NATURE OF CASE: Appeal from reversal of award of reparations in action over the reasonableness of shipping rates set by the Interstate Commerce Commission.

FACT SUMMARY: Atchison, Topeka & Santa Fe Railway (Atchison) (D) contended the Interstate Commerce Commission (ICC) could not require it to pay reparations to Arizona Grocery Co. (P) for overpayment of shipping rates because the rates charged were previously approved by the ICC.

🏛 RULE OF LAW
A rate that is declared by the Interstate Commerce Commission (ICC) to be legal and reasonable must be treated as such by the ICC, so that a carrier charging a rate within the limits of such pronouncement is not liable to shippers for reparations.

FACTS: A 1921 report and order issued by the Interstate Commerce Commission (ICC) declared that $0.96 was a reasonable rate for carriers to charge shippers. Atchison, Topeka & Santa Fe Railway (Atchison) (D) thereafter published and charged Arizona Grocery Co. (P) $0.96 as its shipping rate. Subsequently, the ICC declared Atchison's (D) rate to be unreasonable and ordered it to pay Arizona Grocery (P) reparations in the amount of shipping costs in excess of the newly declared reasonable rate. Atchison (D) contended that the ICC's original pronouncement that $0.96 was reasonable necessarily rendered $0.96 reasonable, and that, therefore, no reparations were due. Arizona Grocery (P) argued that although ICC pronouncements allow the carrier to set charges, such charges are still subject to declarations of unreasonableness in a shipper's suit for reparations. Arizona Grocery (P) sued in federal district court, which returned a judgment for Arizona Grocery (P). The court of appeals reversed, and the United States Supreme Court granted certiorari.

ISSUE: Must a rate that is declared by the ICC to be legal and reasonable be treated as such by the ICC, so that a carrier charging a rate within the limits of such pronouncement is not liable to shippers for reparations?

HOLDING AND DECISION: (Roberts, J.) Yes. A rate that is declared by the ICC to be legal and reasonable must be treated as such by the ICC, so that a carrier charging a rate within the limits of such pronouncement is not liable to shippers for reparations. The Interstate Commerce Act and subsequent amendments delegate congressional power to prescribe a maximum or minimum reasonable rate for shipment. Therefore, when the ICC declares such a rate, it speaks as the legislature, and the

declaration has the force of statute. A carrier therefore may rely on such a declaration in setting its rates without fear of subsequent liability for reparations. In this case, Atchison's (D) rate of $0.96 clearly falls within the rate of $0.96 previously declared reasonable by the ICC. Therefore, no reparations are recoverable. Affirmed.

DISSENT: (Holmes, J.) The ICC should not be precluded from awarding reparations under a previously approved rate as this is in line with the spirit of loose supervision of rates intended by the Interstate Commerce Act.

▶ ANALYSIS

This case recognizes the concept that an agency must follow its own rules. When an agency sets policy under its quasi-legislative power, it cannot subsequently contravene declared policy by exercising its quasi-judicial function. Commonly this concept is articulated by saying that an administrative ruling binds the world and the agency until it is changed. Exceptions have been recognized where the ruling relates to a purely internal agency policy or where a rule is waived to be lenient on a particular person.

■ ▬ ■

Quicknotes

COMMON CARRIER An entity whose business is the transport of persons or property.

RULEMAKING The promulgation of a rule by an administrative agency, acting within the scope of its power pursuant to statute, enacting a rule governing a particular activity.

■ ▬ ■

United States v. Caceres

Federal government (P) v. Criminal defendant (D)

440 U.S. 741 (1979).

NATURE OF CASE: Appeal from reversal of a conviction of attempted bribery of an IRS agent.

FACT SUMMARY: Caceres (D) attempted to exclude evidence gained by the Internal Revenue Service (IRS) in violation of IRS regulations, but not in violation of any constitutional or statutory requirement.

🏛 RULE OF LAW

A criminal defendant cannot exclude evidence gained in violation of administrative regulations.

FACTS: The Internal Revenue Service (IRS) placed Caceres (D) under surveillance and obtained evidence showing him to attempt to bribe an IRS agent. Although IRS regulations required such surveillance be given prior approval of the Justice Department, because of a time shortage, no approval was sought until after the evidence was gained. The evidence was not obtained in violation of any constitutional or statutory requirements. Caceres (D) sought to exclude the evidence. The district court admitted the evidence and Caceres (D) was convicted. The court of appeals reversed, and the United States Supreme Court granted certiorari.

ISSUE: Can a criminal defendant exclude evidence gained in violation of administrative regulations?

HOLDING AND DECISION: (Stevens, J.) No. A criminal defendant cannot exclude evidence gained in violation of administrative regulation. To allow a criminal defendant to enforce administrative regulations by application of the exclusionary rule would have a deterrent effect on the promulgation of standards to govern police and prosecutorial procedures. To require exclusion in each case of the violation of administrative procedure would take away from the executive branch the authority to fashion its own remedies for violation by an executive agency. Therefore, the evidence was properly admitted at trial. Reversed.

DISSENT: (Marshall, J.) Administrative agencies are bound by their rules of operation. One who is being investigated by an agency is legally entitled to insist the agency observe those rules. Due process requires an executive agency to adhere to its standards of conduct where individual interests are at stake, notwithstanding such adherence is not constitutionally or statutorily mandated.

▶ ANALYSIS

In this case, the Court points out that because this was not a case under the Administrative Procedure Act the requirement that agencies follow their own standards would not be enforced. Because the relief sought was not invalidation of agency action, but was a criminal prosecution, the APA did not apply. Some commentators sympathetic to Justice Marshall's position argue that a litigant at least be required to have relied on the agency regulation violated.

■══■

Quicknotes

BRIBERY The unlawful offering or accepting of something of value with the intent of influencing the judgment or actions of a public official in the discharge of his official duties.

EXCLUSIONARY RULE A rule precluding the introduction at trial of evidence unlawfully obtained in violation of the federal constitutional safeguards against unreasonable searches and seizures.

■══■

Schweiker v. Hansen

Secretary of Health (D) v. Social Security beneficiary (D)

450 U.S. 785 (1981).

NATURE OF CASE: Appeal from affirmance of judgment estopping the denial of retroactive Social Security benefits.

FACT SUMMARY: Hansen (P) sued to recover Social Security benefits from the Social Security Administration (SSA) to which she was entitled but erroneously led to believe she was ineligible for by an SSA employee.

🏛 RULE OF LAW
An agency is not estopped from denying retroactive benefits merely because its employee commits a minor breach of the agency's regulations.

FACTS: Hansen (P) was erroneously told by Connelly, an employee of the Social Security Administration (SSA), that she was ineligible for Social Security benefits. She subsequently filed an application for benefits and began to receive them. She then instituted suit against the SSA to recover benefits she would have received had Connelly not given her erroneous information. The Secretary of Health and Human Services, Schweiker (D), argued that under the law Hansen (P) was not legally eligible for benefits until she filed a written application. Hansen (P) responded that the Secretary (D) was estopped from asserting this defense because Connelly violated the internal agency manual in not encouraging her to apply at their initial meeting. The district court held Hansen (P) was substantively eligible upon her initial inquiry and that the Secretary (D) was estopped from denying the retroactive benefits. The court of appeals affirmed, and the United States Supreme Court granted certiorari.

ISSUE: Is an agency estopped from denying retroactive benefits merely because its employee commits a minor breach of the agency's regulations?

HOLDING AND DECISION: (Per curiam) No. An agency is not estopped from denying retroactive benefits merely because its employee violated a purely internal rule. The regulation violated in this case was merely and purely internal in effect, having no force of law. If such a breach could estop the Secretary (D), it would completely destroy the efficacy of the written application requirement as any minor breach could be asserted in support of retroactive benefits. Reversed.

▶ ANALYSIS

This case illustrates that an agency is not necessarily bound by its employee's failure to follow purely internal regulations. The Court overturned the court of appeals, which held that misinformation provided by an agency combined with a showing of misconduct should be sufficient to require estoppel even if the misconduct was not a violation of a legally binding rule.

Quicknotes

ESTOPPEL An equitable doctrine precluding a party from asserting a right to the detriment of another, who justifiably relied on the conduct.

Office of Personnel Management v. Richmond

Human resources office (D) v. Navy welder (P)

496 U.S. 414 (1990).

NATURE OF CASE: Appeal from judgment estopping the government from refusing to pay a disability annuity.

FACT SUMMARY: Richmond (P) retired from his job as a welder for the Navy after the Office of Personnel Management (OPM) (D) approved his application for a disability annuity due to his impaired eyesight, but when his disability benefits were suspended, he contended that the Government (D) was estopped from denying the benefits because he had relied on erroneous advice twice provided by the Navy.

⚖ RULE OF LAW
Estoppel against the government will not lie where payment is requested from the Treasury without appropriations made by law.

FACTS: As a welder for the Navy, Richmond's (P) impaired eyesight qualified him for a disability annuity under 5 U.S.C. § 8337(d). But the statute provided that disability payments would end if the retiree earned an amount fairly comparable to the current rate of pay of the position occupied at the time of retirement. The original measuring period for restoration of earning capacity was two years, but after 1982, the measuring period was changed from two years to one year. Upon retirement, Richmond (P) took a part-time job. Concerned about losing his eligibility if he made too much money, Richmond (P) twice consulted the Navy's Civilian Personnel Department and was given advice based on the former two-year eligibility rule. Richmond (P) then worked overtime in the erroneous belief his eligibility would not be affected, and OPM (D) suspended his disability annuity for six months. The court of appeals ruled that estoppel was properly applied against the federal government and ordered the suspended payments restored to Richmond (P). The United States Supreme Court granted certiorari.

ISSUE: Will estoppel against the government lie where payment is requested from the Treasury without appropriations made by law?

HOLDING AND DECISION: (Kennedy, J.) No. Estoppel against the government will not lie where payment is requested from the Treasury without appropriations made by law. Under the Constitution, "No money shall be drawn from the Treasury, but in consequence of appropriations made by law," (Appropriation Clause, Art. I, § 9, cl. 7). Judicial use of the equitable doctrine of estoppel cannot grant a money remedy that Congress has not authorized. The general purpose of the clause is to prevent fraud and corruption. But the direct purpose relevant to this case is to assure that public funds will be spent according to the letter of the difficult judgments reached by Congress as to the common good, and not according to the individual favor of government agents or the individual pleas of litigants. Estoppel claims based on real or imagined claims of misinformation by disgruntled citizens would impose an unpredictable drain on the public fisc. An assertion of estoppel against the government by a claimant seeking public funds has never been upheld, for courts cannot estop the Constitution. Reversed.

CONCURRENCE: (Stevens, J.) The proper issue is not the Appropriations Clause, but what rules govern administration of an appropriation that has already been made. There are strong equities favoring Richmond's (P) position, but unless the decision in *Federal Crop Ins. Corp. v. Merrill*, 322 U.S. 380 (1947), is repudiated by Congress or this Court, the kind of maladministration seen here must be tolerated.

DISSENT: (Marshall, J.) While the Appropriations Clause is not the proper issue, the facts do merit estoppel.

▶ ANALYSIS

Because of dicta in the Court's more recent cases, the courts of appeals had begun to apply equitable estoppel against the government. In *Richmond*, the Court declared it was not deciding whether an estoppel claim could ever succeed against the government. However, it also declared that it has reversed every finding of estoppel that it has reviewed.

■=■

Quicknotes

ANNUITY The payment or right to receive payment of a fixed sum periodically, for a specified time period.

APPROPRIATION The act of making something one's own or making use of something to serve one own's interest.

ESTOPPEL An equitable doctrine precluding a party from asserting a right to the detriment of another, who justifiably relied on the conduct.

■=■

United States v. Mendoza

Federal government (D) v. Filipino war veterans (P)

464 U.S. 154 (1984).

NATURE OF CASE: Appeal in action seeking naturalization of an alien who had served in the U.S. armed forces. [The procedural posture of the case is not presented in the casebook excerpt.]

FACT SUMMARY: Mendoza (P) contended that collateral estoppel, based on issues decided in prior litigation, required the Government (D) to grant him naturalization, even though he was not a party to the previous litigation.

> **RULE OF LAW**
> Collateral estoppel will be applied to suits against the United States only where the plaintiff was a party to the preceding litigation.

FACTS: In prior litigation, 68 Filipinos petitioned for naturalization based upon their service in the U.S. armed services in World War II. The district court in that action granted the petition, but the Government (D) decided not to appeal. Subsequently, Mendoza (P), not a party to that litigation, sued on identical grounds and argued that collateral estoppel required that his petition be granted. The United States Supreme Court granted certiorari. [The procedural posture of the case is not presented in the casebook excerpt.]

ISSUE: Will collateral estoppel be applied to suits against the United States only where the plaintiff is a party to the preceding litigation?

HOLDING AND DECISION: (Rehnquist, J.) Yes. Collateral estoppel will be applied to suits against the United States only where the plaintiff was a party to the preceding litigation. The variety and quantity of litigation brought against the Government (D), in addition to the changes in policy by new administrations, requires a cap on the use of collateral estoppel. The decision to appeal may be based on existing policies which change over time. Thus, requiring the plaintiff to be a party is necessary to the expeditious administration of justice. Because Mendoza (P) was not a plaintiff in the earlier case, he cannot invoke collateral estoppel here.

▌ *ANALYSIS*

In cases not involving the United States, an identity of party litigants is not necessary for application of collateral estoppel. A distinction was made in this case due to the unusual position the government plays in litigation. This distinction, however, severely limits the application of collateral estoppel against the government by parties who would otherwise benefit from it.

Quicknotes

COLLATERAL ESTOPPEL A doctrine whereby issues litigated and determined in a prior proceeding are binding upon all subsequent litigation between the parties regarding that issue.

NATURALIZATION The process pursuant to which a person becomes a citizen of the United States.

Bowen v. Georgetown University Hospital

Federal department (D) v. Hospital (P)

488 U.S. 204 (1988).

NATURE OF CASE: Appeal of a decision allowing retroactive application of an agency rule.

FACT SUMMARY: The Department of Health and Human Services (D) promulgated a retroactive rule limiting the amount of money Medicare would reimburse hospitals, whereupon several hospitals sought judicial review, claiming the rule was unlawfully retroactive.

🏛 RULE OF LAW
An agency may not exercise its rulemaking authority to promulgate cost limits that are retroactive.

FACTS: The Department of Health and Human Services (HHS) (D) used indices of average wages in calculating the limits it set on the amount of money Medicare would reimburse hospitals. In 1981, HHS (D) promulgated a rule saying it would not look at federally owned hospitals' wages when calculating these indices. In 1983, the D.C. Circuit invalidated the 1981 rule on procedural grounds, and in 1984, HHS (D) held new, procedurally proper rulemaking proceedings and reissued the 1981 rule with retroactive effect. However, because Congress had changed the law in the meantime, the 1984 rule applied only to cost reimbursement for 1981 and 1982. Georgetown Hospital (P), along with several other hospitals that had benefited from the invalidation of the 1981 rule, sought judicial review of the 1984 rule, claiming it was unlawfully retroactive. The lower courts ruled in favor of Georgetown Hospital (P), and this appeal followed. The United States Supreme Court granted certiorari.

ISSUE: May an agency exercise its rulemaking authority to promulgate cost limits that are retroactive?

HOLDING AND DECISION: (Kennedy, J.) No. An agency may not exercise its rulemaking authority to promulgate cost limits that are retroactive. An administrative agency's power to promulgate legislative regulations is limited to the authority delegated by Congress. Congressional enactments and administrative rules will not be construed to have retroactive effect unless their language requires that result. The threshold question is whether the Medicare Act authorizes retroactive rulemaking. While § 1395x(v)(1)(A)(ii) of the Medicare Act on its face permits some form of retroactive action, the structure and language of the statute require the conclusion that the retroactivity provision applies only to case-by-case adjudication, not to rulemaking. The statutory provisions establishing the agency's general rulemaking power contain no express authorization of retroactive rulemaking. Further, a review of legislative intent also indicates that no

such authority was contemplated. Indeed, the House and Senate Committee Reports expressed a desire to forbid retroactive cost-limit rules. Thus, the language and structure of the Medicare Act compels the conclusion that the Secretary (Bowen) (D) has no authority to promulgate retroactive cost-limit rules.

CONCURRENCE: (Scalia, J.) The Administrative Procedure Act (A.P.A.) independently confirms the judgment reached. The only plausible reading of § 551(4) of the A.P.A. is rules have legal consequences only for the future. "The issue is not whether retroactive rulemaking is fair," but rather "whether it is a permissible form of agency action under the particular structure established by the A.P.A." HHS (D) proves nothing that can bring it within that structure.

▶ ANALYSIS

Retroactivity is not favored in the law. Thus, the Court was not willing to read into the statutory provision an implied permission for retroactive application of an agency's cost-limit rules. Further, the Court, deferring to the action of Congress, did not find any express authorization for retroactive cost-limit rules in its examination of legislative history. In fact, the retroactivity of the cost-limit provision was directly addressed in the legislative history, where it was specifically stated that the proposed new authority to set limits on costs would be exercised on a prospective, rather than retrospective, basis.

■=■

Quicknotes

JUDICIAL REVIEW The authority of the courts to review decisions, actions or omissions committed by another agency or branch of government.

LEGISLATIVE INTENT The legislature's motivation or rationale for promulgating a statute.

RULEMAKING The promulgation of a rule by an administrative agency, acting within the scope of its power pursuant to statute, enacting a rule governing a particular activity.

■=■

Procedural Requirements in Agency Decisionmaking

Quick Reference Rules of Law

Londoner v. Denver

Property owner (P) v. City council (D)

210 U.S. 373 (1908).

NATURE OF CASE: Appeal of a tax assessment.

FACT SUMMARY: Londoner (P) contended the Denver City Council (D) denied him due process by imposing an assessment of paving costs without notice and an evidentiary hearing.

🏛 RULE OF LAW
Due process requires that before a tax set by an agency becomes irrevocably fixed, the taxpayers be afforded notice and an opportunity to participate in an oral evidentiary hearing.

FACTS: The Denver City Council (the Council) (D), under statutory authority, approved an assessment on Londoner's (P) property for the costs of paving a public street. Before approving the assessment the Council (D) gave notice to Londoner and afforded an opportunity to file written objections to the assessment. Londoner's (P) objections consisted of allegations that the hearing procedures, precluding the presentation of evidence, denied due process. The Colorado courts rejected Londoner's (P) contentions, and the United States Supreme Court took jurisdiction.

ISSUE: Does due process require that before a tax is irrevocably set by an agency the taxpayers be afforded notice and an opportunity to participate in an oral evidentiary hearing?

HOLDING AND DECISION: (Moody, J.) Yes. Due process requires that before a tax is set by an agency the taxpayers be afforded notice and an opportunity to participate in an evidentiary hearing. While there are few constitutional restrictions on a state legislature's power to tax, there are limitations imposed where this power is delegated to an administrative agency. In such a case, as here, more than an opportunity to tender written objections to the tax is required by due process. The taxpayer must be allowed to present evidence in support of his allegations, and an opportunity to participate in oral argument. The failure to afford such opportunities in this case renders the assessments invalid as adopted through a denial of due process. Reversed.

▶ ANALYSIS

This case illustrates the general requirement that agencies exercising taxation or economic regulation follow formal procedures. This requirement can have several sources including the agency's enabling statute, its own procedural requirements, the Administrative Procedure Act, federal common law, and judicial decisions.

Quicknotes

EVIDENTIARY HEARING Hearing pertaining to the evidence of the case.

NOTICE Communication of information to a person by an authorized person or an otherwise proper source.

PROCEDURAL DUE PROCESS The constitutional mandate that if the state or federal government acts so as to deny a citizen of a life, liberty or property interest the individual is first entitled to notice and the right to be heard.

Bi-Metallic Investment Co. v. State Board of Equalization

Property owner (P) v. State board (D)

239 U.S. 441 (1915).

NATURE OF CASE: Suit to enjoin enforcement of administrative order.

FACT SUMMARY: Bi-Metallic Investment Co. (Bi-Metallic) (P) sued Colorado (D) to enjoin enforcement of an order increasing property taxes in Denver. Bi-Metallic (P) argued that it was entitled to an opportunity to be heard in opposition to the order.

🏛 RULE OF LAW
Where an agency rule will apply to a vast number of people, the Constitution does not require that each be given an opportunity to be heard directly for the purpose of arguing in favor of or against its adoption.

FACTS: The Colorado Tax Commission (D) and the State Board of Equalization (D) ordered a 41 percent increase in the valuation of all taxable property in the city of Denver. Bi-Metallic Investment Co. (Bi-Metallic) (P), the owner of certain real estate in Denver, sought to enjoin enforcement of the order. It argued that it had been afforded no opportunity to be heard in opposition to the order, and was thus threatened with deprivation of property without due process of law. The Supreme Court of Colorado ordered dismissal of Bi-Metallic's (P) claim, and Bi-Metallic (P) appealed to the United States Supreme Court, which granted review.

ISSUE: Where an agency rule will apply to a vast number of people, does the Constitution require that each be given an opportunity to be heard directly for the purpose of arguing in favor of or against its adoption?

HOLDING AND DECISION: (Holmes, J.) No. Where an agency rule will apply to a vast number of people, the Constitution does not require that each be given an opportunity to be heard directly for the purpose of arguing in favor of or against its adoption. Agency orders and rules which will affect vast numbers of people may be adopted without affording every interested party a direct opportunity to be heard. In cases such as the present one, it would be impractical to allow all individuals affected to offer a direct voice in support of or in opposition to an order. Thus, the Constitution is satisfied by the fact that, as voters, the taxpayers involved exercise power, remote or direct, over those responsible for the order. Accordingly, the judgment of the state supreme court dismissing this suit must be affirmed. Affirmed.

▶ ANALYSIS

The result of this case is opposite to that reached in *Londoner v. Denver*, 210 U.S. 373 (1908). However, the apparent conflict between the two cases is explained by the observation that *Bi-Metallic* involved so-called "legislative" facts whereas *Londoner* was a case which presented an issue requiring evaluation of "adjudicative" facts. "Legislative" facts are those which primarily involve determinations of broad policies or principles of general application, e.g., whether every tract of land in a large city has been under-assessed for property tax purposes. In resolving issues pertaining to "legislative" as opposed to "adjudicative" facts, administrative agencies may dispense with the practice of according every interested party an opportunity to be heard.

■=■

Quicknotes

ADMINISTRATIVE ORDER The final disposition of an administrative hearing or the interpretation or application of a statute.

RULEMAKING The promulgation of a rule by an administrative agency, acting within the scope of its power pursuant to statute, enacting a rule governing a particular activity.

■=■

Southern Railway v. Virginia

Railroad company (P) v. State commissioner (D)

290 U.S. 190 (1933).

NATURE OF CASE: Appeal from a decision upholding a state administrative order.

FACT SUMMARY: Southern Railway (P) contended that a Virginia (D) statute, which allowed the State Highway Commissioner to eliminate grade crossings on private land without prior notice, deprived it of constitutional rights not to be deprived of property without due process.

> 🏛 **RULE OF LAW**
> A state statute that allows an administrative officer to make final factual determinations without notice, hearing, or taking evidence violates the Fourteenth Amendment right to due process.

FACTS: The Virginia (D) Highway Commissioner decided to eliminate a grade crossing and directed Southern Railway (Southern) (P) to construct an overhead railroad passage. This decision was made under authority of a Virginia (D) statute which allowed this action to be taken, without prior notice, when in the opinion of the Commissioner the grade required elimination for public safety and convenience. The statute makes no provision for appeal of the Commissioner's determination which is final unless shown to be arbitrary. Southern (P) claimed the statute deprived it of property without due process because of the lack of notice and hearing requirement. The lower courts held for the Commissioner (D), and the United States Supreme Court took jurisdiction.

ISSUE: Does a state statute that allows an administrative officer to make final factual determinations without notice, hearing, or taking evidence violate the Fourteenth Amendment right to due process?

HOLDING AND DECISION: (McReynolds, J.) Yes. A state statute that allows an administrative officer to make final factual determinations without notice, hearing, or taking evidence violates the Fourteenth Amendment right to due process. No officer of government has the power to make a binding, final determination without evidence. Such findings are arbitrary and baseless. The statute in this case allows such findings be made without evidence, or prior notice and hearing. Further, it does not provide for review of such findings. The elimination of the grade crossing and the order to construct an overhead crossing requires an outlay of money. Therefore, the order deprives Southern (D) of its property. The failure to provide prior notice and hearing or to hear evidence constitutes a deprivation of property without due process. Therefore the statute endowing the administrative officer

with such authority violates the Fourteenth Amendment. Reversed.

DISSENT: (Stone, J.) The Commissioner's power in this regard is a valid delegation of authority, as it allows him to abate public nuisances, and the authorizing statute provides adequate review in the event of abuse of the delegated power.

▶ ANALYSIS

Some commentators argue that the opinion in this case can be interpreted as not requiring a hearing if there was a greater opportunity for review of the merits available in state court. If so, there is some debate whether judicial review is an adequate substitute for a prior administrative hearing. Even if judicial review is available, a prior hearing may also be constitutionally required.

∎■∎

Quicknotes

FOURTEENTH AMENDMENT Declares that no state shall make or enforce any law which shall abridge the privileges and immunities of citizens of the United States.

NOTICE Communication of information to a person by an authorized person or an otherwise proper source.

PROCEDURAL DUE PROCESS The constitutional mandate that if the state or federal government acts so as to deny a citizen of a life, liberty or property interest the individual is first entitled to notice and the right to be heard.

∎■∎

Dominion Energy Bayton Point, LLC v. Johnson

Energy company (P) v. Government official (D)

443 F.3d 12 (1st Cir. 2006).

NATURE OF CASE: Appeal in action challenging the Environmental Protection Agency's denial of a request for a variance from requirements under the Clean Water Act.

FACT SUMMARY: Dominion Energy Bayton Point, LLC (Dominion) (P), which operated a power plant, contended that the Environmental Protection Agency (D) had to hold a formal adjudicatory hearing before refusing Dominion's (P) request for a variance from generally applicable requirements under the Clean Water Act.

🏛 RULE OF LAW
The Environmental Protection Agency's (EPA's) conclusion that the term "public hearing" in the Clean Water Act does not require an evidentiary hearing before the EPA issues a National Pollutant Discharge Elimination System (NPDES) permit is entitled to *Chevron* deference where Congress has not spoken directly to the issue and the EPA's interpretation is reasonable.

FACTS: Under the Clean Water Act (CWA), before the Environmental Protection Agency (EPA) (D) either issues or renews a National Pollutant Discharge Elimination System (NPDES) permit, the EPA (D) must provide an "opportunity for public hearing." However, the CWA does not define "public hearing." Dominion Energy Bayton Point, LLC (Dominion) (P), which operated a power plant, sought a variance from generally applicable requirements for thermal discharges. In renewing Dominion's (P) permit, the EPA (D) denied the variance. The EPA (D) had concluded through rulemaking that the CWA did not require a formal hearing, and its denial was made on the basis of written submission. Dominion (P) challenged the EPA's (D) ruling, contending that the EPA (D) had to hold a formal adjudicatory hearing before refusing its request. The court of appeals granted review. [The procedural posture of the case is not presented in the casebook excerpt.]

ISSUE: Is the Environmental Protection Agency's (EPA's) conclusion that the term "public hearing" in the Clean Water Act (CWA) does not require an evidentiary hearing before the EPA issues a National Pollutant Discharge Elimination System (NPDES) permit entitled to *Chevron* deference where Congress has not spoken directly to the issue and the EPA's interpretation is reasonable?

HOLDING AND DECISION: (Selya, J.) Yes. The Environmental Protection Agency's (EPA's) conclusion that the term "public hearing" in the Clean Water Act (CWA) does not require an evidentiary hearing before the EPA issues a National Pollutant Discharge Elimination

System (NPDES) permit is entitled to *Chevron* deference, *Chevron U.S.A., Inc. v. Natural Resources Defense Council*, 467 U.S. 837 (1984), where Congress has not spoken directly to the issue and the EPA's interpretation is reasonable. In *Seacoast Anti-Pollution League v. Costle*, 572 F.2d 872 (1st Cir. 1978), this court held that the CWA does trigger a formal hearing under the Administrative Procedure Act (APA). Since then, the *Chevron* case was decided. Under Supreme Court precedent, if the EPA's (D) interpretation of the CWA merits deference, *Seacoast* cannot be controlling. First, *Seacoast* did not hold that Congress clearly intended the term "public hearing" in the CWA to mean "evidentiary hearing." Instead, the court in *Seacoast*, faced with unclear congressional intent and an opaque statute, determined what it believed to be the best construction of the CWA's "public hearing" language. Such a determination, however, is appropriate under step two of *Chevron*, not under step one. Therefore, under the Supreme Court's precedent in *Brand X Internet Services*, 545 U.S. 967 (2005), *Seacoast* must yield to a reasonable agency interpretation of the CWA's "public hearing" requirement. Here, the EPA's (D) interpretation was reasonable, as it took into account the private interests at stake, the risk of erroneous decision-making, and the nature of the government interest. The EPA's (D) therefore seems reasonable. Contrary to Dominion's (P) assertion, *Seacoast* was not an interpretation of the APA, but clearly interpreted the CWA, and, accordingly, Dominion's (P) argument that the EPA's (D) interpretation is not entitled to deference (since *Chevron* deference is inappropriate vis-à-vis an agency interpretation of the APA's burden-of-proof provision) must be rejected. For these reasons, the EPA (D) was not required to provide an evidentiary hearing on Dominion's (P) permit application and requested variance. [The disposition of this case is not indicated in casebook excerpt.]

▶ ANALYSIS

The circuit courts are split as to the issue presented by the *Dominion* case. In addition to the First Circuit, which decided *Dominion*, the D.C. Circuit has also deferred to the EPA's (D) interpretation that "public hearing" does not require an evidentiary hearing. See *Chemical Waste Management, Inc. v. EPA*, 873 F.2d 1477 (D.C. Cir. 1989). On the other hand, the Ninth Circuit continues to hold that a requirement of a "public hearing" in an adjudicatory context triggers an evidentiary hearing under the APA, but that circuit has also ruled that such an evidentiary hearing need

Continued on next page.

not be a full-blown, trial-type hearing. See *United Farm-workers of America v. EPA,* 592 F.3d 1080 (9th Cir. 2010).

■━■

Quicknotes

EVIDENTIARY HEARING   Hearing pertaining to the evidence of the case.

PUBLIC HEARING   A hearing before anybody in which the parties have the right to appear and present evidence and to call and examine witnesses.

■━■

National Petroleum Refiners Association v. FTC

Trade association (P) v. Federal commission (D)

482 F.2d 672 (D.C. Cir. 1973).

NATURE OF CASE: Appeal from denial of an agency's substantive rulemaking power.

FACT SUMMARY: National Petroleum Refiners Association (P) challenged the Federal Trade Commission's (FTC's) (D) power to promulgate rules governing private business conduct claiming such power was beyond the FTC's (D) statutory authority.

> ## 🏛 RULE OF LAW
> The Federal Trade Commission is empowered under the Federal Trade Act to promulgate substantive rules defining statutory standards of illegality.

FACTS: The Federal Trade Commission Act (the Act) vested in the Federal Trade Commission (FTC) (D) the power to prevent unfair or deceptive acts or practices in commerce, and to make rules to carry out the purpose of the Act. The FTC (D) promulgated a regulation declaring that it was illegal under the Act to fail to post octane rating numbers on gas pumps at service stations. National Petroleum Refiners Association (P) contended the FTC's (D) rulemaking power was limited to specifying nonadjudicatory investigative functions of the agency, and that it did not extend to substantive rulemaking to be used in its adjudicatory function. The district court held the FTC (D) lacked substantive rulemaking power, and the FTC (D) appealed.

ISSUE: Is the FTC empowered under the Federal Trade Act to promulgate substantive rules defining statutory standards of illegality?

HOLDING AND DECISION: (Wright, J.) Yes. The FTC is empowered under the Federal Trade Act to promulgate substantive rules defining statutory standards of illegality. The power of substantive rulemaking is essential to efficient administration. Substantive rulemaking is fairer to regulated parties than total reliance on case-by-case adjudications. The use of notice and public participation in rulemaking proceedings precludes one market participant from being singled out for regulation while all others are free to violate the Act until legal action is brought. As a result, the rules developed here were valid. Reversed.

▌ *ANALYSIS*

Rulemaking involves the promulgation of general standards applicable to all parties regulated under the agency's enabling Act. Adjudication, on the other hand, is a case by case development of agency policy and binds only the parties to the litigation. Some enabling statutes specifically bestow substantive rulemaking power on the agency, while others, such as the Federal Trade Act, merely contain catchall provisions giving the agency power to make rules in furtherance of the statutory purpose. In the latter case, substantive rulemaking power becomes a product of statutory interpretation.

■■■

Quicknotes

ENABLING ACT A statute that confers new powers upon a person or entity.

RULEMAKING The promulgation of a rule by an administrative agency, acting within the scope of its power pursuant to statute, enacting a rule governing a particular activity.

■■■

NLRB v. Wyman-Gordon Co.

Federal agency (D) v. Private company (P)

394 U.S. 759 (1969).

NATURE OF CASE: Appeal from judgment vacating an agency order requiring a company to provide its employees' names and addresses to a labor union.

FACT SUMMARY: The National Labor Relations Board (NLRB) (D) ordered Wyman-Gordon Co. (P) to produce a list of its employees' names and addresses to labor unions. The NLRB (D) based its order on a requirement that the agency had only prospectively applied even though the requirement had arisen during an adjudicative proceeding, not under the statutorily required rulemaking process.

RULE OF LAW

An agency can order parties to comply with an agency requirement even if the requirement is in effect a rule promulgated in violation of the Administrative Procedure Act.

FACTS: The National Labor Relations Board NLRB (D) ordered Wyman-Gordon Co. (P) to provide a list of its employees' names and addresses to labor unions who sought to organize the employees. Supporting the order was a ruling in a recent NLRB (D) adjudication, *Excelsior Underwear, Inc.,* 156 N.L.R.B. 1236 (1966). In *Excelsior,* the NLRB (D) had decided that disclosures of such lists should be required but that the requirement should not be applied retrospectively against the companies that were before the agency in *Excelsior.* Instead, the NLRB (D) decided that its heavily briefed decision in *Excelsior* should apply only prospectively, taking effect thirty (30) days after entry of the order in *Excelsior.* Wyman-Gordon (P) challenged the disclosure order based on *Excelsior,* and the court of appeals vacated the order. The court of appeals reasoned (1) that the requirement arising in *Excelsior* was invalid because it was actually a rule that required compliance with the Administrative Procedure Act's (APA's) rulemaking procedures, not with the procedures governing the adjudicative setting in *Excelsior;* and (2) that the disclosure order against Wyman-Gordon (P) thus was necessarily invalid as it was based on the invalid *Excelsior* requirement. The NLRB (D) petitioned the United States Supreme Court for further review, and the Supreme Court granted certiorari.

ISSUE: Can an agency order parties to comply with an agency requirement even if the requirement is in effect a rule promulgated in violation of the APA?

HOLDING AND DECISION: (Fortas, J.) Yes. An agency can order parties to comply with an agency requirement even if the requirement is in effect a rule promulgated in violation of the APA. An agency may not avoid the APA's procedural rulemaking requirements by in effect making rules through adjudication. *Excelsior*'s prospective requirement was not published in the Federal Register, as the APA requires for rules, and the failure to publish in the Federal Register meant that only a select group of organizations were notified of the rule. The rule in *Excelsior* was therefore clearly invalid. Nonetheless, the order against Wyman-Gordon (P) was just as clearly valid. It was an order, and Wyman-Gordon (P) therefore was required to obey it. Reversed.

CONCURRENCE: (Black, J.) The plurality reached the right result, but it did so under a flawed rationale. The upshot of the plurality's reasoning is that an agency should follow the law for a rulemaking, but that courts are nevertheless required to enforce orders that are based on invalidly adopted rules. Contrary to such reasoning, courts should not reward unlawful agency procedure by permitting agencies to base future action on invalid earlier actions. In this case, however, the underlying *Excelsior* requirement was not improper: it legitimately arose during an adjudication of an individual case, and the NLRB (D) followed all the procedural requirements for adjudication in *Excelsior.* The order against Wyman-Gordon (P) therefore must be valid, too.

DISSENT: (Douglas, J.) The rule in *Excelsior* did not apply to the specific case then before the NLRB (D); it applied only prospectively, to cases in general, and it states policy instead of deciding a particular set of facts. In such cases, the APA requires certain procedures, including a public hearing, before the rule can take effect.

DISSENT: (Harlan, J.) Under the APA, an agency is not adjudicating when it fashions a rule but fails to apply it to the current dispute in an order that imposes a final disposition as to the current parties. Under the APA, therefore, the NLRB's (D) rule arising from *Excelsior* clearly required compliance with the APA's rulemaking procedures. This conclusion leaves no alternative but to affirm the court of appeals' decision to vacate the disclosure order issued against Wyman-Gordon (P). To do otherwise is to permit the NLRB (D) to benefit from what the plurality itself concludes was a clear failure to comply with the APA in *Excelsior.* Given the invalid basis for the disclosure order against Wyman-Gordon (P), *Chenery I,* (*SEC v. Chenery Corp.*, 318 U.S. 80 (1943)), required this Court to remand this case to the NLRB (D) for reconsideration of all appropriate issues.

Continued on next page.

▶ *ANALYSIS*

The student should treat this summary's "rule of law" with care. As a plurality opinion, the first opinion in *Wyman-Gordon* does not have the precedential value usually required for a case to be seen as announcing a "rule of law." See, e.g., *Seminole Tribe of Florida v. Florida,* 517 U.S. 44, 66 (1996) (the precedential value of a plurality opinion is undercut when, as in *Wyman-Gordon,* a majority of the Court disagrees with the plurality's rationale). The plurality's remarkably weak rationale, requiring a company to obey an invalid order for what amounts to no higher value than blind obedience, looks all the weaker in comparison with the reasoning of Justice Harlan, whose conclusion to vacate the disclosure order required only that the plurality follow its own invalidation of the *Excelsior* order to that holding's logical conclusion (i.e., that the order against Wyman-Gordon (P) was also necessarily invalid). Six members of the Court—Justices Fortas, Stewart, White, Douglas, and Harlan, along with Chief Justice Warren—agreed that the *Excelsior* rule was invalid. But only two of those six—Justices Douglas and Harlan—voted to require the agency to pay a price for not following the law.

■═■

Quicknotes

ADJUDICATORY PROCEEDING A hearing conducted by an administrative agency resulting in a final judgment regarding the rights of the parties involved.

JUDICIAL REVIEW The authority of the courts to review decisions, actions or omissions committed by another agency or branch of government.

LABOR UNION A group of employees formed for the purpose of obtaining more favorable working conditions or wages.

RULEMAKING The promulgation of a rule governing a particular activity by an administrative agency, acting within the scope of its power pursuant to statute.

■═■

Morton v. Ruiz

Bureau of Indian Affairs (D) v. Native American (P)

415 U.S. 199 (1974).

NATURE OF CASE: Appeal from reversal of dismissal of action seeking general assistance benefits.

FACT SUMMARY: Ruiz (P), an Indian, was denied general assistance benefits because he did not live on a reservation.

🏛 RULE OF LAW
Before an agency may extinguish the entitlement of potential beneficiaries, it must comply with its own internal procedures.

FACTS: The Bureau of Indian Affairs (BIA) (D) deemed that Indians would not be eligible for general assistance benefits if they did not live on a reservation. Ruiz (P), an Indian, was denied general assistance benefits because he did not live on a reservation. The BIA (D) did not publish its eligibility requirements for general assistance in the federal register. This was the case even though the BIA (D) declared in its Manual that eligibility requirements for benefits were to be published. Ruiz (P) utilized his administrative remedies and then brought suit in the district court, which dismissed the action. The court of appeals reversed, and the United States Supreme Court granted certiorari.

ISSUE: Before an agency may extinguish the entitlement of potential beneficiaries, must it comply with its own internal procedures?

HOLDING AND DECISION: (Blackmun, J.) Yes. Before an agency may extinguish the entitlement of potential beneficiaries, it must comply with its own internal procedures. The congressional intent is not to exclude Indians not living on the reservation from receiving benefits. The congressional appropriation was intended to cover welfare services at least to those Indians residing on or near the reservation. Although the BIA (D) has the power to create reasonable classifications, and has some residual discretion, especially if funding is insufficient to cover all intended beneficiaries, no matter how rational or consistent with congressional intent a particular decision might be, the determination of eligibility cannot be made on an ad hoc basis by the dispenser of the funds. Here, the BIA (D) chose not to publish its eligibility requirements for general assistance in the federal register. The only official manifestation of its policy is in its Manual. Where individuals' rights are at stake, it is incumbent upon agencies to follow their own procedures, even if such procedures are possibly more rigorous than otherwise would be required. Before the BIA (D) may extinguish the entitlement of these otherwise eligible beneficiaries, it must comply, at a minimum, with its own internal procedures. The BIA (D) must promulgate eligibility requirements according to established procedures. Affirmed and remanded.

▶ ANALYSIS

According to Fuchs, this case stands partly for the proposition that "limitations on eligibility may not be newly imposed case by case, even on the basis of reasoned opinions, because the limitations must be made known in advance to persons adversely affected by them." Furthermore, Fuchs says that the development of criteria which seems to conflict with the statutory mandate is a power which is hard to regulate. Moreover, this power is an extremely wide one. Gellhorn, W., *Admin. Law*, 239.

Quicknotes

SNYDER ACT Provides that general assistance benefits shall be available to Native Americans.

APA Provides that administration policies affecting individual rights should follow stated procedures so as not to be arbitrary.

NLRB v. Bell Aerospace Co.

Federal agency (D) v. Private company (P)

416 U.S. 267 (1974).

NATURE OF CASE: Appeal from judgment invalidating an administrative order.

FACT SUMMARY: Bell Aerospace Co. (P) opposed a representation election on the grounds that its buyers were "managerial employees" and were thus not covered by the National Labor Relations Act or entitled to elect union representation.

🏛 RULE OF LAW
The National Labor Relations Board is not precluded from announcing new principles in an adjudicative proceeding.

FACTS: In an unfair-labor-practice adjudication before the National Labor Relations Board (NLRB) (D), Bell Aerospace Co. (P) defended itself by arguing that the buyer-employees opposing the company were "managerial employees" to whom the National Labor Relations Act did not apply. A long line of NLRB (D) adjudicative precedent supported Bell Aerospace's (P) position on this point. The NLRB (D) disagreed with Bell Aerospace (D), however, classifying the buyers as "nonmanagerial employees" and ordering the company to bargain with the buyers' chosen labor union. Bell Aerospace (P) appealed that administrative order, and the court of appeals held that making such a radical change in an adjudication would impose an unfairly retroactive policy upon Bell Aerospace (P); according to the court of appeals, such a change could occur only in a rulemaking proceeding. The NLRB (D) petitioned the United States Supreme Court for further review, and the Supreme Court granted certirorari.

ISSUE: Is the NLRB precluded from announcing new principles in an adjudicative proceeding?

HOLDING AND DECISION: [The judge is not stated in the casebook excerpt.] No. The NLRB (D) is not precluded from announcing new principles in an adjudicative proceeding. The choice between rulemaking and adjudication lies within the NLRB's discretion in the first instance. In this case, there is ample indication that adjudication is particularly appropriate. The duties of buyers vary widely depending on the company or industry; it is doubtful whether any generalized standard could be framed that would have more than marginal utility. The NLRB (D) thus has reason to proceed with caution, developing its standards in a case-by-case manner with attention to the specific character of the buyers' authority and duties in each company. The NLRB's (D) judgment that adjudication best serves this purpose is entitled to great weight and the agency has discretion to decide that the adjudicative procedures in this case may also produce the relevant information necessary for a mature and fair consideration of the issues. Reversed and remanded.

▶ ANALYSIS

When the Taft Harley Act of 1947 was passed, both the U.S. Senate and the House of Representatives voiced concern over the NLRB's (D) broad reading of the term "employee" which then included those clearly within the managerial hierarchy. The Senate noted that unionization of supervisors had hurt productivity, increased the accident rate, upset the balance of power in collective bargaining, and tended to blur the lines between management and labor. The House echoed the concern for reduction of industrial output and noted that unionization of supervisors had deprived employers of loyal representatives to which they were entitled.

■■■

Quicknotes

ADMINISTRATIVE ORDER The final disposition of an administrative hearing or the interpretation or application of a statute.

■■■

FPC v. Texaco, Inc.

Federal agency (D) v. Petroleum company (P)

377 U.S. 33 (1964).

NATURE OF CASE: Appeal from reversal of dismissal of a gas sales application.

FACT SUMMARY: The Federal Power Commission (D) rejected, without a hearing, Texaco's (P) application for a certificate allowing gas sales to pipeline companies.

🏛 RULE OF LAW
The Federal Power Commission can validly deny a hearing on applications if the application does not conform to commission standards promulgated under the rulemaking power.

FACTS: Section 7 of the Natural Gas Act provided that the Federal Power Commission (FPC) (D) had to set hearings on applications for certificates of public necessity which were required before a company could sell natural gas to pipeline companies. Under its rulemaking power, the FPC (D) enacted regulations to preclude escalation of prices. The rules allowed the FPC (D) to dismiss an application, without a hearing, if it contained elements of such escalation provisions. Texaco's (P) application was dismissed without a hearing, and it brought suit claiming it was denied due process. The lower courts held for Texaco (P), and the United States Supreme Court granted certiorari.

ISSUE: Can the FPC validly deny a hearing on an application which does not conform to standards promulgated under the rulemaking power?

HOLDING AND DECISION: (Douglas, J.) Yes. The FPC can validly deny a hearing and dismiss an application which does not conform to standards promulgated under the Commission's rulemaking power. The FPC's (D) rulemaking authority is broad enough for it to condition the acceptance of applications on threshold requirements which it develops in attempting to carry out the provisions of the Natural Gas Act. Requiring a hearing in every case would lead to intolerably numerous proceedings which relitigated the same issues over and over again. Therefore, the FPC (D) may choose to summarily deny nonconforming applications which do not state contentions attacking the validity of the rule, but merely contravene it. Reversed.

▌ ANALYSIS

In this case, the Court declares that the process of promulgating rules, whereby an agency holds hearings and elicits testimony from interested parties, sufficiently protects such parties' due process rights in relation to actions which undeniably fall under the rule's scope. Parties must challenge the validity of the rule when acting in contravention, or no hearing on adverse agency action is required. It is recognized that absent a genuine issue of material fact, an agency, as a quasi-judicial body, may validly deny a hearing based on a summary judgment-type determination.

■=■

Quicknotes

HEARING (ADMINISTRATIVE HEARING) A hearing conducted before an administrative agency.

JUDICIAL REVIEW The authority of the courts to review decisions, actions or omissions committed by another agency or branch of government.

PROCEDURAL DUE PROCESS The constitutional mandate that if the state or federal government acts so as to deny a citizen of a life, liberty or property interest the individual is first entitled to notice and the right to be heard.

RULEMAKING The promulgation of a rule by an administrative agency, acting within the scope of its power pursuant to statute, enacting a rule governing a particular activity.

■=■

Heckler v. Campbell

Regulatory department (D) v. Disabilities beneficiary (P)

461 U.S. 458 (1983).

NATURE OF CASE: Appeal from reversal of judgment upholding an administrative denial of disability benefits.

FACT SUMMARY: Campbell (P) was denied disability benefits when the Department of Health and Human Services (D), using published guidelines, determined that she was not disabled.

🏛 RULE OF LAW
The Department of Health and Human Services may rely on published medical-vocational guidelines to determine a claimant's right to Social Security disability benefits.

FACTS: The Department of Health and Human Services (DHHS) (D) adopted regulations which factored in a disability claimant's age, health, education, and experience and set forth rules regarding whether a significant number of jobs would exist for which the applicant was qualified. If such jobs did exist, then benefits would be denied. Prior to these rules, vocational experts made determinations on a case-by-case basis. Campbell (P) was denied benefits after use of the adopted guidelines. The Social Security Appeals Council and the district court upheld the decision, but the court of appeals reversed, holding that the DHHS (D) must identify specific alternative jobs for an applicant, since the failure to provide such evidence would deprive a claimant of the requisite adjudicatory hearing. The United States Supreme Court granted certiorari.

ISSUE: May DHSS rely on published medical-vocational guidelines to determine a claimant's right to Social Security disability benefits?

HOLDING AND DECISION: (Powell, J.) Yes. DHSS may rely on published medical-vocational guidelines to determine a claimant's right to Social Security disability benefits. Contrary to Campbell's (P) assertions, the findings of DHHS (D) here were individualized. DHHS (D) had to compare her qualifications with the standards adopted and then make the determination. The requirement of individualized treatment does not prohibit an agency from using rulemaking standards not requiring case-by-case treatment. The present method affords claimants ample opportunity to present evidence. Only after considering this evidence was the decision made. There is nothing unacceptable about this procedure. Reversed.

▶ ANALYSIS

The Court, as far as the opinion indicates, did not really address what the court of appeals seemed to think important. The court of appeals held that DHHS (D) must list the specific jobs available to an applicant. The Court did not address this but merely held the DHHS (D) procedure valid.

Quicknotes

HEARING (ADMINISTRATIVE HEARING) A hearing conducted before an administrative agency.

United States v. Florida East Coast Railway

Federal government (D) v. Railroad company (P)

410 U.S. 224 (1973).

NATURE OF CASE: Appeal from reversal of a ratemaking order.

FACT SUMMARY: Florida East Coast Railway (P) contended that the Interstate Commerce Commission (D) could not set a per diem charge on freight cars without a full evidentiary hearing.

🏛 RULE OF LAW

The Administrative Procedure Act does not require a formal evidentiary hearing in a rulemaking determination by the Interstate Commerce Commission.

FACTS: In order to ease the problems created by a shortage of railroad freight cars, the Interstate Commerce Commission (ICC) (D), without a formal hearing, ordered a per diem rate charge on the rental of freight cars. Under § 1(14)(a) of the Interstate Commerce Act, the Commission (D) had the authority to impose such charges "after hearing." Florida East Coast Railway (FECR) (P) challenged the order, claiming that this language required that a formal rulemaking proceeding be held under § 556 of the Administrative Procedure Act (APA), and that, in the absence of such formal hearing, the order was invalid. The ICC (D) defended, contending the language in the Interstate Commerce Act (ICA) did not trigger § 556 of the APA, and that the informal determination, wherein FECR (P) was afforded an opportunity to submit written objections, conformed with § 553(c) of the APA, so that the order was valid. The district court held § 556 applied and invalidated the order, and the ICC (D) appealed. The United States Supreme Court granted certiorari.

ISSUE: Does the Administrative Procedure Act require a formal evidentiary hearing in a rulemaking determination by the Interstate Commerce Commission?

HOLDING AND DECISION: (Rehnquist, J.) No. The Administrative Procedure Act does not require a formal evidentiary hearing in a rulemaking determination by the Interstate Commerce Commission. Previous decisions have clearly stated that the reference to a hearing in § 1(14)(a) of the ICA does not invoke the APA § 553(c) requirement that such proceedings be formal or on-the-record hearings under § 556. As such, no on-the-record hearing is required, and only a notice and comment proceeding need be held. In this case, FECR (P) was given the opportunity to submit written objections to the ICC (D) order. As the hearing requirement of ICA § 1(14)(a) requires merely a notice and comment rulemaking proceeding and not an adjudication of individual rights, this opportunity fulfilled the requirements of the ICA, and the APA, and the order is valid. Reversed.

DISSENT: (Douglas, J.) The majority's decision represents a sharp break with traditional concepts of procedural due process. FECR (P) was "prejudiced" by being limited to written objections to what is essentially a ratemaking order. As such, the informal procedure used by the ICC (D) violated the APA, and the order is invalid.

▶ ANALYSIS

Some commentators argue that as a result of this case, the applicability of APA § 556 is triggered only if a statute uses the key phrase "on the record after opportunity for an agency hearing." As a result, it is argued, the case overly restricts the on-the-record rulemaking requirements. Lower courts have adopted the requirement of the use of the phrase, yet the Court's decision leaves the question open.

■■■

Quicknotes

HEARING (ADMINISTRATIVE HEARING) A hearing conducted before an administrative agency.

RULEMAKING The promulgation of a rule by an administrative agency, acting within the scope of its power pursuant to statute, enacting a rule governing a particular activity.

■■■

United States v. Nova Scotia Food Products Corp.

Federal government (P) v. Food company (D)

568 F.2d 240 (2d Cir. 1977).

NATURE OF CASE: Appeal from decision enjoining smoked fish processing.

FACT SUMMARY: Nova Scotia Food Products Corp. (D) appealed from an order of the district court enjoining them from processing hot-smoked whitefish in violation of regulations promulgated by the Food and Drug Administration (P).

🏛 RULE OF LAW
Agency notice and comment rulemaking proceedings must develop a sufficiently complete administrative record upon which to predicate adequate judicial review.

FACTS: Pursuant to the Food, Drug, and Cosmetic Act, the Food and Drug Administration (FDA) (P) conducted notice and comment rulemaking proceedings to promulgate safety regulations for the fish smoking industry. After the promulgation of such regulations, the FDA (P) sued to enjoin Nova Scotia Food Products Corp. (Nova Scotia) (D) from processing hot-smoked whitefish in violation of the regulations. At this enforcement proceeding, it became clear that no contemporaneous record of the FDA's (P) rulemaking proceedings had been made or certified. The record was reconstructed from FDA (P) files and participants' memories and consisted of comments by outside parties in the proceedings and previously undisclosed scientific data relied on by the FDA (P). Questions addressed to the need and wisdom of applying these regulations specifically to processing whitefish were dealt with in a cursory manner. The district court granted the FDA (P) the requested injunction, and Nova Scotia (D) appealed, challenging the adequacy of the rulemaking procedure in that it failed to disclose the scientific data relied on by the FDA (P), and that it failed to consider questions of commercial feasibility in applying these regulations to the processing of whitefish. The court of appeals granted review.

ISSUE: Must agency notice and comment rulemaking proceedings develop a sufficiently complete administrative record upon which to predicate adequate judicial review?

HOLDING AND DECISION: (Gurfein, J.) Yes. Agency notice and comment rulemaking proceedings must develop a sufficiently complete administrative record upon which to predicate adequate judicial review. The record in the present case showed the proceeding to be completely inadequate. The FDA (P) failed to disclose or even indicate what scientific data were relied on, making it impossible for interested parties to comment. Secondly, the FDA (P) only dealt in a cursory manner with the concerns of Nova Scotia (D) that application of the regulations to processing whitefish was inappropriate, given the low incidence of disease associated with processed whitefish, and the fact that application of these regulations could make whitefish commercially unsalable. Agencies have a good deal of discretion, but they are not at liberty to obscure the reasons for their decisions or to leave vital, relevant questions completely unanswered. Given the inadequate disclosure of data and reasons underlying the FDA's (P) promulgation of these regulations, the procedure followed can be considered no less than arbitrary. Reversed; complaint dismissed.

▶ ANALYSIS

Federal courts have seized upon the inadequacy of the notice and comment requirements of APA § 553 to force agencies to develop far more elaborate "paper records" upon which to base the required judicial "hard look." Some commentators have hailed this development, claiming improved agency rulemaking has developed, while others point to delays in agency rulemaking as making it difficult for agency policies, developed in the fourth year of a presidential administration, to be carried through to a judicially sustainable end.

■═■

Quicknotes

JUDICIAL REVIEW The authority of the courts to review decisions, actions or omissions committed by another agency or branch of government.

RULEMAKING The promulgation of a rule by an administrative agency, acting within the scope of its power pursuant to statute, enacting a rule governing a particular activity.

■═■

Vermont Yankee Nuclear Power Corp. v. Natural Resources Defense Council

Power plant operator (D) v. Community group (P)

435 U.S. 519 (1978).

NATURE OF CASE: Appeal from the invalidation of a grant of a nuclear power plant license.

FACT SUMMARY: The court of appeals invalidated Vermont Yankee Nuclear Power Corp.'s (D) license to operate a nuclear power plant, holding the Atomic Energy Commission had not engaged in adequate rulemaking proceedings under the Administrative Procedure Act in establishing the licensing standards used to grant the license.

🏛 RULE OF LAW
A court may not review and overturn an agency's rulemaking proceeding on the basis of the procedural devices employed (or not employed) by the agency where the agency has employed at least the statutory minima.

FACTS: [The Atomic Energy Commission (Commission) granted Vermont Yankee Nuclear Power Corp. (Vermont Yankee) (D) a license to operate a nuclear power plant. The licensing standard used involved a formula developed by the Commission in a rulemaking proceeding, wherein parties opposed to prevailing methods of disposing of nuclear waste were precluded from rebutting evidence relied upon by the Commission in the findings. The proceedings conformed with § 553 of the Administrative Procedure Act (APA), yet the court of appeals invalidated the formula and the license, holding stricter procedural standards of investigation should have been used by the Commission. The court of appeals also found that the Commission should have required greater elucidation of certain problems raised by the Advisory Committee on Reactor Safeguards (ACRS). Because it determined that the rulemaking proceeding was defective, and, therefore, the resulting rule was invalid, the court of appeals held that the license based upon that rule was equally invalid.] The United States Supreme Court granted certiorari.

ISSUE: May a court review and overturn an agency's rulemaking proceeding on the basis of the procedural devices employed (or not employed) by the agency where the agency has employed at least the statutory minima?

HOLDING AND DECISION: (Rehnquist, J.) No. A court may not review and overturn an agency's rulemaking proceeding on the basis of the procedural devices employed (or not employed) by the agency where the agency has employed at least the statutory minima. It is well established law that, except in rare circumstances, a reviewing court cannot impose upon an agency a more stringent procedural requirement than that articulated in the APA. Agencies must be free to develop their own procedures to allow them to discharge their statutory duties, provided those procedures meet minimum statutory requirements. Here, there is no question that the Commission met this requirement. If agencies had to tailor their procedures to what they anticipated a reviewing court would require, they would engage in full adjudicatory hearings, thus negating all the benefits of informal rulemaking. Further, the court of appeals erroneously believed that there is a correlation between enhanced rulemaking procedures and a more complete record. Given that the agency need not conduct any formal hearing, the adequacy of the record turns not on enhanced procedures, but on whether the agency has followed the APA's mandate. Nonetheless, there remains the issue of whether the challenged rule finds sufficient support in the administrative proceedings—an issue over which the court of appeals judges were split. Accordingly, the case must be remanded for resolution of this issue. Finally, the court of appeals' ruling that the Commission had failed to require adequate elucidation from the ACRS of problems mentioned in the ACRS's report represents another unjustified intrusion into the administrative process. The report referenced publicly available sources, it did not obfuscate the ACRS's position or findings, and the report did not have to contain technical expositions of every issue raised. It was sufficient for the ACRS to have stated its position regarding those issues. For the court of appeals to have required remand on this basis is an example of "judicial intervention run riot." Ultimately, it is up to Congress to determine the policy questions involved, and the courts may not review those policy choices under the guise of agency review where the court is unhappy with the underlying policy. The courts' role is a limited one—only to ensure that the agency acted within its statutory parameters. Reversed and remanded.

▌ *ANALYSIS*

In this case the Court recognized that if reviewing courts could prescribe agency procedures, the scope of judicial review would be unpredictable. Agencies would not know how stringent their procedural requirements would have to be, and as a result, agencies would be forced to conduct full hearings in every case. This would unduly burden the agency in fulfilling its statutory duties.

■■■

Continued on next page.

Quicknotes

HEARING (ADMINISTRATIVE HEARING) A hearing conducted before an administrative agency.

JUDICIAL REVIEW The authority of the courts to review decisions, actions or omissions committed by another agency or branch of government.

RULEMAKING The promulgation of a rule by an administrative agency, acting within the scope of its power pursuant to statute, enacting a rule governing a particular activity.

Long Island Care at Home, Ltd. v. Coke

Former employer (D) v. Former "companionship services" employee (P)

551 U.S. 158 (2007).

NATURE OF CASE: Appeal in action challenging the validity of a Department of Labor regulation. [The procedural posture of this case is not presented in the casebook excerpt.]

FACT SUMMARY: Coke (P) challenged a Department of Labor (DOL) regulation, referred to as a third-party regulation, on the grounds, inter alia, that the DOL's notice-and-comment procedure, which led to the enactment of the third-party regulation, was legally defective because notice had been defective.

🏛 RULE OF LAW
A notice of proposed rulemaking is legally valid where an agency makes clear that it is considering merely a proposal, so that it is reasonably foreseeable that the agency might later withdraw the proposal and replace it with a different final rule.

FACTS: Coke (P) brought suit against her former employer, Long Island Care at Home, Ltd. (Long Island Care) (D), seeking minimum wages and overtime wages that she claimed were owed to her under the Fair Labor Standards Act (FLSA) for work she performed as a "companionship services" employee. The parties agreed that the FLSA required payment of those wages only if the Department of Labor's (DOL's) "companionship services" exemption, contained in a DOL Interpretation (also referred to as a "third-party regulation"), did not apply to workers paid by third-party agencies such as Long Island Care (D), but only applied to workers hired directly by those to whom they provided the services or by their households. Coke (P) contended, inter alia, that the DOL's notice-and-comment procedure, which led to the enactment of the third-party regulation, was legally defective because notice had been defective. The United States Supreme Court granted certiorari. [The procedural posture of this case is not presented in the casebook excerpt.]

ISSUE: Is a notice of proposed rulemaking legally valid where an agency makes clear that it is considering merely a proposal, so that it is reasonably foreseeable that the agency might later withdraw the proposal and replace it with a different final rule?

HOLDING AND DECISION: (Breyer, J.) Yes. A notice of proposed rulemaking is legally valid where an agency makes clear that it is considering merely a proposal, so that it is reasonably foreseeable that the agency might later withdraw the proposal and replace it with a different final rule. Fair notice is the object of the Administrative Procedure Act (APA) requirement that a notice of proposed rulemaking contain "either the terms or substance of the proposed rule or a description of the subjects and issues involved." The courts of appeals have generally interpreted this to mean that the final rule must be a "logical outgrowth" of the rule proposed. Initially, the DOL's proposed regulation would have placed outside the exemption individuals employed by the large enterprise third-party employers. Since that was simply a proposal, however, its presence meant that the DOL was considering the matter and might later choose to keep the proposal or to withdraw it. The DOL finally withdrew it, resulting in a determination exempting all third-party-employed companionship workers from the FLSA, and that possibility was reasonably foreseeable. [The disposition of this case is not indicated in the casebook excerpt.]

▶ *ANALYSIS*

Although the lower courts have long applied the "logical outgrowth" test, this is the first Supreme Court application of that test. When an agency has failed to comply with notice and comment requirements because a final rule is not the "logical outgrowth" of the proposed rule, the error will not be deemed harmless unless the agency offers persuasive evidence that all possible objections to its final rules had already been given sufficient consideration. See *Shell Oil Co. v. EPA,* 950 F.2d 741, 752 (D.C. Cir. 1991). If the agency meets that burden, a party challenging the final rule must show that indeed it would have submitted arguments that were not before the agency had it been given the opportunity to do so.

■━■

Quicknotes

NOTICE Communication of information to a person by one authorized or by an otherwise proper source.

RULEMAKING The promulgation of a rule by an administrative agency, acting within the scope of its power pursuant to statute, enacting a rule governing a particular activity.

■━■

American Hospital Association v. Bowen

Trade organization (P) v. Regulatory department (D)

834 F.2d 1037 (D.C. Cir. 1987).

NATURE OF CASE: [The nature of case is not stated in the casebook excerpt.]

FACT SUMMARY: The Department of Health and Human Services (D) promulgated regulations concerning Peer Review Organizations without following notice and comment procedures.

🏛 RULE OF LAW
The requirement of notice and an opportunity for comment does not apply to interpretative rules, general statements of policy, or rules of agency organization, procedure, or practice.

FACTS: The Department of Health and Human Services (HHS) (D) contracted with Peer Review Organizations (PROs) to oversee the expenditure of Medicare dollars by doctors and hospitals. PROs determined whether the hospitals and doctors were performing in accordance with various standards. If they were not so performing, HHS (D) would deny them Medicare reimbursement funds or impose other sanctions. HHS (D) promulgated its regulations concerning the organization of PROs, their activities, and their enforcement powers without following notice and comment procedures.

ISSUE: Does the requirement of notice and an opportunity for comment apply to interpretative rules, general statements of policy, or rules of agency organization, procedure, or practice?

HOLDING AND DECISION: (Wald, C.J.) No. The requirement of notice and an opportunity for comment does not apply to interpretative rules, general statements of policy, or rules of agency organization, procedure, or practice. (See § 553 of the Administrative Procedure Act (APA).) The rules in question are procedural in nature, and impose no direct substantive obligations upon the hospitals they are intended to regulate. While the terms of the contracts between the PROs and HHS (D) set forth "rules" and "regulations," they also appear to set goals rather than impose definite standards. They are thus "statements of policy" and exempt from the procedural requirements. The perimeters of the exemptions for interpretative announcements and general statements of policy are fuzzy, and turn on the facts of each case. Substantive rules are ones which grant rights, impose obligations, or produce other significant effects on private interests, or which effect a change in existing law or policy. Interpretative rules merely clarify or explain existing law or regulations, while general statements of policy only announce what an agency seeks to establish as policy. An exemption for interpretative rules allows agencies to explain ambiguous terms in legislative enactments without having to undertake cumbersome proceedings, and the exemption for general policy statements allows agencies to announce their tentative intentions for the future without binding themselves. The purpose of the exemption for rules of agency organization, procedure, or practice ensures that agencies retain latitude in organizing their internal operations. In applying the exemption for procedural rules, the focus of inquiry has shifted from asking whether the rule has a substantial impact on parties to asking whether the agency action also encodes a substantive value judgment or puts a stamp of approval or disapproval on a given type of behavior.

▶ ANALYSIS

While it may appear under this ruling that exemptions remove all control from agency actions involving interpretative rules, general statements of policy, or rules of agency organization, procedure, or practice, such is not the case. Many other statutes, court decisions, and regulations control government contracts, sometimes more strictly than the APA. Note, also, that agencies are free to provide notice and comment even where the APA does not require it.

━━■

Quicknotes

ADMINISTRATIVE PROCEDURE ACT (AP) Enacted in 1946 to govern practices and proceedings before federal administrative agencies.

APA Provides that administration policies affecting individual rights should follow stated procedures so as not to be arbitrary.

INTERPRETIVE RULES A rule issued by an administrative agency for the purpose of explaining or interpreting a statute.

RULEMAKING The promulgation of a rule by an administrative agency, acting within the scope of its power pursuant to statute, enacting a rule governing a particular activity.

━━■

Community Nutrition Institute v. Young

Food shipper (P) v. Federal agency (D)

818 F.2d 943 (D.C. Cir. 1987).

NATURE OF CASE: Action seeking condemnation of interstate shipment of food.

FACT SUMMARY: The Food and Drug Administration (D) established the maximum levels of unavoidable contaminants it would permit before taking action to condemn interstate shipments of adulterated food.

🏛 RULE OF LAW
An agency must give notice and an opportunity to comment when the regulations it promulgates have a substantive effect.

FACTS: "Action levels" set by the Food and Drug Administration (FDA) (D) allowed the agency to bring a court action to condemn any interstate shipment of food containing more than the maximum amounts of unavoidable contaminants permitted by regulation. In any such action, the FDA (D) was required to prove the fact of adulteration to the court. The FDA (D) contended that its action levels represented nonbinding statements of agency enforcement policy. Community Nutrition Institute (CNI) (P), on the other hand, argued that the action levels restricted enforcement discretion to such a degree as to constitute legislative (substantive) rules.

ISSUE: Must an agency give notice and an opportunity to comment when the regulations it promulgates have a substantive effect?

HOLDING AND DECISION: (Per curiam) Yes. An agency must give notice and an opportunity to comment when the regulations it promulgates have a substantive effect. Section 553 of the Administrative Procedures Act allows interpretative regulations and general statements of policy to be exempted from the procedural requirements of notice and an opportunity to comment. Applying the principles that a statement of policy (1) must not have a present, binding effect and (2) must leave the agency and its decision-makers free to exercise discretion, it appears that the FDA (D) action levels are legislative rules and thus subject to the notice and comment requirements of § 553. First, the language used by the FDA (D) in creating and describing its action levels suggests that those levels have a present effect and are binding. Further, the FDA (D) requirement that food producers secure exceptions to the action levels also indicates a present, binding effect. Finally, the FDA (D) by its own course of conduct has chosen to limit its discretion. Having accorded such substantive significance to its action levels, the FDA (D) is compelled by the A.P.A. to utilize notice and com-

ment procedures in promulgating them. [The disposition of this case is not indicated in the casebook excerpt.]

DISSENT: (Starr, J.) The applicable test should be that if the pronouncement has the force of law in future proceedings, it is a legislative rule. Action levels offer guidance to the regulated community with respect to what products the FDA (D) deems adulterated. But in an enforcement proceeding in which the FDA (D) seeks to impose sanctions for shipment of an adulterated product or to enjoin shipment of an adulterated product, the agency must first prove the product is adulterated. Thus, the action level does not have the force of law in the subsequent proceeding. Indeed, it has no force at all.

▶ ANALYSIS

In *Mada-Luna v. Fitzpatrick*, 813 F.2d 1006 (9th Cir. 1987), the court noted that the Attorney General's manual described general policy statements as "statements issued by an agency to advise the public prospectively of the manner in which the agency proposes to exercise a discretionary power." The general tenor of this definition seems to comport with the criteria applied by the majority decision in the instant case. Yet it is ambiguous enough to apply as well to the position held by Judge Starr in the dissent.

■=■

Quicknotes

RULEMAKING The promulgation of a rule by an administrative agency, acting within the scope of its power pursuant to statute, enacting a rule governing a particular activity.

■=■

Air Transport Association of America v. Department of Transportation

Trade association (P) v. Federal agency (D)

900 F.2d 369 (D.C. Cir. 1990), *vacated*, 498 U.S.1077 (1991).

NATURE OF CASE: [The nature of case is not stated in the casebook excerpt.]

FACT SUMMARY: Congress enacted a series of amendments to the Federal Aviation Act (the Act) authorizing the Federal Aviation Administration (FAA) (D) to establish a program of administrative civil penalties for violation of the Act. The FAA (D) established its penalty program without notice and opportunity for comment.

> ## 🏛 RULE OF LAW
> The promulgation of regulations governing the adjudication of administrative civil penalty actions is not exempt from the requirements of notice and procedure.

FACTS: Congress enacted a series of amendments to the Federal Aviation Act (the Act) authorizing the Federal Aviation Administration (FAA) (D) to establish a program of administrative civil penalties for violation of the Act. The FAA (D) established its penalty program without notice and opportunity for comment. These "Penalty Rules" established a schedule of civil penalties of fines up to $10,000 per violation of the Act's safety provisions and a comprehensive adjudicatory scheme providing for formal notice, settlement procedures, discovery, an adversary hearing before an administrative law judge (ALJ), and an administrative appeal. The FAA (D) argued that the Penalty Rules were exempt as "rules of organization, procedure, or practice" because they established "procedures" for adjudicating civil penalty actions.

ISSUE: Is the promulgation of regulations governing the adjudication of administrative civil penalty actions exempt from the requirements of notice and comment?

HOLDING AND DECISION: (Edwards, J.) No. The promulgation of regulations governing the adjudication of administrative civil penalty actions is not exempt from the requirements of notice and comment. Cases interpreting § 553(b)(A) of the Administrative Procedure Act (APA) have long emphasized that a rule does not fall within the scope of the exception merely because it is capable of bearing the label "procedural." Where nominally procedural rules contain a substantial value judgment, or substantially alter the rights or interest of regulated parties, the rules must be preceded by notice and comment. The Penalty Rules fall outside the scope of § 553(b)(A) because they substantially affect a civil penalty defendant's right to an administrative adjudication. In implementing its congressional mandate, the FAA (D) made numerous choices as to the type of process civil penalty defendants were due, so that each of those choices contained a significant substantive value judgment as to the appropriate balance between a defendant's adjudicatory rights and the agency's interest in efficiency. Therefore, members of the aviation community had a legitimate interest in participating in the rulemaking process.

DISSENT: (Silberman, J.) The Penalty Rules deal with enforcement or adjudication of claims of violations of the substantive norm, but do not purport to affect the substantive norm. These kinds of rules are, therefore, clearly procedural. Of course, procedure impacts on outcomes and thus can virtually always be described as affecting substance, but to pursue this line of analysis results in the obliteration of the distinction that Congress demanded.

▶ ANALYSIS

Courts will consider the label an agency puts on its own rules, but, as in this case, such labels are not determinative as to the ruling of the court. Rather, courts will also consider whether rules go "beyond formality and substantially affect the rights of those over whom the agency exercises authority." *Pickus v. United States Board of Parole*, 507 F.2d 1107 (D.C. Cir. 1974). Thus, a rule will not be considered procedural if it has a substantive effect on the regulated parties to whom it applies.

■■■

Quicknotes

PROCEDURAL RULE Rule relating to the process of carrying out a lawsuit and not to the substantive rights asserted by the parties.

RULEMAKING The promulgation of a rule by an administrative agency, acting within the scope of its power pursuant to statute, enacting a rule governing a particular activity.

■■■

United States v. Abilene & Southern Ry. Co.

Federal government (D) v. Railway (P)

265 U.S. 274 (1924).

NATURE OF CASE: Appeal from an order to reallocate joint shipping rates.

FACT SUMMARY: Abilene & Southern Railway Co. (P) contended that the Interstate Commerce Commission's (ICC's) (D) order reallocating joint shipping rates was invalid because it was based on evidence not legally before the ICC.

🏛 RULE OF LAW
Administrative orders must be supported by sufficient evidence legally introduced and considered on the record by the agency.

FACTS: The Interstate Commerce Commission (ICC) (D) issued an order granting a new division of joint rates charged when a shipper's goods must travel on more than one line. Orient Express was in receivership and petitioned to have its cost division lowered. Based on financial reports submitted by law annually, the ICC (D) determined the new division. Abilene & Southern Railway Co. (Abilene) (P) challenged the new division order claiming it was invalid because the reports were not offered into evidence at the hearing, and, therefore, the order was not supported by evidence. The district court enjoined the order, and the ICC (D) appealed.

ISSUE: Must administrative orders be supported by sufficient evidence legally introduced and considered on the record by the agency?

HOLDING AND DECISION: (Brandeis, J.) Yes. Administrative orders must be supported by sufficient evidence legally introduced and considered on the record by the agency. Nothing that is not introduced as evidence can be treated as evidence, unless it is judicially noticed. Here, the ICC (D) could not properly take notice of the reports without their introduction into evidence. A finding without evidence is beyond the ICC's (D) power, and the order was properly enjoined. Affirmed.

▶ ANALYSIS

Some commentators disagree with the proposition that nothing can be treated as evidence unless introduced as such. It is argued that in a case such as this, the agency may merely include what evidence was relied upon in its

decision, and allow the parties to petition for rehearing if the evidence is challengeable.

Quicknotes

ADMINISTRATIVE ORDER The final disposition of an administrative hearing or the interpretation or application of a statute.

EVIDENCE Any type of proof offered at a trial in order to prove or disprove a disputed fact or issue.

Ohio Bell Tel. Co. v. Public Utilities Commn.

Telephone company (P) v. Regulatory agency (D)

301 U.S. 292 (1937).

NATURE OF CASE: Appeal from a rate setting order.

FACT SUMMARY: The Public Utilities Commission (PUC) (D) determined the value of Ohio Bell Telephone Co.'s (Ohio Bell) (P) property, for the purpose of setting Ohio Bell's (P) rates, by resorting to evidence not revealed on the record of the rate setting hearing.

🏛 RULE OF LAW
An agency must base its adjudicatory determinations on evidence validly in the record of the proceeding to allow proper examination by the parties and proper review by an appellate court.

FACTS: The Public Utilities Commission (PUC) (D) held ratemaking hearings within which it sought to determine the value of Ohio Bell Telephone Co.'s (Ohio Bell) (P) property. In making this determination, the PUC (D) examined tax values in communities where Ohio Bell (P) held extensive real estate and price indexes in a construction industry magazine. None of this information was examined or identified on the record and Ohio Bell's (P) request to examine, analyze, explain, or rebut it was denied. Based on these unrevealed sources, the PUC (D) ordered Ohio Bell (P) to pay millions of dollars in refunds for charging excessive rates. Ohio Bell (P) sued to invalidate the order, and the PUC (D) defended its decision, stating it had taken judicial notice of the sources, yet it never revealed the sources. The Ohio Supreme Court affirmed, and the United States Supreme Court took jurisdiction.

ISSUE: Must an agency base its adjudicatory determinations on evidence validly in the record of the proceeding to allow proper examination by the parties and proper review by an appellate court?

HOLDING AND DECISION: (Cardozo, J.) Yes. An agency must base its adjudicatory determinations on evidence validly in the record of the proceeding to allow proper examination by the parties and proper review by an appellate court. In this case the evidence relied upon by the PUC (D) was unknown and unknowable by Ohio Bell (P). It was therefore impossible for a trial to be validly held and equally impossible for a reviewing court to do anything more than merely accept the PUC (D) findings. No valid review of the findings could have occurred. Therefore Ohio Bell (P) was denied its fundamental right to a hearing. Reversed.

▶ ANALYSIS

This case illustrates the basic requirement that agencies cannot make determinations which are in effect merely arbitrary denials or grants of rights. The requirement that evidence relied upon in reaching a decision appear on the record ensures a fundamental due process right to confront the evidence and explain or rebut it. The refusal to allow such confrontation is contrary to basic notions of fairness and justice.

■■■

Quicknotes

EVIDENCE Any type of proof offered at a trial in order to prove or disprove a disputed fact or issue.

■■■

Market Street Ry. v. Railroad Commn.

Railway (P) v. State agency (D)

324 U.S. 548 (1945).

NATURE OF CASE: Appeal of Railroad Commission (D) order.

FACT SUMMARY: In order to stimulate commerce, the Railroad Commission (the Commission) (D) ordered Market Street Ry. (Market) (P) to reduce its rates. Market (P) contended it had been denied due process because the Commission's (D) order was based in part on data not available at the time of the Commission's (D) hearing.

🏛 RULE OF LAW
Due process does not preclude an administrative agency from going outside the record of a particular proceeding to base a decision upon predictive inferences from other factual evidence as long as no prejudice is shown to have been incurred by any adverse party as a result.

FACTS: A hearing was held by the state Railroad Commission (the Commission) (D) to determine whether a fare reduction should be ordered for Market Street Railway Co. (Market) (P) and others. The Commission (D) ultimately ordered a reduction in fares from $0.7 to $0.6. Its decision represented the desire to stimulate traffic and commerce. It was based, at least in part, upon the Commission's (D) examination of certain actual traffic survey figures. These figures, however, had not been available at the time of the hearing. Market (P), therefore, challenged the predictive inferences (of increased traffic), which the Commission (D) drew from these statistics and based its decision upon, as violative of due process. Specifically, Market (P) alleged that it was improper for the Commission (D) to deprive them of an opportunity to rebut these figures by simply noticing them. This appeal followed.

ISSUE: Does due process preclude an administrative agency from going outside the record of a particular proceeding to base a decision upon predictive inferences from other factual evidence as long as no prejudice is shown to have been incurred by any adverse party as a result?

HOLDING AND DECISION: (Jackson, J.) No. Due process does not preclude an administrative agency from going outside the record of a particular proceeding to base a decision upon predictive inferences from other factual evidence as long as no prejudice is shown to have been incurred by any adverse party as a result. Due process deals with matters of substance and is not to be trivialized by objections that have no substantial bearing on the ultimate rights of the parties. Here, no contentions were made by Market (P) that the figures examined by the Commission (D) were erroneous, or that its evaluation of them was outside its expertise, or that these figures could have been rebutted or explained away at the hearing. As such, the mere exercise by the agency of its well-established expertise cannot be said to be error. Affirmed.

▶ ANALYSIS

This case points up the well-established rule that expert agency evaluation of extra-record facts does not violate due process. Practically, this means that the range of potentially "noticed" facts in administrative decisions is as broad as the concept of relevance permits. Note, however, that the Federal Rules of Evidence (Federal Rules), while not expressly applicable to agency proceedings, proscribes a somewhat more limited scope of notice. Under Rule 201, notice can be taken only of facts "not subject to reasonable dispute." In *Market* this rule would probably have invalidated the agency's notice of the traffic figures since statistics are almost always vulnerable to some kind of methodical attack. Note, however, that the Federal Rules are only applicable to proceedings to determine "adjudicative" facts, not legislative ones. As such, the *Market* decision is probably not inconsistent with the rationale of the Federal Rules. Professor Davis suggests that the adjudicative-legislative distinction for notice purposes should turn on whether or not the agency is engaged in determining facts which involve the immediate parties to the action. If they do, then the facts are adjudicative and "notice" is limited.

Quicknotes

ADMINISTRATIVE ORDER The final disposition of an administrative hearing or the interpretation or application of a statute.

DUE PROCESS The constitutional mandate requiring the courts to protect and enforce individuals' rights and liberties consistent with prevailing principles of fairness and justice and prohibiting the federal and state governments from such activities that deprive its citizens of life, liberty, or property interest.

Boston Edison Co. v. FERC

Electric company (P) v. Regulatory agency (D)

885 F.2d 962 (1st Cir. 1989).

NATURE OF CASE: Not stated in the casebook excerpt.

FACT SUMMARY: The Federal Energy Regulatory Commission (D) adjusted Boston Edison Co.'s (P) rate of return downward, and Boston Edison (P) contested the adjustment.

> 🏛 **RULE OF LAW**
> When an agency decision rests on official notice of a material fact not appearing in the evidence in the record, a party is entitled, on timely request, to an opportunity to show the contrary.

FACTS: Because interest rates had fallen and stock prices had risen, the Federal Energy Regulatory Commission (the Commission) (D) adjusted Boston Edison Co.'s (P) rate of return downward. The Commission (D) based the reduction on Treasury bond interest rates, and then raised the adjustment to the lower bound of the "zone of reasonableness." Boston Edison (P) argued that the Commission's (D) decision to use the Treasury bond data after the close of the record violated § 556(e) of the Administrative Procedure Act (APA).

ISSUE: When an agency decision rests on official notice of a material fact not appearing in the evidence in the record is a party entitled, on timely request, to an opportunity to show the contrary?

HOLDING AND DECISION: [The judge is not stated in the casebook excerpt.] Yes. When an agency decision rests on official notice of a material fact not appearing in the evidence in the record, a party is entitled, on timely request, to an opportunity to show the contrary. The Commission (D) frequently adjusts the return on equity when warranted by changing circumstances in the financial markets after the close of the record, since such information is not typically subject to dispute. Boston Edison (P) did not dispute the accuracy of the "material fact" in question, that is, the relevant Treasury bond interest rates. Moreover, the Commission (D) gave Boston Edison (P) an adequate opportunity to argue against the adjustment or any other factual matter in its petition for rehearing. Additionally, in light of the significant drop in interest rates, it was not unreasonable for the Commission (D) to make a relatively small downward adjustment in the rate of return, even if, as Boston Edison (P) contends, utility investors do not react precisely the same way as Treasury bond holders to changes in interest rates. In sum, the result reached was reasonable, so it is irrelevant if the Commission's (D) methodology was imperfect. [The

disposition of this case is not indicated in the casebook excerpt.]

▶ ANALYSIS

Section 556(e) of the APA also states that the transcript of testimony and exhibits, together with all papers and requests filed in the proceeding, constitute the exclusive record for decision in accordance with § 557 of the APA. When the record is formally closed, the administrative law judge cannot add to it, and the parties can reopen it only through petition to the judge. However, it appears that in certain circumstances, such as the ones of this case, "material facts" which are not typically subject to dispute, are within a range of reasonableness, and are entered after the close of the record, will be allowed.

Quicknotes

APA § 556 Provides that the testimony transcript constitutes the exclusive record for decision. Provides that rule proponent has burden of proof.

MATERIAL FACT A fact without the existence of which a contract would not have been entered.

Union Electric Co. v. FERC

Electric company (P) v. Regulatory agency (D)

890 F.2d 1193 (D.C. Cir. 1990).

NATURE OF CASE: Not stated in the casebook excerpt.

FACT SUMMARY: The Federal Energy Regulatory Commission (the Commission) (D) reduced the figure for Union Electric Co.'s (Union's) (P) equity rate of return, and Union (P) claimed the Commission (D) violated its rights under the Administrative Procedure Act.

> ## 🏛 RULE OF LAW
> When an agency decision rests on official notice of a material fact not appearing in the evidence in the record, a party is entitled, on timely request, to an opportunity to show the contrary.

FACTS: A two-year time lag existed between the administrative law judge's (ALJ's) development of a record, and the issuance of the Federal Energy Regulatory Commission's (the Commission's) (D) own decision. During this period, the yield on 10-year Treasury bonds dropped 4.09 percent, and the Commission (D) reduced the ALJ's figure for the equity rate of return by the same amount. In its petition for rehearing, Union Electric Co. (Union) (P) argued that the Commission (D) could and should have taken into account two later months. The Commission (D) accordingly reduced the adjustment from 4.09 percent to 3.65 percent. The Commission (D) ultimately approved a rate of 12.15 percent, rather than the 15.08 percentage rate recommended by the staff and found reasonable by the ALJ. Union (P) argued that the Commission's (D) refusal to let it challenge the use of the Treasury bond data violated its rights under § 556(e) of the Administrative Procedure Act (APA).

ISSUE: When an agency decision rests on official notice of a material fact not appearing in the evidence in the record is a party entitled, on timely request, to an opportunity to show the contrary?

HOLDING AND DECISION: [The judge is not stated in the casebook excerpt.] Yes. When an agency decision rests on official notice of a material fact not appearing in the evidence in the record, a party is entitled, on timely request, to an opportunity to show the contrary. Two prerequisites have been established for use of official evidence. First, the information noticed must be appropriate for official notice. Second, the agency must follow proper procedures in using the information, disclosing it to the parties and affording them a suitable opportunity to contradict it or "parry its effect." Official notice is broader than judicial notice, allowing an agency to notice technical or scientific facts that are within the agency's area of

expertise. Thus, the Commission (D) properly took notice of a change in the rate on 10-year Treasury bonds. The Commission's (D) procedures in using the Treasury interest rates for inferences concerning the cost of equity, however, did not adequately protect Union's (P) right to "parry their effect," that is, to challenge the Commission's (D) inferences. Section 556(e)'s assurance that parties must have "an opportunity to show the contrary" includes a chance not only to dispute the facts noticed, but also to offer evidence or analysis contesting the Commission's (D) inferences. Union (P) was allowed a partial opportunity "to show the contrary," but the Commission (D) did not seriously address Union's (P) broader attack on its use of the Treasury bond rates. Instead of responding to Union (P) on the merits, the Commission (D) dismissed Union's (P) claim out of hand, thereby violating the APA. Instead, the Commission (D) should either have accepted Union's (P) proof, or adequately refuted it. The Commission's (D) summary dismissal of the proof fell short of the Commission's (D) obligations under the APA.

▶ ANALYSIS

Official notice, like judicial notice, allows certain well known facts to become a part of the record without going through the formal process of proof. The parties must be informed of an agency's intention to take official notice of a material fact, so that the parties may be afforded an opportunity to comment. Here, the Commission's (D) dismissal of Union's (P) claim failed to provide Union (P) with the "opportunity to show the contrary" required by § 556(e) of the APA.

■━■

Quicknotes

APA § 556 Provides that rule proponent has burden of proof.

MATERIAL FACT A fact without the existence of which a contract would not have been entered.

■━■

Professional Air Traffic Controllers Org. v. Federal Labor Relations Auth.

Professional organization (P) v. Federal agency (D)

685 F.2d 547 (D.C. Cir. 1982).

NATURE OF CASE: Challenge to agency decertification proceeding.

FACT SUMMARY: While seeking judicial review of the Federal Labor Relations Authority's (FLRA's) (D) decision revoking the union certification of the Professional Air Traffic Controllers Organization (PATCO) (P), a hearing was held to determine the effects of ex parte contacts with the FLRA (D) during the consideration of the revocation of PATCO's (P) certification, and PATCO (P) appealed from a decision upholding the decertification in spite of the ex parte contacts.

⚖ RULE OF LAW
The improper ex parte communications of an interested party does not require the vacating of an agency decision on a particular issue if it can be shown that the decision with respect to the issue was made on the basis of the evidence in the record and not improperly influenced by the ex parte communication.

FACTS: In 1981, Professional Air Traffic Controllers Organization (PATCO) (P) called a strike, and the Federal Aviation Authority (FAA) immediately sought to have PATCO's (P) union certification revoked by applying to the Federal Labor Relations Authority (FLRA) (D). The FLRA (D) granted revocation, and PATCO (P) immediately sought judicial review. Prior to oral arguments, the Department of Justice raised allegations of impropriety, claiming that the decision of the FLRA (D) may have been marred by ex parte contacts and communications between FLRA (D) members and interested parties. Communications proving most troublesome were phone calls placed by Lewis of the Department of Transportation to FLRA (D) members, and a dinner conversation between an FLRA (D) member and Shanker, president of the American Federation of Teachers. The evidentiary hearing convened to consider these allegations concluded that there was no evidence that the FLRA's (D) final decision was in any way affected by these ex parte communications. The district court agreed in most part with the administrative law judge of the evidentiary hearing, but found the phone calls and the dinner conversation more troubling. PATCO (P) appealed from a decision holding that the vacating of the FLRA's (D) revocation decision was not required.

ISSUE: Do the improper ex parte communications of an interested party require the vacating of an agency decision on a particular issue if it can be shown that the

decision with respect to the issue was made on the basis of the evidence in the record and not improperly influenced by the ex parte communication?

HOLDING AND DECISION: (Edwards, J.) No. The improper ex parte communications of an interested party do not require the vacating of an agency decision on a particular issue if it can be shown that the decision with respect to the issue was made on the basis of the evidence in the record and not improperly influenced by the ex parte communication. The disclosure of the presence of ex parte communications serves two purposes: first, it prevents the appearance of impropriety in a decision required to be decided on the record, and secondly, it insures that interested parties will have an opportunity to respond to all relevant arguments made in the course of the agency's decision. The mere presence of ex parte communications, even if improper, does not invalidate an agency's decision. The courts will look for evidence that the decision has been improperly influenced by the communications or if an interested party has benefited from the decision before it will decide to vacate the agency's decision. In the present case, the phone calls, while probably ill-advised, were not improper, since the evidence indicated that Lewis expressly refrained from discussing the merits of the case. The dinner between Shanker and the FLRA (D) member was clearly improper, however. Although for a majority of the conversation, the merits of the case were not discussed, the conversation closed with a discussion of various approaches to public employee strikes on the state and federal levels. Clearly, Shanker's position as the president of a union sympathetic to PATCO (P) showed he was an interested party, and a discussion of public employee strikes directly addressed the merits of the FLRA (D) decision. The evidence on the record also indicated, however, that the FLRA (D) decision was not improperly influenced by this conversation, and the ultimate decision of the FLRA (D), adverse to PATCO's (P) position, removes the inference of any improper influence. Since it appeared that the FLRA's (D) decision was not affected by these ex parte communications, its decision need not be vacated. FLRA (D) decision affirmed.

▶ ANALYSIS

The court in the present case, when it discusses "interested parties," seems to indicate that this is a straw man with no real substance. It suggests that it is improper for "any

Continued on next page.

person" to attempt to directly influence an agency decision outside of formal, public hearings. Such a holding, not required in the present case, completely ignores the presence of the "interested party" standard in the prohibition against ex parte communications.

■━■

Quicknotes

EX PARTE A proceeding commenced by one party.

■━■

Sangamon Valley Television Corp. v. United States

Television Company (P) v. Federal government (D)

269 F.2d 221 (D.C. Cir. 1959).

NATURE OF CASE: Appeal of an Federal Communications Commission order granting a broadcast channel.

FACT SUMMARY: Sangamon (P) challenged a Federal Communications Commission (D) order switching a VHF channel to St. Louis, contending the decision was improperly influenced by a prospective licensee.

> **RULE OF LAW**
> Administrative proceedings involving the allocation of services by licensing or the resolution of conflicting private claims must be carried on in the open to be valid.

FACTS: Tenebaum sought a VHF television license in St. Louis. In pursuit thereof, he took Federal Communications Commission (FCC) (D) members to lunch, sent them gifts, and sent them letters, in private, arguing that a VHF channel in Illinois be switched to St. Louis. Sangamon (P), who wanted the VHF license for Illinois, opposed the switch. The FCC (D) set a hearing giving all parties ample notice and inviting written comments to be filed no later than November 15, 1956, and no others would be accepted. During the pendency of the hearing and after the deadline, Tenenbaum sent each FCC (D) member a private letter which contained factual data supporting his being granted the license and the switch of the channels. This letter was never made public, and Sangamon (P) was not given a chance to rebut it or given knowledge of it. The FCC (D) ordered the switch to St. Louis, and Sangamon (P) sought review, claiming the order was invalid because of improper influence.

ISSUE: Must administrative proceedings involving the allocation of services by licensees or the resolution of conflicting private claims be carried on in the open to be valid?

HOLDING AND DECISION: (Edgerton, C.J.) Yes. Administrative proceedings involving the allocation of services by licensing or the resolution of conflicting private claims must be carried on in the open to be valid. When an agency, such as the FCC (D), makes such decisions, it is exercising its quasi-judicial power, and any attempts to influence it strike at the very core of the validity of that power. Even when the activity is rulemaking in nature, fundamental fairness requires open proceedings. The private approaches to the Commissioners rendered its order invalid because the basis for the order could be subjective and not subject to public debate and rebuttal. Further, allowing Tenenbaum's letter after the cut-off date for submitting such information was in derogation of its own rules and is, therefore, an invalidating factor in its own regard. Reversed and remanded.

▶ ANALYSIS

Ex parte communications generally are allowed only in informal proceedings and not in formal, on the record hearings. This is so because informal hearings are generally held as quasi-legislative fact-finding proceedings while formal hearings are adversarial in nature. Prior to this case, it was felt that all rulemaking proceedings were quasi-legislative and, therefore, did not prohibit ex parte communications. This was so especially if the hearings were merely notice and comment rulemaking proceedings.

Quicknotes

QUASI-JUDICIAL Function of administrative officers to hear and determine matters.

Home Box Office, Inc. v. FCC

Cable television company (P) v. Regulatory agency (D)

567 F.2d 9 (D.C. Cir. 1977), *cert. denied*, 434 U.S. 829, *rehearing denied*, 434 U.S. 988 (1977).

NATURE OF CASE: Appeal from an order limiting the content of cable television programming.

FACT SUMMARY: The Federal Communications Commission (D) issued an order regulating the content of cable television broadcasting after commissioners admittedly met with interested parties on an ex parte basis without revealing the substance of these ex parte meetings in the record of the rulemaking proceeding.

🏛 RULE OF LAW
An agency must include in the record of its rulemaking proceedings the information and materials upon which it relied in making its decision so as to allow a reviewing court an opportunity to review the proceeding to ensure the determinations made were not arbitrary.

FACTS: Home Box Office, Inc. (HBO) (P), a cable television company, challenged a Federal Communications Commission (FCC) (D) order limiting the content of cable broadcasts. The order was issued following a notice and comment rulemaking procedure, wherein interested parties could file written comments and participate in oral argument. Apart from the rulemaking proceeding, the FCC (D) commissioners engaged in extensive ex parte discussions with interested persons concerning the rules to be promulgated. HBO (P) challenged the validity of such proceedings and sought judicial review of the order.

ISSUE: Must an agency include in the record of its rulemaking proceedings the information and materials upon which it relied in making its decision so as to allow a reviewing court an opportunity to review the proceeding to ensure the determinations made were not arbitrary?

HOLDING AND DECISION: (Per curiam) Yes. An agency must include in the record of its rulemaking proceedings the information and materials upon which it relied in making its decision so as to allow a reviewing court an opportunity to review the proceeding to ensure the determination made as not arbitrary. This requirement is imposed not only to ensure against arbitrariness, but also to allow all evidence relied upon to be subjected to adversarial scrutiny and rebuttal. Once a notice of proposed rulemaking has been issued, however, any agency official or employee who is or may reasonably be expected to be involved in the decisional process of the rulemaking proceeding, should refuse to discuss matters relating to the disposition of the rulemaking with any interested person. In this case, the failure to include the ex parte exchanges in the record does not allow a reviewing court to assume that the ex parte meetings had no effect on the decisions made. As a result the order based upon such an incomplete record must be vacated.

▶ ANALYSIS

This case recognizes that the need for effective judicial review and adversary scrutiny of evidence compel an agency not to make decisions on secret facts. Both Congress, in "Government in the Sunshine Act" (Pub. Law No. 94-409, § 2) and the President, in Executive Order 11920, address the issue of ex parte contacts with decision-makers. Both actions recognize the detrimental impact of such contacts on fundamental fairness in decision-making which cannot be tolerated consistent with an effective and just administrative scheme.

■=■

Quicknotes

ARBITRARY AND CAPRICIOUS STANDARD Standard imposed in reviewing the decision of an agency or court when the decision may have been made in disregard of the facts or law.

EX PARTE A proceeding commenced by one party.

NOTICE AND COMMENT Informal rulemaking.

RULEMAKING The promulgation of a rule governing a particular activity by an administrative agency, acting within the scope of its power pursuant to statute.

■=■

Action for Children's Television v. FCC

Nonprofit public interest organization (P) v. Regulatory agency (D)

564 F.2d 458 (D.C. Cir. 1977).

NATURE OF CASE: Appeal from Federal Communications Commission decision not to regulate children's television programming.

FACT SUMMARY: Action for Children's Television (P) challenged a Federal Communications Commission (D) refusal to regulate children's programming, claiming the agreement voluntarily entered into by broadcasters to self-regulate was not subject to public input.

🏛 RULE OF LAW
An agency need not provide public participation at every stage of a determination so long as adequate notice of the proceeding is given, sufficient opportunity for public comment is provided, and the decision issued identifies the evidence and factors relied upon so as to ensure a complete record for review.

FACTS: Action for Children's Television (ACT) (P) petitioned the Federal Communications Commission (FCC) (D) to ban advertising on children's television programming and to regulate the amount and content of such programming. The FCC (D) issued notice and held a comment rulemaking hearing. It also received and considered comments from broadcasters and other interested parties. Prior to a determination, broadcasters voluntarily agreed to regulate the programming privately. Subsequently, the FCC (D) refused to issue regulations because of the self-regulation by the broadcasters. ACT (P) challenged the decision not to regulate, contending that the agreement entered into by the broadcaster could not serve as a basis for an FCC (D) decision because it was not subject to public comment.

ISSUE: Does an agency need to provide public participation at every stage of a determination so long as adequate notice of the proceeding is given, sufficient opportunity for public comment is provided, and the decision issued identifies the evidence and factors relied upon so as to ensure a complete record for review?

HOLDING AND DECISION: (Tamm, J.) No. An agency need not provide public participation at every stage of a determination so long as adequate notice of the proceeding is given, sufficient opportunity for public comment is provided, and the decision issued identifies the evidence and factors relied upon so as to ensure a complete record for review. Although the case might be different if private conflicting claims were at stake, a case such as this does not require public input at every stage because the issues in-

volved are of general applicability. Therefore, one side's interests are not necessarily prejudiced by adverse action. Requiring every piece of information be made public would present unmanageable problems which are not necessary for the protection of the public interest. Affirmed.

▶ ANALYSIS

The decision here is distinguished by the court from previous holdings in *Sangamon Valley Television Corp. v. U.S.*, 269 F.2d 221 (1959), and *Home Box Office, Inc. v. FCC*, 567 F.2d 9, (1977). Those cases prohibited an agency from relying on ex parte communications. Those cases involved private claims in conflict. It is unclear whether the decisions there are based on constitutional due process requirements or merely statutory authority under the Administrative Procedure Act. Further, there is no clear standard for determining when private conflicting rights are at stake and ex parte communications are not to be relied upon, and where public rights are exclusively involved.

■=■

Quicknotes

NOTICE AND COMMENT Informal rulemaking.

■=■

Sierra Club v. Costle

Environmental organization (P) v. Regulatory agency administrator (D)

657 F.2d 298 (D.C. Cir. 1981).

NATURE OF CASE: Appeal from decision denying relief in a challenge to an agency rule.

FACT SUMMARY: The Sierra Club (P) and the Environmental Defense Fund (P) challenged the Environmental Protection Agency's (EPA) (D) adoption of an emission standard for power plants using coal fuel to generate power, contending that post-comment communications between the EPA (D) and government officials, in particular the President and a Senator, should have been docketed.

RULE OF LAW
The Clean Air Act requires that all documents that become available after a proposed rule has been published and which the Administrator determines are of central relevance to the rulemaking shall be placed in the docket as soon as possible after their availability.

FACTS: The Environmental Defense Fund (EDF) (P) and the Sierra Club (P) challenged a rule promulgated by the Environmental Protection Agency (EPA) (D) that adopted an emission standard for power plants using coal fuel to generate power; in the plaintiffs' opinion, the standard was too low. The EDF (P) contended that comments regarding the adopted standard were filed after the official comment period closed, and that meetings between EPA (D) officials and various government and private parties interested in the outcome of the final rule took place after the comment period closed. The EDF (P) also alleged that some post-comment communications, particularly those involving the President and a Senator, were not docketed by the EPA (D) as required by the Clean Air Amendments of 1977 (the Act), and the EDF (P) thus argued that it could not adequately respond to all the communications that informed the EPA's (D) rulemaking process.

ISSUE: Does the Clean Air Act require that all documents that become available after a proposed rule has been published and which the Administrator determines are of central relevance to the rulemaking shall be placed in the docket as soon as possible after their availability?

HOLDING AND DECISION: [The judge is not stated in the casebook excerpt.] Yes. The Clean Air Act requires that all documents that become available after a proposed rule has been published and which the Administrator determines are of central relevance to the rulemaking shall be placed in the docket as soon as possible after their availability. This requirement, however, does not prohibit all off-the-record face-to-face contacts in the informal rulemaking process. The Act requires only that a promulgated rule may not be based on information or data that has not been placed in the docket. That statutory requirement is consistent with face-to-face post-comment contacts that are not placed in the docket. Indeed, the Act does not expressly prohibit oral face-to-face discussions anywhere, anytime, and the judiciary cannot properly fashion its own prohibition on such contacts under *Vermont Yankee*'s limitations on judicial review, *Vermont Yankee Nuclear Power Corp. v. Natural Resources Defense Council*, 435 U.S. 519 (1978). The statutory requirement for docketing "centrally relevant" documents includes written summaries of similarly relevant oral communications, and the Act vests the EPA (D) with the discretion to decide whether documents, including summaries of oral communications, are "centrally relevant." There might well be occasions when oral communications between agencies and the President would need to be docketed to guarantee basic due process. This is not such a case because the EPA (D) did not base its rule on its meetings with the President. Moreover, the meeting with the Senator also did not constitute undue congressional influence. Congressional representative may vigorously represent their constituents' interest so long as they do so in a manner that is consistent with statutory and procedural requirements. In such situations, the agencies are expected to balance congressional pressure against pressure from all other sources. To hold otherwise would deprive agencies of valuable input and call into question the validity of any controversial ruling. In sum, the EPA's (D) adoption of the emissions standard was free from procedural error.

▌ ANALYSIS

In the above case, the comment period regarding the proposed emissions ceiling ran from September 19, 1978 to January 15, 1979. After January 15, the EPA (D) received almost 300 written submissions on the proposed rule which were accepted by the EPA and entered on its administration docket. EPA (D) did not officially reopen the comment period nor did it notify the public through the Federal Register that it had received and was entering "late" comments. Of the late comments, the EDF (P) claimed that at least 30 were from representatives of the coal or utility industries and 22 were submitted by Congressmen as advocates of those interests. The EDF (P) characterized such comments and meetings which took place after the comment period closed as an "ex parte

Continued on next page.

blitz" by the coal industry to force the EPA to adapt a higher emissions ceiling.

■━■

Quicknotes

COMMENT PERIOD Official period of time set by a governmental body permitting comments by the public to be submitted in approval or disapproval of proposed new rules and regulations, or statutes to be adopted as law after the proscribed period ends.

EX PARTE A proceeding commenced by one party.

PROCEDURAL DUE PROCESS The constitutional mandate that if the state or federal government acts so as to deny a citizen of a life, liberty or property interest the individual is first entitled to notice and the right to be heard.

RULEMAKING The promulgation of a rule governing a particular activity by an administrative agency, acting within the scope of its power pursuant to statute.

■━■

Bailey v. Richardson

Government employee (P) v. Regulatory commission (D)

182 F.2d 46 (D.C. Cir. 1950), *aff'd* 341 U.S. 918 (1951).

NATURE OF CASE: Appeal from denial of order directing a government employee's reinstatement.

FACT SUMMARY: Bailey (P) claimed that she was denied due process of law when her government employment was terminated without a quasi-judicial hearing.

🏛 **RULE OF LAW**
There is no due process right to a quasi-judicial hearing prior to termination of government employment.

FACTS: Bailey (P) was hired by the federal government and was subject to removal if an investigation by the Civil Service Commission disclosed disqualification based on reasonable grounds to believe she was disloyal to the government of the United States. The Commission sent her a letter stating its investigation indicated she had some affiliation with communist organizations. Bailey (P) denied most of the charges and vigorously asserted her loyalty. She demanded and was given an administrative hearing, after which the Commission found reasonable grounds to believe she was disloyal, and dismissed her. Bailey (P) sued in federal court for declaratory relief and an order directing her reinstatement, claiming she was entitled to a quasi-judicial hearing prior to termination and, therefore, was denied due process of law. The district court denied the order, and Bailey (P) appealed. The court of appeals granted review.

ISSUE: Is there a due process right to a quasi-judicial hearing prior to termination of government employment?

HOLDING AND DECISION: (Prettyman, J.) No. There is no due process right to a quasi-judicial hearing prior to termination of government employment. Such employment is not property, liberty, or life, therefore, the due process clause does not apply to it. Further, the merit classification system, along with over 160 years of history, expressly denies the right to such a hearing. The only constitutional criterion for termination is the confidence of superior executive officials, because such confidence is necessary to the smooth functioning of government. Therefore, in this case, Bailey (P) was not entitled to a hearing and her termination was valid. Affirmed.

▌ *ANALYSIS*

In support of the holding in this case, it has been argued that to recognize government employment as constitutionally protected would require judicial hearings not only for termination, but also for demotion, transfer, failure to hire, or failure to promote. This would put an insurmountable burden on the federal judiciary. Further, it is argued that civil service seniority rules already make dismissal too difficult, and imposing a hearing requirement would further inhibit dismissal of ineffective government employees.

■■■

Quicknotes

HEARING (ADMINISTRATIVE HEARING) A hearing conducted before an administrative agency.

PROCEDURAL DUE PROCESS The constitutional mandate that if the state or federal government acts so as to deny a citizen of a life, liberty or property interest the individual is first entitled to notice and the right to be heard.

■■■

Greene v. McElroy

Defense contractor (P) v. Government department (D)

360 U.S. 474 (1959).

NATURE OF CASE: Appeal of the revocation of a defense contractor's security clearance.

FACT SUMMARY: The Department of Defense (DOD) (D) claimed that legislation implicitly empowered the DOD (D) to revoke security clearances based on confidential information.

RULE OF LAW

Acquiescence or implied ratification by Congress or the President is insufficient to show delegation of authority to a department of government enabling it to take actions which are constitutionally questionable.

FACTS: The Department of Defense (DOD) (D) revoked Greene's (P) security clearance to work on government military contracts, basing its decision on confidential information, undisclosed to Greene (P), that he had associated with communists. Revocation of Greene's (P) security clearance meant that he had to forgo an annual income of $18,000 for a job that paid $4,700 per year. According to the DOD (D), the authority to base such a seriously injurious decision on information that Greene (P) could not possibly refute was implicitly delegated to the DOD (D) by legislation. The court of appeals upheld the revocation of Greene's (P) security clearance, and Greene (P) appealed. The United States Supreme Court granted certiorari.

ISSUE: Is acquiescence or implied ratification by Congress or the President sufficient to show delegation of authority to a department of government enabling it to take actions which are constitutionally questionable?

HOLDING AND DECISION: (Warren, C.J.) No. Acquiescence or implied ratification by Congress or the President is insufficient to show delegation of authority to a department of government enabling it to take actions which are constitutionally questionable. It is deeply rooted in law that where government actions injure an individual, and the basis for such actions depends upon findings of fact, the evidence proving such facts must be disclosed to the individual to allow him an opportunity for rebuttal. Because this requirement of confrontation and cross-examination is so widely protected, before a department of government may circumvent it there must be an explicit delegation of that power, either statutorily or by Executive Order. Without such express delegation, important constitutional decisions would be made by administrators who are unauthorized to do so. Therefore, given the absence of an express delegation here, the DOD's (D) revocation of

Greene's (P) security clearance was not authorized. Reversed.

▶ **ANALYSIS**

It has been argued that this case directly conflicts with the holding in *Bailey v. Richardson*, 182 F.2d 46 (1951), where it was held that the government could discharge an employee without a hearing. The difference, however, is that in *Bailey*, a specific statute expressly denied the right to such a hearing while in this case the holding was based on the absence of such express denial.

▬▬■

Quicknotes

DELEGATION The authorization of one person to act on another's behalf.

EXECUTIVE BRANCH The branch of government responsible for the administration of the laws.

LEGISLATIVE BRANCH The branch of government charged with the promulgation of laws.

PROCEDURAL DUE PROCESS The constitutional mandate that if the state or federal government acts so as to deny a citizen of a life, liberty or property interest the individual is first entitled to notice and the right to be heard.

▬▬■

Cafeteria Workers v. McElroy

Government workers (P) v. Administrative committee (D)

367 U.S. 886 (1961).

NATURE OF CASE: Appeal from action contesting the revocation of a security clearance.

FACT SUMMARY: Brawner (P) contended she was denied due process when her security clearance was revoked, preventing her from working on Navy premises, without being advised of the grounds for revocation or affording her a hearing.

> 🏛 **RULE OF LAW**
> Due process does not require notice and a hearing prior to the revocation of a security clearance that results in the loss of employment if such revocation does not impair the person's future ability to gain employment.

FACTS: Brawner (P) worked as a short order cook at a cafeteria privately operated on the premises of the Naval Gun Factory in Washington. Navy officials revoked her security clearance for failure to meet base requirements. This prevented Brawner (P) from entering the premises and therefore prevented her from working at this particular cafeteria. However, her employer offered her a similar position in a different location, but Brawner (P) declined such employment because she found it inconvenient. Brawner (P) contested the revocation, contending she was entitled to be informed of the specific grounds for her exclusion and to be afforded an opportunity to be heard to refute those grounds. She argued that a failure to provide her these constituted a deprivation of due process of law.

ISSUE: Does due process require notice and a hearing prior to the revocation of a security clearance that results in the loss of employment if such revocation does not impair the person's future ability to gain employment?

HOLDING AND DECISION: (Stewart, J.) No. Due process does not require notice and a hearing prior to the revocation of a security clearance that results in the loss of employment if such revocation does not impair the person's future ability to gain employment. In this case, Brawner's (P) interest in pursuing a chosen profession was not infringed by the revocation. The Constitution does not require a trial-type hearing in every conceivable instance of governmental impairment of private interests. She would have been entitled to such a hearing if she was barred from employment at the base for unconstitutional reasons, such as discrimination based on her religion, but here she was prevented from working at the base because she was a security risk. She was free and able to seek employment elsewhere. She was merely denied the opportunity to practice her trade at one particular place. It is clear that the Navy has the power to manage the internal operations of its establishments, and it has long been held that government employees are subject to summary dismissal. Because the reason for such dismissal here was not unconstitutional, but rather clearly within the Navy's authority, no due process violation occurred. Affirmed.

DISSENT: (Brennan, J.) The rule announced by the majority will allow government officials to deny citizens protectable liberty and property rights without notice or a hearing merely by stating the grounds as security reasons. This violates the fundamental right of freedom from arbitrary injury by the government, a right protected by the Due Process Clause of the Fifth Amendment. Without the charges against Brawner (P) being specified, how can it be determined that in fact she was not barred from employment for unconstitutional reasons? Moreover, by labeling Brawner (P) as a "security risk," the government has effectively attached a "badge of infamy" to her without specifying the charges against her and without affording her the opportunity to reply. The Court should not permit that.

▶ **ANALYSIS**

Once it is established that a person has a protectable liberty or property interest to trigger due process protection, it must be determined what process is in fact due the interests involved. In *Board of Regents v. Roth*, 408 U.S. 654 (1972), it was held that notice and a hearing are required where the loss of government employment would result in a stigma foreclosing future employment. This principle was followed in *Greene v. McElroy*, 360 U.S. 474 (1959), where the Defense Department was prevented from revoking a security clearance without notice and a hearing where such would prevent Greene, an engineer, from practicing his profession.

■=■

Quicknotes

HEARING (ADMINISTRATIVE HEARING) A hearing conducted before an administrative agency.

NOTICE Communication of information to a person by an authorized person or an otherwise proper source.

PROCEDURAL DUE PROCESS The constitutional mandate that if the state or federal government acts so as to deny a citizen of a life, liberty or property interest the individual is first entitled to notice and the right to be heard.

■=■

North American Cold Storage Co. v. Chicago

Warehouse (P) v. Health officials (D)

211 U.S. 306 (1908).

NATURE OF CASE: Appeal from the denial of injunctive relief.

FACT SUMMARY: Chicago health officials (D) summarily seized North American Cold Storage Co.'s (P) frozen poultry, declaring without a hearing that it was unfit for human consumption.

🏛 RULE OF LAW
Due process does not require a prior hearing where administrative action is required to be immediate in nature.

FACTS: North American Cold Storage Co. (North American) (P), a storage warehouse, was ordered by Chicago health officials (D) to surrender for destruction poultry deemed by the officials (D) as unfit for human consumption. North American (P) refused, and the officials (D) threatened summary seizure and destruction of the poultry and prohibited further deliveries to North American (P). North American (P) sued to enjoin the destruction and the prohibition on deliveries, contending it was entitled to prior notice and hearing, and also asserting that since the food was in cold storage and would not change in nature, there was ample time for such a hearing. The district court dismissed for lack of jurisdiction, and the court of appeals affirmed. The United States Supreme Court took jurisdiction.

ISSUE: Does due process require a prior hearing where administrative action is necessarily immediate in nature?

HOLDING AND DECISION: (Peckham, J.) No. Due process does not require a prior hearing where administrative agency action is required to be immediate in nature. Putrid or unfit food presents an immediate health hazard to those coming in contact with it or digesting it. Therefore, the power to seize such food is inherent in the power of a public health official. Such seizure does not require a prior hearing because the owner of the product can sue after the fact and be made whole should it be determined the food was in fact wholesome. To allow storage of unfit food pending a dispositional hearing would present increased health hazards and not confer any benefit on the owner. Affirmed.

▶ ANALYSIS

Some commentators criticize this decision on several grounds. First, it is argued that impounding the food is an adequate means of protecting public health pending a hearing. Second, it is argued that a tort action after seizure would not adequately compensate the owner for the destruction of his property. Even if the suit is successful, it is questionable any recovery on the judgment could be collected.

■═■

Quicknotes

■═■

Goldberg v. Kelly

Welfare officials (D) v. Welfare recipients (P)

397 U.S. 254 (1970).

NATURE OF CASE: Appeal from judgment holding the termination of welfare benefits absent a pretermination hearing to be unconstitutional.

FACT SUMMARY: Kelly (P) and other welfare recipients alleged that they were deprived of due process of law because they were afforded no hearing prior to the decision of welfare authorities (D) to terminate their benefits.

🏛 RULE OF LAW
The Due Process Clause requires that welfare benefits may be terminated only after a hearing at which the recipient is afforded at least minimal procedural safeguards, including the opportunity to be heard on his own behalf.

FACTS: Kelly (P) and other recipients (P) of welfare assistance, under either the federal Aid to Families with Dependent Children (AFDC) plan or New York State's general Home Relief program, brought suit alleging that welfare officials (D) had deprived them of due process of law by deciding to terminate their benefits without first conducting a hearing concerning their continuing eligibility for aid. Subsequent to the filing of the action, welfare officials (D) of both the city and state adopted procedures which provided for limited notice and hearings prior to termination of assistance. Both procedures were designed to afford notice of the reasons for termination of benefits. However, although both procedures permitted the submission of written statements by the recipient, neither provided for a pretermination hearing at which the recipient might appear. The district court found the procedures to be constitutionally inadequate, and rendered judgment in favor of the aggrieved recipients. The case eventually was appealed to the United States Supreme Court, which granted certiorari.

ISSUE: Does the Due Process Clause require that welfare benefits may be terminated only after a hearing at which the recipient is afforded at least minimal procedural safeguards, including the opportunity to be heard on his own behalf?

HOLDING AND DECISION: (Brennan, J.) Yes. The Due Process Clause requires that welfare benefits may be terminated only after a hearing at which the recipient is afforded at least minimal procedural safeguards, including the opportunity to be heard on his own behalf. Welfare benefits are a matter of statutory entitlement for those eligible to receive them, and the desperate need of recipients for such benefits clearly outweighs the government's interest in summary adjudication of ineligibility. In fact, the conducting of hearings prior to termination of benefits may further governmental interests by increasing the capacity of assistance programs to "promote the general welfare." Therefore, some type of pretermination hearing must be afforded welfare recipients threatened with discontinuance of benefits, although such a hearing need not incorporate all the formalities of a judicial trial. A hearing may be deemed sufficient if it is conducted pursuant to a notice which fairly apprises the recipient of the reasons for the proposed termination of benefits, offers the recipient an opportunity to be heard on his own behalf, to confront adverse witnesses, to present arguments and evidence, and to be represented by counsel. And, needless to say, the hearing must be conducted before an impartial decision-maker. Since the procedures adopted by the welfare officials (D) of the City and State of New York fall short of guaranteeing the incidents of procedural due process herein prescribed, the judgment in favor of the complaining recipients must be affirmed. Affirmed.

DISSENT: (Black, J.) It is probable that many welfare recipients do not meet the eligibility requirements for receipt of benefits. If the government may not suspend aid to these individuals pending ultimate determination of their ineligibility, it will lose a lot of money, which it will probably be unable to recoup. Moreover, the majority's opinion will ultimately be detrimental to eligible recipients of public assistance, since it will inevitably lead to pretermination hearings of such formality and expense that welfare agencies will hesitate to award benefits to anyone for fear that it will be too costly to terminate aid which is eventually determined to be unnecessary.

▶ ANALYSIS

Goldberg v. Kelly was significant in that it established that an individual may not be deprived of property rights without a prior hearing. This proposition has been adopted and expanded by subsequent cases. The effect of *Goldberg v. Kelly* is actually to guarantee two hearings—an initial determination of eligibility prior to termination, and a final resolution after benefits have been discontinued. Note that the procedures prescribed by the case are in some ways more extensive than those compelled by § 554 of the Administrative Procedure Act.

Continued on next page.

Quicknotes

GENERAL WELFARE Governmental interest or concern for the public's health, safety, morals, and well-being.

HEARING (ADMINISTRATIVE HEARING) A hearing conducted before an administrative agency.

NOTICE Communication of information to a person by an authorized person or an otherwise proper source.

PROCEDURAL DUE PROCESS The constitutional mandate that if the state or federal government acts so as to deny a citizen of a life, liberty or property interest the individual is first entitled to notice and the right to be heard.

■══■

Board of Regents of State Colleges v. Roth

School board (D) v. Professor (P)

408 U.S. 564 (1972).

NATURE OF CASE: Appeal from a grant of summary judgment for wrongful dismissal without due process of law.

FACT SUMMARY: Roth (P) contended that the Board of Regents (D) denied him due process when they failed to rehire him as an assistant professor without giving him a reason or affording him an opportunity for a hearing.

🏛 RULE OF LAW
There is no Fourteenth Amendment liberty or property interest denied a nontenured professor at a public university at the expiration of his contract that triggers procedural due process rights when the professor is not rehired.

FACTS: Roth (P) was hired as an assistant professor at Wisconsin State University. His contract was for one year and did not require cause be shown for nonrenewal. At the end of the year, Roth (P) was not rehired and no reason was given for this. Subsequently, Roth (P) sued in federal court claiming the Board of Regents (D) had violated procedural due process by failing to give him reasons for his nonretention or to afford him an opportunity for a hearing on the rehiring issue. The district court granted Roth's (P) motion for summary judgment, and the court of appeals affirmed. The United States Supreme Court granted certiorari.

ISSUE: Is a Fourteenth Amendment liberty or property interest denied a nontenured professor at a public university at the expiration of his contract that triggers procedural due process rights when the professor is not rehired?

HOLDING AND DECISION: (Stewart, J.) No. There is no Fourteenth Amendment liberty or property interest denied a nontenured professor at a public university at the expiration of his contract that triggers procedural due process rights when the professor is not rehired. In failing to rehire Roth (P), the state did not impugn his good name, reputation or honor, nor did it in any way stigmatize him in a manner that would preclude his future advancement within his profession. Therefore, he was not deprived of liberty when he was not rehired. Further, his employment lapsed at the conclusion of the contract term. No property interest was denied as he was not entitled to being rehired. Because Roth (P) was not denied liberty or property, no procedural due process rights to a hearing or to a revelation of cause accrued.

Therefore summary judgment was invalidly granted. Reversed and remanded.

DISSENT: (Marshall, J.) Every citizen applying for a government job is entitled to it unless the government has a legitimate reason for denying it. The property right exists in the entitlement and the liberty interest is the liberty to work, and so due process safeguards apply.

▶ *ANALYSIS*

This case illustrates the applicability of procedural due process rights. Before such rights accrue, the party asserting their existence must establish they have been deprived of a liberty or property interest. If such interest exists, a second inquiry is made as to what process is due. This is determined by weighing the interest in question against the governmental interest involved.

■=■

Quicknotes

FOURTEENTH AMENDMENT Declares that no state shall make or enforce any law which shall abridge the privileges and immunities of citizens of the United States.

PROCEDURAL DUE PROCESS The constitutional mandate that if the state or federal government acts so as to deny a citizen of a life, liberty or property interest the individual is first entitled to notice and the right to be heard.

WRONGFUL DISCHARGE Unlawful termination of an individual's employment.

■=■

Perry v. Sindermann

School board (D) v. Professor (P)

408 U.S. 593 (1972).

NATURE OF CASE: Appeal from reversal of a grant of summary judgment for defendant in action claiming a denial of due process rights.

FACT SUMMARY: Sindermann (P) claimed that an informal implied tenure system at Odessa Junior College which gave him a property interest in his continued employment was protected by due process requirements.

RULE OF LAW
An interest is a property interest for due process purposes if there are mutual understandings supporting a claim of entitlement to a benefit which may be invoked at a hearing.

FACTS: Sindermann (P) was employed by the Texas state college system for 10 years, under one-year contracts. The College had no formal tenure system, yet the Faculty Guide stated in effect that tenure was assumed so long as the employment was mutually beneficial to the college and the employee. Further, the Coordinating Board of the Texas College and University System (D) promulgated rules bestowing upon employees, who were employed over seven years, job tenure. When the Board (D) voted not to offer him a contract for the following year without holding a hearing or stating reasons Sindermann (P) sued in federal court. He claimed that he was not rehired in retaliation for his exercise of his First Amendment free speech rights. He also claimed that the implied tenure system gave him a property interest in his continued employment which could not be denied him without his due process rights. The district court granted the Board (D) summary judgment, the court of appeals reversed, and the United States Supreme Court granted certiorari.

ISSUE: Is an interest a property interest for due process purposes if there are mutual understandings supporting a claim of entitlement to a benefit which may be invoked at a hearing?

HOLDING AND DECISION: (Stewart, J.) Yes. An interest is a property interest for due process purposes if there are mutual understandings supporting a claim of entitlement to a benefit which may be invoked at a hearing. First, if Sindermann (P) was not rehired in retaliation for his exercise of his First Amendment free speech rights, it does not matter whether he had a property interest in being rehired, as the failure to renew would be an unconstitutional deprivation of "liberty," which Sindermann (P) is entitled to prove at a hearing. Second, while a written contract calling for tenure clearly establishes a property

right in continued employment, the absence of an express agreement will not necessarily invalidate a property right claim. Based on his extended employment and the implied expectations of tenure on both sides, it can be said that Sindermann (P) had a property interest in his continued employment. As a property interest it could not be taken from him without due process, which would at least include a hearing. However, because "property" interests are not constitutionally defined, it is up to the Texas courts to determine if a property right existed in this case. The holding in this case is limited to the concept that an implied contract right may be defined by a state as a property right under the federal constitution, and, therefore, Sindermann (P) must be given an opportunity to prove the legitimacy of his claim. If upon showing such legitimacy a property right is found, this would entitle Sindermann (P) to a hearing on his reinstatement. Affirmed.

ANALYSIS

In dealing with procedural due process problems, one must engage in a two-tier method of analysis. First it must be determined whether the interest at stake is the type eligible for due process protection as involving liberty or property. If such an interest is found, an inquiry must be made into what process is due this interest. This is a weighing process pitting the interest in question against the governmental interest involved. The more important the interest the greater the due process protection must be.

Quicknotes

ENTITLEMENT A right or interest that may not be denied without due process.

HEARING (ADMINISTRATIVE HEARING) A hearing conducted before an administrative agency.

PROCEDURAL DUE PROCESS The constitutional mandate that if the state or federal government acts so as to deny a citizen of a life, liberty or property interest the individual is first entitled to notice and the right to be heard.

PROPERTY RIGHT INTEREST A legal right in specified personal or real property.

Arnett v. Kennedy

Federal official (D) v. Federal employee (P)

416 U.S. 134 (1974).

NATURE OF CASE: Appeal from the entry of summary judgment holding a statute unconstitutional.

FACT SUMMARY: Kennedy (P) contended he could not be terminated from his federal civil service job without pretermination trial-type hearings.

🏛 RULE OF LAW
The holder of a protectable property right is entitled only to that level of due process protection afforded by the statutory scheme within which the property right was created.

FACTS: Kennedy (P), an employee at the Office of Economic Opportunity (OEO), was discharged from his federal civil service job on the grounds that he had falsely accused his supervisor of bribery. Kennedy (P) was given notice of his right to respond to the charges orally and in writing, and to submit affidavits. Kennedy (P) failed to file written objections to the charges against him and instead sued in federal court, claiming the Lloyd-La Follette Act gave him a protectable property interest in his continued employment and therefore his termination without an evidentiary hearing before an impartial official deprived him of due process of law. The district court held the Lloyd-La Follette Act unconstitutional in that it created the property right asserted by Kennedy (P), yet its explicit denial of a right to an evidentiary hearing deprived Kennedy (P) of his right without due process. The United States Supreme Court granted certiorari.

ISSUE: Is the holder of a protectable property right entitled only to that level of due process protection afforded by the statutory scheme within which the property right was created?

HOLDING AND DECISION: (Rehnquist, J.) Yes. The holder of a protectable property right is entitled only to that level of due process protection afforded by the statutory scheme within which the property right was created. Prior to the Lloyd-La Follette Act civil service employment was a matter of patronage. None had an expectancy or protectable interest in continued employment. The Act established such right but by the same token created the procedural protections to be afforded that right. In other words, "[W]here the grant of substantive right is inextricably intertwined with the limitations on the procedures which are to be employed in determining that right, a litigant in the position of appellee must take the bitter with the sweet." A court cannot overrule the intent of Congress by imposing greater procedural requirements. Therefore, Kennedy (P) was afforded his statutory

protection and that protection was constitutional. Reversed and remanded.

CONCURRENCE IN PART: (Powell, J.) The right to procedural due process is bestowed by and subject only to the limits of the Constitution. The right is not limited in protection to that given by the statute unless the statute is valid, judged on constitutional grounds. In this case, however, procedural due process does not require an evidentiary hearing, and therefore, the Court's conclusion is correct.

DISSENT: (Marshall, J.) The Constitution requires a pretermination hearing. It is wrong to assert that because Kennedy's (P) entitlement arose from statute it could be conditioned on a statutory limitation of procedural due process protections. Protection would be rendered inapplicable to the taking away of any statutory benefit where a statute prescribed a termination procedure. Also, the government's interest in avoiding a pre-termination hearing is far less substantial than Kennedy's (P) interest in obtaining such a hearing.

▶ ANALYSIS

This case illustrates the scope of procedural due process of a statutorily created right. A majority of the justices do not clearly agree either with Justice Rehnquist's argument that the scope of protection is that conferred by the statute, or with Justice Powell's argument that the scope is always measured in constitutional terms. As a result it is unclear whether the case has persuasive precedential value other than on cases with strong factual similarities.

■=■

Quicknotes

ENTITLEMENT A right or interest that may not be denied without due process.

EXPECTANCY INTEREST The expectation or contingency of obtaining possession of a right or interest in the future.

PROCEDURAL DUE PROCESS The constitutional mandate that if the state or federal government acts so as to deny a citizen of a life, liberty or property interest the individual is first entitled to notice and the right to be heard.

■=■

Meachum v. Fano

Prison superintendent (D) v. Prisoner (P)

427 U.S. 215 (1976).

NATURE OF CASE: Appeal in action by prisoners challenging a hearing as lacking in due process.

FACT SUMMARY: Fano (P) and other prisoners (P) contended they had been deprived due process where they were transferred from a medium-security prison to a maximum-security prison on the basis of a hearing at which they could submit evidence but not confront adverse witnesses.

RULE OF LAW

The Due Process Clause does not entitle a convicted state prisoner to a factfinding hearing when he is transferred to a prison the conditions of which are substantially less favorable to him, absent a state law or practice conditioning such transfers on proof of serious misconduct or the occurrence of other specified events.

FACTS: Fano (P) and other prisoners were transferred from a medium-security prison to a maximum-security prison on the basis of a hearing on their responsibility for arson at the medium-security prison. The prisoners (P) were permitted to testify and submit supporting evidence, but not to confront adverse witnesses, including the prison's superintendent, Meachum (D). On appeal from the court of appeals, the Unites States Supreme Court granted certiorari. [The procedural posture of the case is not presented in the casebook excerpt.]

ISSUE: Does the Due Process Clause entitle a convicted state prisoner to a factfinding hearing when he is transferred to a prison the conditions of which are substantially less favorable to him, absent a state law or practice conditioning such transfers on proof of serious misconduct or the occurrence of other specified events?

HOLDING AND DECISION: (White, J.) No. The Due Process Clause does not entitle a convicted state prisoner to a factfinding hearing when he is transferred to a prison the conditions of which are substantially less favorable to him, absent a state law or practice conditioning such transfers on proof of serious misconduct or the occurrence of other specified events. Once there has been a valid criminal conviction, the criminal defendant has been constitutionally deprived of his liberty to the extent that the State may confine him and subject him to the rules of its prison system so long as the conditions of confinement do not otherwise violate the Constitution. Moving the prisoner from one prison to another does not implicate any remaining liberty interest the prisoner might have, even where the prisoner is transferred to an institution

with more severe rules. Here the State did not create any rights entitling the prisoner to remain in any given prison, and transfers of prisoners were not conditioned by the State on any occurrence of specified events. To the contrary, the discretion to effect a transfer is vested in prison officials. Whatever expectation the prisoner may have in remaining at a particular prison so long as he behaves himself is too ephemeral and insubstantial to trigger procedural due process protections as long as prison officials have discretion to transfer him for any reason whatsoever or for no reason at all. [The disposition of the case is not indicated in the casebook excerpt.]

DISSENT: (Stevens, J.) Liberty interests are created by the Constitution, not by state law. Here, the prison transfer constituted a significant deprivation of those liberties that prisoners retain even after they are convicted and incarcerated, thus warranting due process safeguards for the prison transfer hearing.

ANALYSIS

The Court has since held that claimed inmate entitlements based on regulations constraining the disciplinary discretion of prison officials should no longer be recognized as creating a constitutionally protected liberty interest. See *Sandin v. Conner,* 515 U.S. 472 (1995). Notwithstanding its ruling in *Sandin,* the Court has held that prisoners have a liberty interest protectable by due process rights where conditions of imprisonment are extremely harsh—as where a prisoner is placed in a "supermax" prison and potentially deprived of any significant human contact indefinitely, along with other harsh conditions. See *Wilkinson v. Austin,* 545 U.S. 209 (2005). Thus, it seems that only the most extreme prison conditions will be deemed to trigger due process rights, regardless of the existence, or absence, of state or federal prison regulations.

Quicknotes

DUE PROCESS CLAUSE Clauses found in the Fifth and Fourteenth Amendments to the United States Constitution, providing, that no person shall be deprived of "life, liberty, or property, without due process of law."

DUE PROCESS RIGHTS The constitutional mandate requiring the courts to protect and enforce individuals' rights and liberties consistent with prevailing principles of fairness and justice, and prohibiting the federal and state

Continued on next page.

governments from such activities that deprive its citizens of a life, liberty or property interest.

PROCEDURAL DUE PROCESS The constitutional mandate that if the state or federal government acts so as to deny a citizen of a life, liberty or property interest the individual is first entitled to notice and the right to be heard.

■═■

Mathews v. Eldridge

Secretary of Health (D) v. Social Security beneficiary (P)

424 U.S. 319 (1976).

NATURE OF CASE: Appeal from affirmance of decision declaring unconstitutional the termination of Social Security benefits.

FACT SUMMARY: Eldridge (P) contended that he was denied due process when his Social Security benefits were terminated without an evidentiary hearing.

🏛 RULE OF LAW
An evidentiary hearing is not required prior to adverse administrative action if the administrative procedures provided adequate safeguards against error.

FACTS: Eldridge's (P) Social Security disability benefits were terminated without an evidentiary hearing. The administrative procedures set out by the Secretary of Health, Education, and Welfare (D) to be used prior to termination included an initial determination of ineligibility by a committee of both medical and lay members, followed by giving the beneficiary an opportunity to review the evidence relied upon and to submit additional evidence. The beneficiary has a right to review and then a right to a nonadversarial evidentiary hearing before a Social Security Administration administrative law judge. Eldridge (P) sued, contending he was denied procedural due process because the proceedings did not require an evidentiary hearing prior to termination of benefits. The district court held for Eldridge (P), the court of appeals affirmed, and the Secretary (D) appealed.

ISSUE: Is an evidentiary judicial hearing required prior to adverse administrative action if the administrative procedures provide adequate safeguards against error?

HOLDING AND DECISION: (Powell, J.) No. An evidentiary judicial hearing is not required prior to adverse administrative action if the administrative procedures provide adequate safeguards against error. In evaluating the sufficiency of an administrative proceeding for purposes of due process, the important issue is the nature of the inquiry required before action is taken. In this case, the termination of benefits could occur only after a medical evaluation of the case and after the beneficiary is afforded an opportunity to review the evidence and submit written evidence on his behalf. The evaluations and written submissions are subject to the same questions of credibility and veracity as any evidence presented in a judicial hearing. Procedural due process rests on the risk of error which is no more apparent from these proceedings than they would be in a judicial hearing. Therefore, in striking the appropriate due process balance, a judicial evidentiary hearing, requiring large administrative and judicial expenditures, is not required here. Reversed.

DISSENT: (Brennan, J.) Due process requires a trial-type hearing for any deprivation of benefits because any termination of benefits may cause serious harm to the person receiving the benefits.

▶ ANALYSIS

Although Justice Powell determines that the sole function of procedural due process is the attainment of accuracy in decision-making, the opinion suggests a formula for stronger procedural safeguards. The formula would balance the increased accuracy of additional procedures, such as evidentiary hearings, and the interest of the beneficiary, against the increased burden of such proceedings on the government. This has been criticized as it is viewed as impossible to quantify an individual's liberty or property interest in relation to the governmental interest in efficient administrative proceedings.

Quicknotes

EVIDENTIARY HEARING Hearing pertaining to the evidence of the case.

JUDICIAL HEARING A proceeding before a court in order to resolve issues of fact or law based on the presentation of evidence.

PROCEDURAL DUE PROCESS The constitutional mandate that if the state or federal government acts so as to deny a citizen of a life, liberty or property interest the individual is first entitled to notice and the right to be heard.

PROPERTY INTEREST A legal right in specified personal or real property.

Walters v. National Association of Radiation Survivors

Government official (D) v. Veterans' association (P)

473 U.S. 305 (1985).

NATURE OF CASE: Appeal in challenge to a statutory limitation on attorneys' fees in a veteran's benefits proceeding.

FACT SUMMARY: A veterans' association (P) challenged an 1862 statute that limited to $10 the fee that may be paid an attorney who represents a veteran seeking benefits from the Veterans Administration (VA) (D) for service-connected death or disability, contending that this limitation deprived veterans of due process.

RULE OF LAW

A statute that severely limits attorneys' fees in veterans' benefits proceedings is not unconstitutional as a deprivation of due process where Congress has designed the benefits process to be informal and non-adversarial so that veterans would not have to share their benefits with attorneys.

FACTS: Under longstanding law, Congress has provided veterans with pensions and benefits for service-related deaths and disabilities. To claim these benefits, a veteran files a claim with a regional "rating" board that determines whether the veteran qualifies. A claimant may appear before the board, and the process is not adversarial. The board must resolve all reasonable doubt in favor of the claimant. If the board denies the claim, the claimant may appeal to the Board of Veterans Appeals, at which level the proceedings are also nonadversarial and informal. Veterans' organizations may supply the help of a specially trained agent at no charge to assist the claimant. A veterans' association (P) challenged an 1862 statute that limited to $10 the fee that may be paid an attorney who represents a veteran seeking benefits from the Veterans Administration (VA) (D) for service-connected death or disability, contending that this limitation deprived veterans of due process. The United States Supreme Court granted certiorari in the case. [The procedural posture of the case is not presented in the casebook excerpt.]

ISSUE: Is a statute that severely limits attorneys' fees in veterans' benefits proceedings unconstitutional as a deprivation of due process where Congress has designed the benefits process to be informal and nonadversarial so that veterans would not have to share their benefits with attorneys?

HOLDING AND DECISION: (Rehnquist, J.) No. A statute that severely limits attorneys' fees in veterans' benefits proceedings is not unconstitutional as a deprivation of due process where Congress has designed the benefits process to be informal and nonadversarial so that

veterans would not have to share their benefits with attorneys. The marginal gains from affording an additional procedural safeguard often must be weighed against the societal cost of providing such a safeguard. Here, invalidation of the fee limitation would frustrate Congress's principal goal of wanting the veteran to get the entirety of the benefits award without having to divide it with an attorney. Invalidation would also complicate a process that Congress wished to be as informal and nonadversarial as possible, and might disrupt unnecessarily the very effective network of nonattorney resources that has evolved in the absence of significant attorney involvement in VA (D) claims matters. Because the fundamental fairness of a particular procedure does not turn on the result obtained in any individual case, but rather on the risk of error inherent in the truth-finding process as applied to the generality of cases, it would take an extraordinarily strong showing of probability of error under the present system—and the probability that the presence of attorneys would sharply diminish that possibility—to warrant a holding that the fee limitation denies claimants due process of law. Here, such a showing has not been made. The record instead shows that in the vast majority of cases the presence of attorneys adds no value to the veteran's case. [The disposition of the case is not indicated in the casebook excerpt.]

DISSENT: (Stevens, J.) The statute at issue is unconstitutional because it denies the right of an individual to consult an attorney of his choice in connection with a controversy with the government. Such a right is protected by the Due Process Clause. The governmental interests that the majority concludes support its decision are legitimate interests, but they do not justify the restraint on liberty imposed by the $10-fee limitation. Here, there is no cost to the government; the issue is whether an individual can spend his own money to obtain the advice and assistance of independent counsel in the individual's dispute with the government. "The citizen's right to consult an independent lawyer and to retain that lawyer to speak on his or her behalf is an aspect of liberty that is priceless. It should not be bargained away on the notion that a totalitarian appraisal of the mass of claims processed by the Veterans Administration does not identify an especially high probability of error."

ANALYSIS

Congress ultimately eliminated any fee limitation on attorney pay in veterans' benefits proceedings. Nonetheless,

Continued on next page.

the VA (D) retains the authority to directly review, and modify, private fee arrangements. Under the VA's (D) regulations, fees charged by attorneys must be "reasonable," and a fee that is 20 percent or less of the benefits awarded is presumed reasonable.

■══■

Quicknotes

DUE PROCESS The constitutional mandate requiring the courts to protect and enforce individuals' rights and liberties consistent with prevailing principles of fairness and justice and prohibiting the federal and state governments from such activities that deprive its citizens of life, liberty, or property interest.

■══■

Ingraham v. Wright

School children (P) v. School official (D)

430 U.S. 651 (1977).

NATURE OF CASE: Appeal in class action for denial of due process arising from the administration of corporal punishment without a hearing.

FACT SUMMARY: School children (P) claimed they were denied due process when they were given corporal punishment by school officials without a judicial hearing.

🏛 RULE OF LAW
There is no due process right to a judicial hearing prior to the imposition of corporal punishment on school children where the burden such hearings would place on government outweighs the child's interest in being free from unjustified punishment.

FACTS: Under Florida law, school teachers and principals could decide on the propriety of corporal punishment under the circumstances of individual cases, subject only to liability after the fact if it was judicially declared such punishment was unwarranted or excessive. School children (P) who were given corporal punishment brought a class action contending they had a due process right to a judicial hearing prior to imposition of such punishment.

ISSUE: Is there a due process right to a judicial hearing prior to the imposition of corporal punishment on school children where the burden such hearings would place on government outweighs the child's interest in being free from unjustified punishment?

HOLDING AND DECISION: (Powell, J.) No. There is no due process right to a judicial hearing prior to the imposition of corporal punishment on school children where the burden such hearings would place on the government outweighs the child's interest in being free from unjustified punishment. It is recognized that reasonable corporal punishment is justified based on the common-law balancing of the child's interest in personal security against the necessity of corporal punishment in some situations. There is no deprivation of rights as long as the corporal punishment stays within the limits of this common-law privilege. Although a child has a substantial interest in procedural safeguards against unjustified punishment, this interest is adequately protected by the allowance of an action of tort if the punishment is later shown to be wrongful. It is improbable that a significant number of cases will occur where such punishment is unjustified given the fact that most misconduct is personally witnessed by the teacher, and given the threat of civil or criminal punishment for abuse. Therefore, requiring a judicial hearing prior to any corporal punishment would impose a burden on the government which would greatly outweigh any additional procedural safeguards it would provide. Due process does not require such a hearing.

DISSENT: (White, J.) Because state law allows recovery in these cases only where the punishment was knowingly wrongful, a student who is mistakenly punished has no civil cause of action to protect his due process right. Because the Court holds there is no right to a prior judicial hearing, such students are wholly deprived of due process. Further, even if such a cause of action existed, the physical punishment has already been suffered and cannot be undone in a subsequent proceeding.

▶ ANALYSIS

In *North American Cold Storage Co. v. Chicago*, 211 U.S. 306 (1908), the Court found a need for administrative proceedings before deprivation of a protectable interest occurred, even though there existed state law court remedies available after the fact. It has been argued that this decision is no longer good law after the decision in this case. It is unsettled what data a court would require to evaluate whether post-punishment court remedies adequately protect a party's constitutional interests in liberty or property.

■=■

Quicknotes

ENTITLEMENT A right or interest that may not be denied without due process.

JUDICIAL HEARING A proceeding before a court in order to resolve issues of fact or law based on the presentation of evidence.

PROCEDURAL DUE PROCESS The constitutional mandate that if the state or federal government acts so as to deny a citizen of a life, liberty or property interest the individual is first entitled to notice and the right to be heard.

■=■

Brock v. Roadway Express, Inc.

Government official (D) v. Employer (P)

481 U.S. 252 (1987).

NATURE OF CASE: Appeal from judgment invalidating reinstatement provisions of a federal retaliatory discharge law.

FACT SUMMARY: Roadway Express, Inc. (P) challenged portions of the 1982 Surface Transportation Assistance Act providing for summary reinstatement of a discharged worker pending a full hearing, contending it was deprived of procedural due process by being forced to retain the employee until it was determined at a hearing whether the employee had in fact been a whistleblower.

RULE OF LAW
Those portions of the 1982 Surface Transportation Assistance Act providing for summary reinstatement of a discharged worker pending a full hearing are constitutional.

FACTS: Roadway Express, Inc. (Roadway) (P) discharged Hufstetler, allegedly for misconduct. Hufstetler claimed he had been discharged for "whistleblowing" activities by reporting company safety violations, and he petitioned the Occupational Safety and Health Administration (OSHA) for a reinstatement hearing under the 1982 Surface Transportation Assistance Act (the Act). Per the Act's provisions, a nonadversarial investigation was held by an OSHA official. Although Roadway (P) could present evidence to OSHA, it could not obtain other evidence OSHA relied on. Finding Hufstetler's allegations to be substantial, OSHA ordered Hufstetler reinstated pending a full hearing, which was held over a year later. Roadway (P) challenged the Act, contending that its summary, pre-hearing reinstatement provisions violated procedural due process by forcing it to retain an employee until it was determined at a hearing whether the employee had in fact been a whistleblower. A federal district court ruled the Act was unconstitutional, and the United States Supreme Court granted certiorari.

ISSUE: Are those portions of the 1982 Surface Transportation Assistance Act providing for summary reinstatement of a discharged worker pending a full hearing constitutional?

HOLDING AND DECISION: (Marshall, J.) Yes. Those portions of the 1982 Surface Transportation Assistance Act providing for summary reinstatement of a discharged worker pending a full hearing are constitutional. The amount of process due with respect to any law depends on the competing interests involved. In this case, the interests were the government's, in promoting highway safety and protecting employees from retaliatory discharge;

Hufstetler's in not being improperly discharged; and Roadway's (P) in its rights to discharge an employee for cause. Here, the Act attempted to balance these interests by allowing quick reinstatement, but following this by an expedited full hearing. These procedures are constitutionally adequate, and a full pre-reinstatement hearing was not constitutionally mandated. Reversed as to this issue. [Although the Court ruled that the lack of an evidentiary hearing before ordering reinstatement did not to violate due process, the Court also ruled that not providing Roadway (P) with the evidence supporting Hufstetler's complaint was unconstitutional, as it deprived Roadway (P) of an opportunity to prepare a meaningful response. The Court affirmed as to this issue.]

CONCURRENCE AND DISSENT: (Brennan, J.) Because there is no guaranty that OSHA will promptly hold a full hearing, it will not be able to compensate for inadequacies in the pre-reinstatement procedures. Accordingly, the employer must be given an opportunity to confront its accuser and take evidence before a preliminary reinstatement is ordered.

CONCURRENCE AND DISSENT: (White, J.) Withholding adverse witnesses' names and statements prior to temporary reinstatement did not violate Roadway's (D) due process rights.

DISSENT: (Stevens, J.) Due process must not be sacrificed to accommodate an agency's needs. Unless a case falls within an accepted exception, the presumption should be that government may not take away life, liberty, or property before making a meaningful hearing available. Even if the plurality were correct that the possibility of delay might outweigh the value of confrontation, the employer should at a minimum be supplied with a list of witnesses and a summary of those witnesses' statements, so as to be able to make oral or written arguments about why the investigator should not credit the witness' testimony. This alone would not cause undue delay.

▌ ANALYSIS

No opinion here was able to muster a majority of signatures, so one must examine the various opinions to find a rule. This is difficult to do in this case; the various opinions conflict with each other to an unusual degree. It does not seem clear that the Court has said that the Act's provisions not calling for cross-examination prior to temporary reinstatement are valid.

■=■

Continued on next page.

Quicknotes

COLLECTIVE BARGAINING Negotiations between an employer and employee that are mediated by a specified third party.

CROSS-EXAMINATION The interrogation of a witness by an adverse party either to further inquire as to the subject matter of the direct examination or to call into question the witness's credibility.

HEARING (ADMINISTRATIVE HEARING) A hearing conducted before an administrative agency.

CHAPTER 7

Agency Decisionmaking Structure

Quick Reference Rules of Law

Wong Yang Sung v. McGrath

Chinese national (P) v. Government (D)

339 U.S. 33 (1950).

NATURE OF CASE: Habeas corpus appeal from a deportation order.

FACT SUMMARY: Wong Yang Sung (P) challenged the immigration proceeding that resulted in his ordered deportation, claiming the judicial and prosecutorial functions of the agency were merged in violation of the Administrative Procedure Act.

🏛 RULE OF LAW
The Administrative Procedure Act precludes the Immigration Service from allowing the exercise of its judicial and prosecutorial functions by the same person.

FACTS: Wong Yang Sung (P), a native of China, was arrested and charged with being in the United States illegally. He was provided a hearing before a "presiding inspector," whose duties included the investigation and preparation for prosecution of cases like Sung's (P). The inspector prepared a summary of the evidence and proposed findings of fact, conclusions of law, and an order of deportation. The Acting Commissioner approved the order, the Board of Immigration Appeals affirmed, and Sung (P) brought an action for a writ of habeas corpus in federal court, contending that the proceeding improperly merged the judicial and prosecutorial functions of the agency in violation of the Administrative Procedure Act (APA). The Government (D) admitted the merger, yet claimed the APA did not apply in deportation hearings. The United States Supreme Court granted certiorari.

ISSUE: Does the Administrative Procedure Act preclude the Immigration Service from allowing the exercise of its judicial and prosecutorial functions by the same person?

HOLDING AND DECISION: (Jackson, J.) Yes. The Administrative Procedure Act precludes the Immigration Service from allowing the exercise of its judicial and prosecutorial functions by the same person. The constitutional validity of a deportation order is based upon the conduct of the hearing. As a result, a hearing is required to be held to meet procedural due process standards. Therefore, the APA, which applies wherever a hearing is required, applies in deportation proceedings. As a result, the requirement that an impartial hearing be afforded applied. In this case, the presiding inspector also investigated like cases, and it is clear that he will be the prosecuting official in a case where he will also effectively serve as judge. This inevitably biases his judgment in that he is involved in the prosecution of like cases. Therefore, the judicial and prosecutorial functions have effectively merged, violating the Act. Moreover, there is nothing in the Act that exempts deportation hearings held before immigrant inspectors from the Act's due process safeguards. The writ of habeas corpus is sustained. Reversed.

▶ ANALYSIS

After the Court handed down this decision, Congress passed the Supplemental Appropriations Act of 1951, which specifically exempted deportation proceedings from the requirements of the Administrative Procedure Act. Subsequently, this was repealed by the Immigration and Nationality Act, which provided specific procedures to be used in deportation proceedings. It is clear that the separation of functions doctrine applies only where a hearing is compelled either by statute or as here by the Constitution.

■━■

Quicknotes

ADMINISTRATIVE HEARING A hearing conducted before an administrative agency.

PROCEDURAL DUE PROCESS The constitutional mandate that if the state or federal government acts so as to deny a citizen of a life, liberty or property interest the individual is first entitled to notice and the right to be heard.

■━■

Hercules Inc. v. EPA

Company (P) v. Federal agency (D)

598 F.2d 91 (D.C. Cir. 1978).

NATURE OF CASE: Action to invalidate an Environmental Protection Agency regulation.

FACT SUMMARY: Hercules (P) claimed an Environmental Protection Agency (EPA) (D) regulation was invalid because there had been improper contact between EPA (D) staff members and the EPA (D) judicial officer who promulgated the rule.

🏛 RULE OF LAW

There is no legal requirement of complete separation of administrative and judicial functions in agency rulemaking proceedings.

FACTS: The Environmental Protection Agency (EPA) (D) promulgated regulations limiting the discharge of certain chemicals into rivers and waterways. During the rulemaking proceedings in which these regulations were developed, Marple, the chief EPA (D) judicial officer, aided the administrator in making his final decision on the regulation, as the EPA's (D) procedural rules, which previously had banned such ex parte communication, no longer did so. During this period, Marple consulted with various EPA (D) administrative staff members who were involved in the hearings advocating the EPA's (D) position on the proposed regulations. Hercules (P), virtually the only company to be affected by the regulation, challenged the validity of the regulation due to these ex parte consultations between EPA (D) administrators and the judicial officers ultimately making the regulations.

ISSUE: Is there a legal requirement of complete separation of administrative and judicial functions in agency rulemaking proceedings?

HOLDING AND DECISION: (Tamm, J.) No. There is no legal requirement of complete separation of administrative and judicial functions in agency rulemaking proceedings. The nature of the rulemaking process requires that those persons responsible for fact gathering and development of proposed rules be allowed to counsel those ultimately responsible for promulgation. It would greatly hamper reasoned rulemaking if the administrator were completely cut off from other agency functionaries. In this case, the contacts were made in good faith, and the legislative history sanctions such contacts. Therefore, the regulation cannot be invalidated on these grounds.

▶ *ANALYSIS*

Under the Administrative Procedure Act, all rulemaking procedures are exempt from the separation of functions provisions applicable to other functions. However, in *Home*

Box Office, Inc. v. FCC, 185 U.S. App. D.C. 142 (1977), ex parte contracts between agency decision makers and private parties was held to be improper, if wide ranging. Some commentators believe the intra-agency exemption is too broad especially where decision-makers are allowed to consult with agency attorneys directly involved in the case.

■■■

Quicknotes

ENABLING ACT A statute that confers new powers upon a person or entity.

RULEMAKING The promulgation of a rule by an administrative agency, acting within the scope of its power pursuant to statute, enacting a rule governing a particular activity.

■■■

Nash v. Bowen

Administrative judge (P) v. Federal agency (D)

869 F.2d 675 (2d Cir. 1989).

NATURE OF CASE: Appeal from judgment that agency policies did not infringe on independence of administrative law judges.

FACT SUMMARY: As an administrative law judge (ALJ), Nash (P) contended that policies implemented by the Office of Hearings and Appeals (D) interfered with the decisional independence of ALJs.

🏛 RULE OF LAW
Agency policies designed to insure a reasonable degree of uniformity among administrative law judges' (ALJs') decisions do not infringe on the decisional independence of ALJs.

FACTS: Nash (P) had 30 years of experience as an administrative law judge (ALJ) in the Social Security Administration (the Agency) (D). By 1975, the Agency (D) was faced with an administrative crisis due to a backlog of over 100,000 cases. To eliminate the backlog, a series of reforms were instituted, reforms which Nash (P) contended interfered with the decisional independence of ALJs under the Administrative Procedure Act (APA), the Social Security Act, and the Due Process Clause of the Fifth Amendment. In his complaint, Nash (P) alleged that the Agency Secretary's (D) newly instituted Peer Review Program, monthly production goals, and Quality Assurance System infringed upon the "quasi-judicial" status of ALJs. The district court held that the Peer Review Program was intended to respond to the "wide disparity in legal and factual determinations among ALJs." The district court also determined that "although the defendants may have engaged in some questionable practices ... they did not infringe on the decisional independence of ALJs." The court of appeals granted review.

ISSUE: Do agency policies designed to insure a reasonable degree of uniformity among ALJs' decisions infringe on the decisional independence of ALJs?

HOLDING AND DECISION: (Altimari, J.) No. Agency policies designed to insure a reasonable degree of uniformity among ALJ's decisions do not infringe on the decisional independence of ALJs. The Secretary's (D) efforts through peer review to ensure that ALJ decisions conformed to his interpretation of relevant law and policy were permissible so long as such efforts did not directly interfere with "live" decisions. The efforts complained of here for promoting quality and efficiency do not infringe upon ALJs' decisional independence. As for the policy of setting a minimum number of dispositions an ALJ must decide in a month, such reasonable efforts to increase the production levels of ALJs are not an infringement of decisional independence. In view of the significant backlog of cases, it was not unreasonable to expect ALJs to perform at minimally acceptable levels of efficiency. Simple fairness to claimants awaiting benefits required no less. Thus, decisional independence of ALJs was not in any way usurped by the setting of monthly production goals. The "reversal" rate policy embodied in the Quality Assurance System, however, is cause for concern, and could constitute a clear infringement of decisional independence. But the Agency (D) maintains that there was no goal to reduce reversal rates. The goal was to improve decisional quality and consistency, which is assumed to have as one effect a reduction of the reversal rate. It was entirely within the Secretary's (D) discretion to adopt reasonable administrative measures in order to improve the decision-making process. The policy in this regard did not infringe upon the decisional independence of the ALJs. [Affirmed.]

▶ ANALYSIS

An overall concern exists that the functions of those responsible for setting policy remain separate from the functions of the ALJ. The concern, as shown in this case, focuses on maintaining the integrity and independence of the ALJs in the decision-making process. Certain agencies have gone so far as to completely separate the ALJs from the other functions of the agency in an effort to ensure their integrity.

■■■

Quicknotes

ADMINISTRATIVE HEARING A hearing conducted before an administrative agency.

QUASI-JUDICIAL Function of administrative officers to hear and determine matters.

■■■

Withrow v. Larkin

Medical board (D) v. Physician (P)

421 U.S. 35 (1975).

NATURE OF CASE: Appeal from a license revocation order.

FACT SUMMARY: The district court held that the Wisconsin Medical Examining Board's (D) suspension of Larkin's medical license at its own hearing on charges evolving from its own investigation constituted a denial of procedural due process as the agency was performing both adjudicative and investigative functions on the same case.

🏛 RULE OF LAW
The performance of both prosecutorial and adjudicative functions by the same agency officials is not per se a denial of due process.

FACTS: The Wisconsin Medical Examining Board (the Board) (D) held an investigative hearing to determine whether Larkin (P) had committed certain proscribed acts within his medical practice. As a result of the investigation, the Board (D) notified Larkin (P) that it would hold a contested hearing to determine whether his medical license should be suspended. Larkin (P) brought suit to enjoin the contested hearing on the basis that it was improper for the Board (D) to adjudicate the same case it had investigated. The district court granted the injunction holding that the Board (D) could not properly rule on the same charges it investigates. The Board (D) appealed, and the United States Supreme Court granted review.

ISSUE: Is the performance of both investigatory and adjudicative functions by the same agency officials per se a denial of due process?

HOLDING AND DECISION: (White, J.) No. The performance of both investigatory and adjudicative functions by the same agency officials is not per se a denial of due process. There is a presumption of honesty and integrity in adjudicators. As a result, the performance of these two functions is not a denial of due process unless this presumption is overcome by a showing of bias on the part of those performing the dual functions of investigation and adjudication. Such bias will not be implied merely by the performance of these functions by the same entity. In this case, the only evidence offered of the impropriety of the contested hearing was the performance of both functions by the same officials. This was insufficient to constitute a denial of due process. Reversed and remanded.

▶ ANALYSIS

Some commentators argue that combining adjudicatory and prosecutorial functions, even if not inherently unconstitutional, is fundamentally unfair. An empirical study conducted by Professor Richard Posner, "The Behavior of Administrative Agencies," 1 *J. Legal Stud.* 305 (1972), found that dismissed rates did not reflect a reluctance of agencies to dismiss complaints when performing both prosecutorial and adjudicative functions. Regardless of this empirical evidence, veteran administrators continue to argue that dual functions inhibit an agency reaching a just conclusion.

■■■

Quicknotes

LICENSE A right that is granted to a person allowing him or her to conduct an activity that without such permission he or she could not lawfully do, and which is unassignable and revocable at the will of the licensor.

PER SE An activity that is so inherently obvious that it is unnecessary to examine its underlying validity.

PROCEDURAL DUE PROCESS The constitutional mandate that if the state or federal government acts so as to deny a citizen a life, liberty or property interest the individual is first entitled to notice and the right to be heard.

■■■

Association of National Advertisers v. FTC

Trade association (P) v. Federal agency (D)

627 F.2d 1151 (D.C. Cir. 1979), *cert. denied*, 447 U.S. 921 (1980).

NATURE OF CASE: Appeal from a decision disqualifying an agency chairman from presiding in a rule making procedure.

FACT SUMMARY: The district court disqualified Pertschuk, the Federal Trade Commission (D) chairman, from participating in a rulemaking proceeding concerning a subject upon which he had publicly stated personal views.

🏛 RULE OF LAW
A commissioner should be disqualified from participating in a rulemaking proceeding only when there has been a clear and convincing showing he has an unalterably closed mind on dispositive matters to be determined.

FACTS: Pertschuk, chairman of the Federal Trade Commission (FTC) (D), gave a speech wherein he argued that advertising sugared food on children's programs was harmful to children. Subsequently, the FTC (D) issued a Notice of Proposed Rulemaking which considered prohibiting advertising of sugared foods on children's programs. The Association of National Advertisers (ANA) (P) moved for Pertschuk's disqualification. After he refused, the ANA (P) sought judicial review. The district court held that Pertschuk had prejudiced the issue and therefore must be disqualified. The FTC (D) appealed.

ISSUE: Should a commissioner be disqualified from a rulemaking proceeding only when there has been a clear and convincing showing he has an unalterably closed mind on dispositive matters?

HOLDING AND DECISION: (Tamm, J.) Yes. A commissioner should be disqualified from participating in a rulemaking proceeding only when there has been a clear and convincing showing he has an unalterably closed mind on dispositive matters. While engaged in rulemaking, administrators are performing a legislative function delegated by Congress. As such, administrators have the same leeway as congressmen in conducting legislative fact-finding proceedings. Therefore, it is necessary they be allowed to prejudge factual and policy issues in order to facilitate the exchange of ideas. Only where the agency is engaged in an adjudicatory function will prejudgment disqualify a commissioner. In contrast rulemaking necessarily requires commissioners to use their expertise and judgment to guide the development of policy. Therefore, Pertschuk should not be disqualified in this case as his statements did not constitute an unalterably closed mind. Reversed.

CONCURRENCE: (Leventhal, J.) Commissioners are appointed to carry out legislative policy, with the expectation that they carry predispositions concerning policy. This is in stark contrast to judicial officers who are to exercise calculated impartiality. Therefore, the strict standards of disqualification used for judicial officers cannot be used for administrators exercising rulemaking powers.

DISSENT: (MacKinnon, J.) Pertschuk's comments are biased even under the strict test set forth by the court. Therefore, he should be disqualified.

▶ ANALYSIS

In *Cinderella Career and Finishing Schools v. Federal Trade Commission*, 425 F.2d 583 (D.C. Cir. 1970), the court held that a commissioner would be disqualified for prejudgment when engaged in an adjudicatory function. The court in the present case draws a distinction between adjudicatory and rulemaking decisions. Some commentators argue that administrators are not as politically responsible as elected congressmen, and therefore should not enjoy as wide a latitude on bias as members of Congress.

■■■

Quicknotes

DELEGATION The authorization of one person to act on another's behalf.

LEGISLATIVE BRANCH The branch of government charged with the promulgation of laws.

RULEMAKING The promulgation of a rule by an administrative agency, acting within the scope of its power pursuant to statute, enacting a rule governing a particular activity.

■■■

Gibson v. Berryhill
Optometrists (P) v. State board (D)

411 U.S. 564 (1973).

NATURE OF CASE: Appeal from injunction against an administrative hearing.

FACT SUMMARY: Gibson (P) and other individual optometrists brought this action seeking to enjoin members of the state Board of Optometry (D) from conducting a hearing on the ground that the Board (D) was biased.

▦ RULE OF LAW
The rule that those with substantial pecuniary interest in legal proceedings should not adjudicate these disputes applies with equal force to administrative adjudicators.

FACTS: The Alabama Board of Optometry (the Board) (D), which was composed entirely of independent optometrists, filed disciplinary charges in state court against various optometrists who were salaried, licensed optometrists of Lee Optical Company. The charges alleged that the employed optometrists and Lee Optical were engaging in the unlawful practice of optometry. Gibson (P) and the other charged optometrists filed an action in federal district court against the Alabama Board of Optometry (D). The optometrists alleged that the Board (D) was biased and thus could not give the optometrists a fair and impartial hearing: if the Board's (D) disciplinary action against Gibson (P) and the other employed optometrists succeeded, Gibson (P) argued, the employed optometrists' licenses would be revoked, and optometric business thus could quite conceivably redound to the personal benefit of the independent optometrists who sat on the Board (D). The district court agreed, and the Board (D) appealed.

ISSUE: Does the rule that those with substantial pecuniary interest in legal proceedings should not adjudicate these disputes apply with equal force to administrative adjudicators?

HOLDING AND DECISION: (White, J.) Yes. The rule that those with substantial pecuniary interest in legal proceedings should not adjudicate these disputes applies with equal force to administrative adjudicators. It is sufficiently clear from this Court's cases that those with substantial pecuniary interest in legal proceedings should not adjudicate these disputes. Disqualification because of interest applies with equal force to administrative adjudicators. Here, the pecuniary interest of the members of the Board (D) had sufficient substance to constitutionally disqualify the Board (D) from hearing the charges filed against Gibson (P) and the other optometrists. The aim of the Board (D) according to the district court was to revoke the licenses of all optometrists in the state who were employed by business corporations such as Lee Optical. Since all members of the Board (D) are in private practice, the Board's efforts could result in pecuniary rewards for its members. This type of bias is not allowed. Affirmed.

▶ ANALYSIS

In *Goldberg v. Kelly*, 397 U.S. 254 (1970), the Court held that an impartial decision-maker is essential. *Withrow v. Larkin*, 421 U.S. 35 (1975), held that a fair trial in a fair tribunal is a basic requirement of due process. Not only is a biased decision-maker constitutionally unacceptable but our system of law has always endeavored to prevent even the probability of unfairness.

Quicknotes

ADMINISTRATIVE HEARING A hearing conducted before an administrative agency.

BIAS Predisposition; preconception; refers to the tendency of the judge to favor or disfavor a particular party.

INJUNCTION A court order requiring a person to do or prohibiting that person from doing, a specific act.

PECUNIARY INTEREST A monetary interest.

Morgan v. United States (Morgan I)

Livestock trader (P) v. Government official (D)

298 U.S. 468 (1936).

NATURE OF CASE: Appeal from an order fixing rates for livestock trading.

FACT SUMMARY: Morgan (P) and others whose cases were consolidated for trial challenged the validity of an order of the Secretary of Agriculture (D) which set rates for livestock trading, on the basis that the Secretary (D) failed to consider any of the evidence or findings made at the hearings in issuing the order.

🏛 **RULE OF LAW**
An agency order is valid only where, in a case where a hearing is required, the official making the decision has heard and considered the evidence and arguments presented at the hearing.

FACTS: The Acting Secretary of Agriculture conducted an evidentiary hearing concerning the appropriate maximum rate to be set by market agencies for the buying and selling of livestock. Such hearing was required by statute before a valid order could be issued. Subsequently, the Secretary of Agriculture (D) issued an order setting the rate without hearing or considering the arguments or briefs submitted by Morgan (P) and other plaintiffs. The order was based solely on information about the hearing received by the Secretary (D) through consultation with employees of the Department of Agriculture, out of the presence of any of the plaintiffs or their representatives. Morgan (P) challenged the validity of the order because of the Secretary's (D) failure to consider the hearing evidence. The district court dismissed the suit for failure to state a cause of action, and Morgan (P) appealed.

ISSUE: Is an agency order valid only where, in a case where a hearing is required, the official making the decision has heard and considered the evidence and arguments presented at the hearing?

HOLDING AND DECISION: (Hughes, C.J.) Yes. An agency order is valid only where, in a case where a hearing is required, the official making the decision has heard and considered the evidence and arguments presented at the hearing. The requirement of a hearing inherently includes the process by which the trier of fact considers evidence and argument in making his decision. The purpose in requiring a hearing is to ensure that decisions are made based solely on the evidence and argument presented therein. The failure to consider the evidence and argument constitutes the failure to conduct a hearing. An agency cannot make determinations as an agency, where one person hears evidence and another makes decisions.

Therefore, the failure to conduct a valid hearing renders the validity of the order questionable. Reversed and remanded.

▶ **ANALYSIS**

This case illustrates the requirements of separation of agency functions within adjudicatory proceedings. While the same official may not perform both prosecutorial and adjudicative functions, the distinct function of adjudication requires that the same official hear and consider the arguments and evidence at hearings be the same one who ultimately makes the decisions. The problem occurs in that a great deal of time is involved in attending and conducting hearings. As a result, it has been suggested that agencies rely less on case by case adjudications and attempt to deal with problems by general rulemaking.

■=■

Quicknotes

ADMINISTRATIVE HEARING A hearing conducted before an administrative agency.

AGENCY ORDER The final disposition of a hearing before a public agency or the agency's interpretation or application of a statute.

CAUSE OF ACTION A fact or set of facts the occurrence of which entitle a party to seek judicial relief.

■=■

National Nutritional Foods Association v. FDA

Trade association (P) v. Federal agency (D)

491 F.2d 1141 (2d Cir. 1974).

NATURE OF CASE: Discovery motion in action for review of promulgated administrative regulations.

FACT SUMMARY: National Nutritional Foods Association (P) contended it was entitled to depose Schmidt, the Commissioner of the Food and Drug Administration (D), concerning whether he had personally reviewed objections to proposed regulations before he put them into effect.

🏛 **RULE OF LAW**
There must be a strong showing of improper behavior or bad faith before a court can require administrative officials who participated in a decision to testify in explanation of their actions.

FACTS: The Food and Drug Administration (FDA) (D) published tentative final orders revising the regulations on food labeling. The orders were based on a 12-year series of rulemaking proceedings which produced over 32,000 pages of testimony, thousands of exhibits, and thousands of pages of objections to the rules. Before the rules were finalized, the Commissioner of the FDA resigned and Schmidt was appointed. Within 13 days after taking office, Schmidt signed the rules. National Nutritional Foods Association (P) petitioned for review of the regulations and moved the court to allow it to depose Schmidt, claiming it was impossible for him to review the objections prior to promulgating the rules. The court of appeals granted review.

ISSUE: Must there be a strong showing of improper behavior or bad faith before a court can require administrative officials who participated in a decision to testify in explanation of their actions?

HOLDING AND DECISION: (Friendly, J.) Yes. There must be a strong showing of improper behavior or bad faith before a court can require administrative officials who participated in a decision to testify in explanation of their actions. It is reasonable to assume, in the absence of contrary evidence, that Schmidt could have read summaries of the objections prepared by his staff. There being no showing of bad faith or improper conduct, there is no basis for further inquiry, and the Secretary cannot be compelled to testify. The motion to allow such testimony to be taken is denied.

▌ *ANALYSIS*

It has been observed that most commissioners' opinions are actually written by staff members. It has been argued that such practice gives rise to the use of less qualified commissioners since they are not expected to render personal opinions. On the other hand, the sheer amount of work to be done in producing an opinion makes personal decision-making in all cases impractical. In response to this, it is suggested that cases be categorized in order of importance and that only major cases be fully decided by commissioners with the minor ones subject to staff disposition with cursory overseeing by the commissioner.

■■■

Quicknotes

ADMINISTRATIVE OFFICIAL An official of the executive branch of the government.

■■■

The Availability and Timing of Judicial Review

Quick Reference Rules of Law

American School of Magnetic Healing v. McAnnulty

Mail order business (P) v. Postmaster General (D)

187 U.S. 94 (1902).

NATURE OF CASE: Appeal of an order of the Postmaster General precluding delivery of mail.

FACT SUMMARY: McAnnulty (D), the Postmaster General, after a hearing, ordered the Post Office to stop delivering mail to American School of Magnetic Healing (American) (P), finding that American's (P) mail order business was fraudulent.

🏛 RULE OF LAW
A court may review a determination of an administrative officer which goes beyond the officer's statutory power.

FACTS: American School of Magnetic Healing (American) (P) ran a mail order business purporting to teach people how to use the faculty of the brain and mind. After a hearing, McAnnulty (D), the Postmaster General, acting under a statute, determined that the business was fraudulent, and ordered the Post Office to refuse to deliver any mail to American (P) and to return any mail sent by the sender stamped "fraudulent." American (P) sued, claiming the actions of the Postmaster General exceeded his statutory power, and that the courts could grant relief by way of injunction. McAnnulty (D) demurred, and the trial court entered judgment in his favor. American (P) appealed, and the United States Supreme Court granted review.

ISSUE: May a court review a determination of an administrative officer which goes beyond the officer's statutory power?

HOLDING AND DECISION: (Peckham, J.) Yes. A court may review a determination of an administrative officer which goes beyond the officer's statutory power. In this case, the Postmaster, McAnnulty (D), could not have concluded that American's (P) business was fraudulent as a matter of law merely because it was based on an untested area of science, the mind. Therefore, American's (P) mail was stopped without even violating a federal law. If American (P) cannot seek redress in the courts, it must suffer an irreparable injury without hope of a remedy. Therefore, the court can review and remedy, through appropriate action, the determination made by McAnnulty (D) which exceeded his power. As there is no adequate remedy at law, the court may order the requested injunction. Reversed.

▶ ANALYSIS

This case represents the prevailing attitude concerning the reviewability of administrative determinations. Commentators have suggested that the courts grant a presumption of reviewability. This is codified in the Administrative Proce-dure Act, providing a person suffering a legal wrong due to agency action is entitled to judicial review of the action.

■=■

Quicknotes

ADMINISTRATIVE OFFICIAL An official of the executive branch of the government.

DEMURRER The assertion that the opposing party's pleadings are insufficient and that the demurring party should not be made to answer.

JUDICIAL REVIEW The authority of the courts to review decisions, actions or omissions committed by another agency or branch of government.

■=■

Switchmen's Union v. National Mediation Board

Labor union (P) v. Administrative board (D)

320 U.S. 297 (1943).

NATURE OF CASE: Appeal from affirmance of judgment upholding an agency ruling in an action to cancel certification of a union election.

FACT SUMMARY: Switchmen's Union (P) sought judicial review of the National Mediation Board's (D) certification of a union election.

> ### RULE OF LAW
> Judicial review of an administrative determination is unavailable where the determination is intended, by its authorizing statute, to terminate the dispute and to be judicially unreviewable.

FACTS: Switchmen's Union (Switchmen's) (P) and the Brotherhood of Railroad Trainmen (the Brotherhood) (D), a rival union, had a dispute over the classification of certain railroad employees for purposes of voting eligibility in union elections. The Brotherhood (D) contended all should be eligible, while the Switchmen's (P) contended only some should be. They asked the National Mediation Board (the Board) (D) to settle the dispute. The Board (D) made the determination under authority of §2 of the Railway Labor Act that all the employees were eligible to vote. The Brotherhood (D) was elected the collective bargaining agent, and the Board (D) certified the election. Switchmen's (P) sought review in the district court. The district court upheld the Board's (D) decision. The court of appeals affirmed, and the United States Supreme Court granted certiorari.

ISSUE: Is judicial review of an administrative determination unavailable where the determination is intended, by its authorizing statute, to terminate a certain type of dispute and to be judicially unreviewable?

HOLDING AND DECISION: (Douglas, J.) Yes. Judicial review of an administrative determination is unavailable where the determination is intended, by its authorizing statute, to terminate a certain type of dispute and to be judicially unreviewable. Where Congress is silent as to the judicial reviewability of a particular administrative determination, the relevant inquiry surrounds the intent of the statute authorizing the determination. Section 2 of the Railway Labor Act (the Act) was enacted to deal with jurisdictional disputes between rival unions. It was felt that, due to the highly controversial nature of these disputes, the prestige of the Board (D) would be seriously undermined if judicial review of its determinations were allowed. Therefore, it can be seen that the statute intended the Board's (D) determination to terminate the dispute and not be subject to judicial review. Further, Congress specifically granted reviewability of other determinations made under the Act's

authority. If it had intended to do so in this situation, it would have expressed such. Therefore, the district court erred in accepting jurisdiction of this case on appeal. Reversed.

DISSENT: (Reed, J.) The legislative history of the Act does not indicate that the courts should be deprived of reviewability of this administrative action.

▶ ANALYSIS

Courts have not, for the most part, followed the holding of this case. In *Leedom v. Kyne*, 358 U.S. 184 (1958), the Supreme Court determined that an administrative determination of the National Labor Relations Board (NLRB) was judicially reviewable, even though the authorizing statute strongly suggested the unreviewability of the determination. The Court held review was available because the NLRB's decision was egregiously mistaken and contrary to the provisions of the statute. Usually, silence as to reviewability will not preclude it.

■==■

Quicknotes

ADMINISTRATIVE HEARING A hearing conducted before an administrative agency.

JUDICIAL REVIEW The authority of the courts to review decisions, actions or omissions committed by another agency or branch of government.

■==■

Block v. Community Nutrition Institute

Federal agency (D) v. Milk producer (P)

467 U.S. 340 (1984).

NATURE OF CASE: Appeal of a reversal of a dismissal of an action challenging certain milk pricing regulations.

FACT SUMMARY: The Community Nutrition Institute (P) challenged the Department of Agriculture's (D) minimum milk price regulations.

🏛 RULE OF LAW
Consumers do not have standing to challenge regulations promulgated under the Agricultural Marketing Agreement Act of 1937.

FACTS: In 1937, Congress enacted the Agricultural Marketing Agreement Act, which provided, among other things, for extensive rulemaking authority in the Department of Agriculture (Department) (D) to prevent dairy price collapses. Pursuant to this authority, the Department (D) promulgated rules fixing minimum prices on various classes of milk products. These rules were challenged by individual consumers, several milk handlers, and a consumer organization, the Community Nutrition Institute (P). The district court dismissed for lack of standing and failure to exhaust administrative remedies. The court of appeals reversed as to the consumers, holding that the statutory scheme did not expressly prohibit consumer challenges. The United States Supreme Court granted certiorari.

ISSUE: Do consumers have standing to challenge regulations promulgated under the Agricultural Marketing Agreement Act of 1937?

HOLDING AND DECISION: (O'Connor, J.) No. Consumers do not have standing to challenge regulations promulgated under the Agricultural Marketing Agreement Act of 1937. The Administrative Procedure Act gives rise to a presumption of such standing, but it is only a presumption. Where such standing is contrary to the legislative scheme or expressly prohibited, it will not be found. Contrary to the holding of the court of appeals, an explicit prohibition on such standing need not be found. Here, Congress envisioned a complex administrative procedure and to allow consumer suits would bypass this procedure. Therefore, an express preclusion of consumer suits in the statute was unnecessary. The congressional intent to preclude judicial review is "fairly discernable" from the details of the statutory scheme. Reversed.

▶ ANALYSIS

Prior to this decision, some courts tended to hold, as the court of appeals did here, that congressional desire to prevent citizen standing in challenges to regulations had

to be explicit. This was described as "clear and convincing evidence." The Supreme Court, in this opinion, quite clearly rejected this standard.

Quicknotes

ADMINISTRATIVE REMEDIES Relief that is sought before an administrative body as opposed to a court.

STANDING Whether a party possesses the right to commence suit against another party by having a personal stake in the resolution of the controversy.

Bowen v. Michigan Academy of Family Physicians

Government official (D) v. Trade association (P)

476 U.S. 667 (1986).

NATURE OF CASE: Appeal from affirmance of judgment as to the validity of regulations promulgated by an administrative agency.

FACT SUMMARY: Bowen (D), Secretary of Health and Human Services, appealed a decision by the lower courts that his regulations under the Medicare program were irrational and invalid, contending that his ruling was not subject to judicial review.

> ## 🏛 RULE OF LAW
> Judicial review of final agency actions should not be denied in the absence of persuasive reason to believe that such was the purpose of Congress.

FACTS: The Michigan Academy of Family Physicians (P) challenged the validity of a Medicare regulation which authorized the payment of benefits in different amounts for similar physicians' services depending on whether a physician was board certified or not, contending that the regulation violated the Medicare Act as well as the Fifth Amendment to the Constitution. [The district court, finding that the segregation of allopathic family physicians was not rationally related to any legitimate purpose of the Medicare statute, held that the regulation contravened several provisions of the statute governing the Medicare program. The court of appeals agreed that the regulation was obviously inconsistent with the plain language of the Medicare statute and held that the regulation was irrational and invalid. Bowen (D), Secretary of Health and Human Services, sought review of the decision, contending that Congress had forbidden judicial review of all questions affecting the amount of benefits payable under Part B of the Medicare program.] The United States Supreme Court granted certiorari.

ISSUE: Should judicial review of final agency actions be denied in the absence of persuasive reason to believe that such was the purpose of Congress?

HOLDING AND DECISION: (Stevens, J.) No. Judicial review of final agency actions should not be denied in the absence of persuasive reason to believe that such was the purpose of Congress. Only upon a showing of clear and convincing evidence of a contrary legislative intent should the courts restrict access to judicial review. Subject to constitutional constraints, Congress can make exceptions to the historic practice whereby courts review agency action. Careful analysis of the governing statutory provisions and their legislative history reveals that Congress intended to bar judicial review only of determinations of the amount of benefits to be awarded, but not of the method by which reimbursement amounts are determined. Since a challenge

to a regulation such as the one at issue is not a challenge to an "amount determination," and challenges to the validity of the Secretary's (D) instructions and regulations are not impliedly insulated from judicial review by 42 U.S.C. §1395ff, there was no congressional intent to insulate the regulation at issue from judicial review. The presumption of judicial review of agency decisions has not been surmounted here. Affirmed.

▶ ANALYSIS

In *National Labor Relations Board v. United Food & Commercial Workers*, 484 U.S. 112 (1987), the Court reaffirmed this opinion. The Court declared that the statutory preclusion of judicial review must be demonstrated clearly and convincingly. In the absence of statutory language expressly precluding APA review, the court must examine the structure and history of the statute to determine whether the requisite congressional intent to bar judicial review is clearly established.

■■■

Quicknotes

CONGRESSIONAL INTENT Congress's motivation or rationale for promulgating a statute.

JUDICIAL REVIEW The authority of the courts to review decisions, actions or omissions committed by another agency or branch of government.

■■■

Johnson v. Robison

Conscientious objector (P) v. Government official (D)

415 U.S. 361 (1974).

NATURE OF CASE: Appeal in action to declare unconstitutional a veterans' benefits statute.

FACT SUMMARY: A conscientious objector challenged the constitutionality of veterans' benefits legislation, and the Veterans Administration argued that its denial of the objector's claim for benefits was not subject to judicial review.

🏛 RULE OF LAW
A statute prohibiting judicial review of the decisions of the Administrator of Veterans Affairs does not bar federal courts from deciding the constitutionality of veterans' benefits legislation.

FACTS: A draftee accorded Class I-O conscientious objector status, and who subsequently performed the required alternate civilian service, did not qualify as an "eligible veteran" entitled to veterans' benefits provided by the Veterans Administration. Johnson (P), who was such a conscientious objector, was therefore denied veterans' benefits, and he challenged the pertinent statutes as unconstitutional. The Veterans Administration (D) countered that, under Section 211(a), the Administrator of Veterans Affairs' (Administrator's) (D) decisions on benefit claims were not subject to judicial review. The district court rejected the Administrator's (D) reviewability argument, and the United States Supreme Court granted certiorari.

ISSUE: Does a statute prohibiting judicial review of the decisions of the Administrator of Veterans Affairs bar federal courts from deciding the constitutionality of veterans' benefits legislation?

HOLDING AND DECISION: (Brennan, J.) No. A statute prohibiting judicial review of the decisions of the Administrator of Veterans Affairs does not bar federal courts from deciding the constitutionality of veterans' benefits legislation. As a statute barring judicial review of the constitutionality issue would itself raise questions of its constitutionality, this Court will abide by one of its cardinal principles and first determine whether a construction of the statute is fairly possible by which the constitutional question may be avoided. The statute here plainly does not bar Johnson's (P) constitutional claims. The statute instead addresses itself to the non-reviewability of decisions of the Administrator (D) relating to veterans' benefits under the statutes, not to the non-reviewability of the statutes themselves as congressional enactments. Moreover, the legislative history, too, does not indicate congressional intent to preclude judicial review of the constitutionality of the statutes. Thus, there is no preclusion of the judicial review that Johnson (P) here seeks. Affirmed as to the reviewability issue.

▶ ANALYSIS

In 1972, there was a challenge to the "no-review clause" at issue in this case as it applied to the Administrator's decisions. The court held it did not violate due process. Thus, in the absence of constitutional claims, VA decisions remain immune from judicial review.

■══■

Quicknotes

DECLARATORY JUDGMENT A judgment of the rights between opposing parties that is binding, but does not coercive relief (i.e. damages.)

JUDICIAL REVIEW The authority of the courts to review decisions, actions or omissions committed by another agency or branch of government.

■══■

Heckler v. Chaney

Federal agency (D) v. Death row inmate (P)

470 U.S. 821 (1985).

NATURE OF CASE: Appeal of a reversal of summary judgment in an action to compel drug law enforcement.

FACT SUMMARY: Chaney (P), a death row inmate, brought an action to compel the Federal Drug Administration (FDA) (D) to enforce its drug approval requirements with respect to lethal injections.

> ⚖ **RULE OF LAW**
> An agency decision to not enforce regulations is not subject to judicial review where the agency is acting within its discretion and there is nothing in the substantive statute involved that mandates such enforcement.

FACTS: Chaney (P), a death row inmate in Texas, petitioned the Federal Drug Administration (FDA) (D) to enforce, as to the drugs used in lethal injection executions, certain drug approval regulations, which would have had the practical effect of barring the use of lethal injections. The FDA (D), in its discretion, declined the petition. Chaney (P) brought suit to compel the FDA (D) to enforce the regulations under the Food, Drug, and Cosmetics Act (FDCA). The district court granted summary judgment in favor of the FDA (D). The court of appeals reversed, finding "law to apply," and the United States Supreme Court granted certiorari.

ISSUE: Is an agency decision to not enforce regulations subject to judicial review where the agency is acting within its discretion and there is nothing in the substantive statute involved that mandates such enforcement?

HOLDING AND DECISION: (Rehnquist, J.) No. An agency decision to not enforce regulations is not subject to judicial review where the agency is acting within its discretion and there is nothing in the substantive statute involved that mandates such enforcement. The FDA has discretion in enforcing the approval requirements of the FDCA. The Administrative Procedure Act (APA) allows for judicial review of agency action or inaction, but not of agency functions "committed to agency discretion." The decision not to enforce a regulation is a decision which will generally be based on a complicated balancing of factors particularly within the agency's expertise. Further, unlike enforcement, a decision not to enforce does not involve coercion upon an individual's liberty or property. For this reason, judicial interest in a failure to enforce is not intense. Under the APA, the presumption is that an agency non-enforcement decision is not reviewable. Thus, unless something in the relevant act requires enforcement of its provisions or agency regulations,

the agency will not be held under a duty to enforce it. Here, nothing in the FDCA mandates such enforcement, and the presumption of no reviewability is not surmounted. Reversed.

CONCURRENCE: (Marshall, J.) An agency's refusal to enforce is, like other agency action, reviewable in the absence of clear and convincing congressional intent to the contrary, but such refusal merits judicial deference where there is no indication that the agency has abused its discretion, especially where the agency's decision reflects a choice as to how to best allocate finite enforcement resources. However, the majority's presumption of non-reviewability relies too much on positive law, i.e., statute or the Constitution. Instead, reviewability of non-enforcement decisions should also rest on common-law concerns as to whether the agency's decision is, for example, the product of a conflict of interest, a bribe, retaliation, or some other form of corruption. In such instances, judicial review should also be available.

▶ **ANALYSIS**

The Court borrowed its analysis from the concept of prosecutorial discretion. Traditionally, the prosecutorial function has been considered the sole province of the executive branch, and considered not subject to judicial review. The Court analogized an agency decision not to enforce with a prosecutor's decision not to prosecute. Justice Marshall was not happy with the analogy, contending public interest in agency enforcement was higher than in criminal prosecution.

■■■

Quicknotes

JUDICIAL REVIEW The authority of the courts to review decisions, actions or omissions committed by another agency or branch of government.

SUMMARY JUDGMENT Judgment rendered by a court in response to a motion by one of the parties, claiming that the lack of a question of material fact in respect to an issue warrants disposition of the issue without consideration by the jury.

■■■

Norton v. Southern Utah Wilderness Alliance

Secretary of the Interior (D) v. Environmental group (P)

542 U.S. 55 (2004).

NATURE OF CASE: Suit for declaratory and injunctive relief requiring a federal agency to take a required action that it allegedly was failing to take.

FACT SUMMARY: The Bureau of Land Management (BLM) (D) permitted the use of off-road vehicles on federal lands in Utah. The Southern Utah Wilderness Alliance (P) sued the BLM (D) and others for an alleged failure to satisfy the BLM's (D) statutory mandate to manage such lands in a way that did not impair their suitability as wilderness.

RULE OF LAW

The Administrative Procedure Act, 5 U.S.C. §706(1), does not provide a right of action for an agency's failure to take a general action that it is not required to take.

FACTS: The Bureau of Land Management (BLM) (D) permitted users of federal lands in Utah to operate off-road vehicles (ORVs) for recreational purposes on those lands. ORVs cause significant damage to the lands themselves, to wildlife, and to wilderness enthusiasts. To try to stop such detrimental impacts, Southern Utah Wilderness Alliance (SUWA) (P) filed suit against the BLM (D) and others, requesting declaratory and injunctive relief requiring the BLM (D) to take action, by changing its management of the use of ORVs, in order to manage its Wilderness Study Areas (WSAs) in Utah "in a manner so as not to impair the suitability of such areas for preservation as wilderness," 43 U.S.C. §1782(c). SUWA (P) challenged two other alleged failures to act on the part of the BLM (D) in its suit. [The district court ordered dismissal on all three alleged failures to act, and the court of appeals reversed.] The BLM (D) petitioned the United States Supreme Court for further review, and the Supreme Court granted certiorari.

ISSUE: Does the Administrative Procedure Act, 5 U.S.C. §706(1), provide a right of action for an agency's failure to take a general action that it is not required to take?

HOLDING AND DECISION: (Scalia, J.) No. The Administrative Procedure Act (APA), 5 U.S.C. §706(1), does not provide a right of action for an agency's failure to take a general action that it is not required to take. Sections 702, 704, and 706(1) of the APA all require an "agency action" as the basis for suit, and the APA defines these litigable "agency actions" as discrete actions, not as general, amorphous goals or directives. Even where the APA permits suit for failures to act, the failures must be failures to take "agency actions," which are, by statute, necessarily discrete actions. Moreover, Section 706(1) permits suit to compel agency action only

when the action is required. Accordingly, there is no right of action even as against discrete agency action if the agency action is not required by law. The first basis of SUWA's (P) suit against the BLM (D) in this case, 42 U.S.C. §1782(c)—which is indicative of the other two bases because all three challenge alleged failures to act—mandates a goal for the BLM (D), but it also grants broad discretion to the BLM (D) for deciding how to achieve the mandated goal. The total exclusion of ORVs, for example, certainly is not mandated by the non-impairment statute—certainly, at any rate, not with the clarity required by §706(1). These limitations imposed by the APA serve the legislative purpose, as they do in this case, of prohibiting the courts from interfering with the discretion vested in administrative agencies. Reversed.

ANALYSIS

Principles of separation of powers and judicial restraint pervade administrative law. Here the Court defers to Congressional requirements for reviewability, as established by 5 U.S.C. §706(1), and the Administrative Procedure Act itself in turn exists largely to protect executive-branch agencies from what Justice Scalia calls "undue judicial interference with their lawful discretion." The Court's unanimity in *Southern Utah Wilderness Alliance* demonstrates how clearly those fundamental principles apply in this case.

■■■

Quicknotes

DISCRETION The authority conferred upon a public official to act reasonably in accordance with his own judgment under certain circumstances.

INJUNCTIVE RELIEF A court order issued as a remedy, requiring a person to do, or prohibiting that person from doing, a specific act.

JUDICIAL RESTRAINT Self-imposed discipline by judges making decisions without indulging their own personal views or ideas that may not be consistent with existing law.

SEPARATION OF POWERS The system of checks and balances preventing one branch of government from infringing upon exercising the powers of another branch of government.

■■■

Webster v. Doe

CIA director (D) v. CIA employee (P)

486 U.S. 592 (1988).

NATURE OF CASE: Review of challenge to agency dismissal of an employee.

FACT SUMMARY: Doe (P) challenged his dismissal from the Central Intelligence Agency (CIA) by Webster (D), the CIA's director, on account of his homosexuality, contending his dismissal exceeded Webster's (D) statutory authority and was unconstitutional.

🏛 RULE OF LAW
A dismissal from the CIA is not judicially reviewable on statutory grounds.

FACTS: Doe (P), a Central Intelligence Agency (CIA) employee, was dismissed on account of his homosexuality. He filed an action against Webster (D), the director of the CIA, alleging that the dismissal exceeded Webster's (D) statutory authority, as well as constitutional violations. The court of appeals held the dismissal reviewable on statutory grounds. Webster (D) petitioned for United States Supreme Court review, and the Court granted certiorari.

ISSUE: Is a dismissal from the CIA judicially reviewable on statutory grounds?

HOLDING AND DECISION: (Rehnquist, C.J.) No. A dismissal from the CIA is not judicially reviewable on statutory grounds. In deciding upon the reviewability of any agency action, a court must look to the statutory authority under which the agency acted. Here, the National Security Act gives the director discretion to terminate any employee whenever he deems such termination advisable in the interests of the United States. This standard fairly exudes deference to the director: the dismissed party need not actually be a threat to U.S. security—he only must be one in the eyes of the director. It is difficult to see how any judicial review under this standard is possible. Consequently, no such review is available. [The Court went on to hold that the dismissal was reviewable on a constitutional level.] Affirmed in part; reversed in part.

CONCURRENCE AND DISSENT: (Scalia, J.) Although the discretion granted to the CIA director (D) by the National Security Act is broad, it is not unlimited contrary to the Court's reasoning in this case. The "no law to apply" test sometimes explains non-reviewability, but certainly not always. Any governmental decision is susceptible to several legal constraints that permit judicial review, first among them being the requirement to base decisions on a public purpose instead of on mere private, personal interest (notwithstanding the courts' reluctance to review a prosecutor's decision to prosecute against claims of personal animosity). The majority's "committed to agency discretion by law" rationale, grounded in §701(a)(2) of the Administrative Procedures Act (APA), requires a further contrast with the "statutes preclude judicial review" requirement of §701(a)(1). It is clear under our precedents that §701(a)(2)'s "committed to agency discretion by law" requirement equates with the comparatively broad standard "of the sort that is traditionally unreviewable." In this case, the language of §102(c) of the National Security Act prohibits, at a minimum, dismissing a CIA employee out of personal vindictiveness, or nepotism, and such a dismissal would be reviewable under §§102(c) and 701(a)(2). The "no law to apply" test and the correct test, defining the reviewability of agency discretion by traditional standards of reviewability, will be a pivotal issue if and when the Court decides the issue it leaves unresolved in this case.

▶ ANALYSIS

The success of a statutory challenge to an agency act is wholly dependent upon the statute authorizing the agency in question. Some statutes list in detail what is expected of an agency in executing the law. Others like the law in question are quite permissive in granting discretion. A plaintiff has a much better chance of success under the former type of statute.

Quicknotes

ABSOLUTE DISCRETION The authority conferred upon a public agency by law to act reasonably in accordance with its own judgment under certain circumstances.

JUDICIAL REVIEW The authority of the courts to review decisions, actions or omissions committed by another agency or branch of government.

Alabama Power Co. v. Ickes

Utility company (P) v. Government official (D)

302 U.S. 464 (1938).

NATURE OF CASE: Appeal from an action to declare federal financial aid grants unconstitutional.

FACT SUMMARY: Alabama Power Co. (P) claimed that federal financial aid grants to municipal electric companies would be financially injurious to it and that the grants violated the Constitution.

RULE OF LAW
In order to have federal standing to sue, the proposed plaintiff must show some direct injury suffered or threatened by the abridgement of a protectable legal right.

FACTS: Ickes (D), the Federal Energy Administrator, made federal grants to municipal power companies under a congressionally enacted federal works program. Alabama Power Co. (P), a private company, challenged the grants as unconstitutional, asserting standing to sue as a federal taxpayer and contending it would be financially injured by the grants in that the municipal companies would enjoy a competitive advantage.

ISSUE: In order to have federal standing to sue, must the proposed plaintiff show some direct injury suffered or threatened by the abridgement of a protectable legal right?

HOLDING AND DECISION: (Sutherland, J.) Yes. In order to have federal standing to sue, the proposed plaintiff must show some direct injury suffered or threatened by the abridgement of a protectable legal right. Standing is not established merely by being a federal taxpayer, and although Alabama Power (P) may be severely injured economically, it has no legal right to protection from competition, as it does not have an exclusive franchise, and the municipalities are legally engaged in the competitive activities. Therefore, the grants to the municipalities do not abridge any legal right of Alabama Power (P), and any injury suffered, no matter how directly or severely, does not confer standing to sue.

▶ ANALYSIS

Article III of the Constitution requires that, in order for federal courts to have jurisdiction over a dispute, it must be a "case or controversy." A part of the determination whether such a case or controversy is presented is to establish whether the party bringing suit has the power to invoke federal jurisdiction over the dispute. This power is called standing to sue. In order to have standing, the person must have suffered a direct injury or be immediately threatened by such. This ensures that the party has a strong enough interest in the outcome of the dispute so as to induce full and vigorous litigation of all issues presented.

■■■

Quicknotes

CASE OR CONTROVERSY Constitutional requirement in order to invoke federal court jurisdiction that the matter present a justiciable issue.

JURISDICTION The authority of a court to hear and declare judgment in respect to a particular matter.

STANDING Whether a party possesses the right to commence suit against another party by having a personal stake in the resolution of the controversy.

■■■

FCC v. Sanders Brothers Radio Station

Federal agency (D) v. Radio licensees (P)

309 U.S. 470 (1940).

NATURE OF CASE: Appeal in an action seeking judicial review of an FCC's grant of a radio license.

FACT SUMMARY: The Federal Communications Commission (FCC) (D) contended that Sanders Brothers Radio Station's (Sanders Brothers) (P) potential loss of earnings due to an FCC (D) determination was an insufficient injury to bestow federal standing to challenge the FCC's (D) grant of a radio license to Sanders Brothers' (P) competitor.

> **RULE OF LAW**
> Federal standing exists based on mere economic loss due to an agency's action regarding a competitor where a statute provides for review of such action.

FACTS: Sanders Brothers Radio Station (Sanders Brothers) (P), radio licensees in Dubuque, Iowa, challenged a Federal Communications Commission (FCC) (D) order granting the Telegraph Herald newspaper a radio license in the same city. They claimed that the city could not provide sufficient advertising revenue to support two stations and, therefore, granting a second license would bankrupt both stations. Sanders Brothers (P) sought judicial review of the licensing under the Federal Communications Act (FCA). That statute provided that any person whose interests are adversely affected by any decision of the FCC (D) granting or refusing a license could have such decision judicially reviewed in federal court. The FCC (D) contended Sanders Brothers (P) lacked standing to challenge the issuance of a license. The court of appeals set aside the FCC (D) order and the United States Supreme Court granted certiorari.

ISSUE: Does federal standing exist based on mere economic loss due to an agency's action regarding a competitor where a statute provides for review of such action?

HOLDING AND DECISION: (Roberts, J.) Yes. Federal standing exists based on mere economic loss due to an agency's action regarding a competitor where a statute provides for review of such action. Although general mere economic loss due to a competitive advantage is not sufficient to support standing to sue, Congress in the FCA has specifically provided a right of review to all adversely affected parties. Unless that specific language is to be viewed as mere surplusage, it must be interpreted to grant standing to those able to seek review. Therefore, Sanders Brothers (P) had standing to seek review. However, on review of the merits, the FCC (D) was within its authority in granting the license to the Telegraph Herald.

ANALYSIS

Some commentators have argued that the holding in this case grants Sanders Brothers (P) standing to protect its own economic interest from the complexities of the free market system. The Court recognizes the peculiarities of the broadcast industry and the need therefore for extraordinary regulation. It would seem that rules regarding determinations in this area cannot be viewed as analogous to other areas where standing requirements are stricter.

Quicknotes

ECONOMIC LOSS RULE for products liability losses, economic losses can include repair and replacement costs as well as lost profits and the commercial value lost due to inadequate use.

JUDICIAL REVIEW The authority of the courts to review decisions, actions or omissions committed by another agency or branch of government.

LICENSE A right that is granted to a person allowing him or her to conduct an activity that without such permission he or she could not lawfully do, and which is unassignable and revocable at the will of the licensor.

STANDING Whether a party possesses the right to commence suit against another party by having a personal stake in the resolution of the controversy.

Association of Data Processing Service Organizations v. Camp

Trade association (P) v. Government official (D)

397 U.S. 150 (1970).

NATURE OF CASE: Appeal from dismissal of suit challenging a ruling of the Comptroller of the Currency.

FACT SUMMARY: The Association of Data Processing Service Organizations (the Association) (P) challenged a ruling of the Comptroller of the Currency (the Comptroller) (D) that national banks could perform data processing services for customers and other banks. The Comptroller (D) attacked the Association's (P) standing to prosecute the suit.

🏛 RULE OF LAW
Standing to challenge an order of an administrative agency is established by a showing that the interest sought to be protected is arguably within the zone of interests to be regulated by the statute or the constitutional guarantee in question.

FACTS: The Association of Data Processing Service Organizations (the Association) (P) challenged a ruling by the Comptroller of the Currency (D) that allowed national banks, as an incident to their banking services, to make their data processing services available to other banks and to bank customers. The court of appeals dismissed the suit, holding that the Association (P) lacked standing to prosecute the action. The United States Supreme Court granted certiorari.

ISSUE: Is standing to challenge an order of an administrative agency established by a showing that the interest sought to be protected is arguably within the zone of interests to be regulated by the statute or the constitutional guarantee in question?

HOLDING AND DECISION: (Douglas, J.) Yes. Standing to challenge an order of an administrative agency is established by a showing that the interest sought to be protected is arguably within the zone of interests to be regulated by the statute or the constitutional guarantee in question. Administrative orders may be challenged by anyone who alleges an injury to an interest that is arguably within the zone of interests intended to be protected or regulated by the statute or the constitutional guarantee in question. Section 4 of the Bank Service Corporation Act prohibits any bank from engaging in the performance of any activity other than that of providing banking services. It is apparent from the legislative history of this enactment that it was intended in part to protect entities that, like the Association (P) here, would suffer financial or other harm were the banks permitted to engage in non-banking activities. Accordingly, as a competitor, the Association (P) arguably asserts claims within the zone of interest protected by Section 4. The merits of those claims must be decided on remand. Remanded.

▶ ANALYSIS

Issues of standing are almost always determined in favor of the party whose right to bring a suit is being challenged. More and more, standing is being accorded plaintiffs whose interests are non-monetary, indirect, or minimal. Frequently, determination of the standing issue will depend upon the availability of other plaintiffs whose interests in pursuing an action are more concrete than are those of the party presently before the court. But, the fact that a party is not the best of all possible plaintiffs will not alone justify a ruling that he lacks standing to prosecute an action. It is anticipated that the evident judicial tendency to confer standing upon even the more dubious plaintiffs will result in the formulation of ever more imaginative bases upon which standing might be predicated.

■=■

Quicknotes

ADMINISTRATIVE HEARING A hearing conducted before an administrative agency.

STANDING Whether a party possesses the right to commence suit against another party by having a personal stake in the resolution of the controversy.

■=■

Clarke v. Securities Industry Association

Government official (D) v. Trade association (P)

479 U.S. 388 (1987).

NATURE OF CASE: Review of order reversing administrative decision regarding financial services.

FACT SUMMARY: Clarke (D), the Comptroller of the Currency, argued that the Securities Industry Association (P) did not have standing to challenge his decision allowing national banks to offer discount brokerage services.

🏛 RULE OF LAW
Where a class of plaintiffs itself is not the subject of the contested regulatory action, the essential inquiry under the "zone of interest" test is whether Congress intended for that particular class of plaintiffs to be relied upon to challenge agency disregard of the law.

FACTS: Clarke (D), the Comptroller of Currency (the Comptroller), issued a regulation permitting national banks to open offices selling discount brokerage services to the public. The Securities Industry Association (SIA) (P), an organization made up of securities dealers, challenged the ruling as contrary to law, particularly the McFadden Act, which placed limitations on the activities in which bank branches could engage. The court of appeals invalidated the decision. The United States Supreme Court granted review, and first addressed the Comptroller's (D) argument that the SIA (P) lacked standing.

ISSUE: Where a class of plaintiffs itself is not the subject of the contested regulatory action, is the essential inquiry under the "zone of interest" test whether Congress intended for that particular class of plaintiffs to be relied upon to challenge agency disregard of the law?

HOLDING AND DECISION: (White, J.) Yes. Where a class of plaintiffs itself is not the subject of the contested regulatory action, the essential inquiry under the "zone of interest" test is whether Congress intended for that particular class of plaintiffs to be relied upon to challenge agency disregard of the law. Whether a party has standing to challenge an administrative decision is largely governed by the "zone of interests" test. Under this test, if a party is within the zone of interests protected by any statute relevant to the agency action, standing will exist. If a party's interests are so marginally related to or inconsistent with the statute, standing will be held not to exist. Here, the SIA (P) has standing to challenge a Comptroller of Currency (D) decision allowing national banks to offer discount brokerage services. The McFadden Act was largely concerned with excessive accumulation of power by national banks through branching, and the SIA (P) and its constituent members would seem to be within the zone of interests here. [The Court went on to address the merits, and held for the comptroller.]

CONCURRENCE: (Stevens, J.) SIA (P) so clearly has standing under the McFadden Act that the Court did not need to belabor its standing analysis.

▶ ANALYSIS

When all is said and done, standing is a matter of congressional intent. The zone of interests test is merely the Court's formulation of a manner of ascertaining such intent. If a party falls within the zone, but is still not within Congress's contemplation of who should be a plaintiff, the test could not be applied by the reviewing court to grant standing.

■▬■

Quicknotes

ADMINISTRATIVE HEARING A hearing conducted before an administrative agency.

JUDICIAL REVIEW The authority of the courts to review decisions, actions or omissions committed by another agency or branch of government.

STANDING Whether a party possesses the right to commence suit against another party by having a personal stake in the resolution of the controversy.

ZONE OF INTERESTS The range or category of interests that a constitutional guarantee or statute is intended to protect.

■▬■

National Credit Union Administration v. First National Bank & Trust Co.

Federal agency (D) v. Banks (P)

522 U.S. 479 (1998).

NATURE OF CASE: Appeal from petition for federal court review of agency interpretation of a statute.

FACT SUMMARY: First National Bank & Trust Co. (P) and other banks alleged that the National Credit Union Administration (D), the agency which administers the Federal Credit Union Act, had erred in permitting multiple unrelated employer groups to participate in the same federal credit union.

🏛 RULE OF LAW
(1) As competitors of federal credit unions, banks have an interest in limiting the markets that federal credit unions can serve.
(2) This interest is sufficient to confer standing on banks to seek federal court review of the National Credit Union Administration's interpretation of the Federal Credit Union Act where such interpretation has potentially expanded credit union's markets.

FACTS: Since 1982, the National Credit Union Administration (NCUA) (D) has interpreted provisions of the Federal Credit Union Act (FCUA) to allow groups of unrelated employers having a common bond of the same occupation to belong to the same credit union. First National Bank & Trust Co. (First National) (P) and other banks alleged that they had standing to seek federal court review of this interpretation. The challenged interpretation was found impermissible and the appellate court affirmed. The United States Supreme Court granted certiorari.

ISSUE:
(1) As competitors of federal credit unions, do banks have an interest in limiting the markets that federal credit unions can serve?
(2) If so, is this interest sufficient to confer standing on banks to seek federal court review of the NCUA's interpretation of the FCUA where such interpretation has potentially expanded credit union's markets?

HOLDING AND DECISION: (Thomas, J.)
(1) Yes. As competitors of federal credit unions, banks have an interest in limiting the markets that federal credit unions can serve.
(2) Yes. This interest is sufficient to confer standing on banks to seek federal court review of the NCUA's interpretation of the FCUA where such interpretation has potentially expanded credit union's markets. Since the interest sought to be protected by the complainant is arguably within the zone of interest to be protected by the statute, First National (P) had standing under the

Administrative Procedure Act to challenge the NCUA's (D) interpretation. [The regulation was impermissible under step one of *Chevron*, 467 U.S. 837 (1984).] Affirmed.

DISSENT: (O'Connor, J.) Competitive injury to commercial interests does not arguably fall within the zone of interests sought to be protected by the common bond provision of the FCUA, and the majority's application of the zone-of-interest test all but eviscerates the zone-of-interest requirements. Under the majority's approach, any party that establishes injury in fact under Article III will automatically satisfy the zone-of-interest requirements, thus rendering that test ineffectual. Under a proper zone-of-interest analysis, First National (P) fails to establish standing. The judgment of the court of appeals should be vacated and the case should be remanded with instructions that it be dismissed.

▌ ANALYSIS

The Court here found that the banks had standing to challenge the NCUA's interpretation of federal law. It also concluded that the NCUA's interpretation was erroneous. By applying the canons of construction of statutes, the agency's interpretation was found lacking.

■═■

Quicknotes

JUDICIAL REVIEW The authority of the courts to review decisions, actions or omissions committed by another agency or branch of government.

ZONE OF INTERESTS The range or category of interests that a constitutional guarantee or statute is intended to protect.

■═■

Sierra Club v. Morton

Environment organization (P) v. Federal agency (D)

405 U.S. 727 (1972).

NATURE OF CASE: Appeal from reversal of an order enjoining the commercial development of a recreational wilderness area.

FACT SUMMARY: The United States Forest Service (USFS) (D) contended that the Sierra Club (P) did not suffer direct injury from the proposed development of a recreation area so as to endow it with standing to sue to enjoin the development.

RULE OF LAW
Although an injury need not be economic in nature, it must be suffered by the plaintiff in order for him to have standing to sue.

FACTS: The Sierra Club (P), an environmental protection organization, sued to enjoin the commercial development of a recreational wilderness area by Walt Disney Enterprises, Inc. It alleged standing on the basis that a destruction of the wilderness would adversely affect the scenery, natural and historic objects, and wildlife of the park. The United States Forest Service (USFS) (D), which solicited bids on the project, contended the Sierra Club (P) lacked standing to sue as the injury alleged was common to the general public and was not economic in nature. The district court granted a preliminary injunction, but the court of appeals reversed, finding the Sierra Club (P) lacked standing. The United States Supreme Court granted certiorari.

ISSUE: Although an injury need not be economic in nature, must it be suffered by the plaintiff in order for him to have standing to sue?

HOLDING AND DECISION: (Stewart, J.) Yes. Although an injury need not be economic in nature, it must be suffered by the plaintiff in order for him to have standing to sue. Although the change in use of the wilderness land which would result in aesthetic injury is a sufficient injury in fact to support standing, the Sierra Club (P) has not established it would suffer the injury. The impact of the development will be felt only by those who have used the wilderness area. There being no allegation in Sierra Club's (P) pleadings or affidavits that any of its members actually use or used the area, it cannot be said that the Sierra Club (P) will be directly injured by the development. As a result, it lacks standing to sue. Affirmed.

DISSENT: (Douglas, J.) Environmental cases should carry a unique test of standing whereby suit could be maintained on behalf of the inanimate object to be affected. The environment should be allowed to sue for its own preservation. Those with a meaningful relationship to the object such as hikers, fishermen, and zoologists could seek review on behalf of the object.

DISSENT: (Blackmun, J.) The issue presented in the case should be considered unique because of the immediate need to protect the environment. The Sierra Club (P) should either be granted leave to amend its complaint, or the traditional standing rules should be relaxed in environmental cases.

ANALYSIS

Following the decision in this case, the Court reaffirmed its holding in *United States v. SCRAP*, 412 U.S. 669 (1973). In that case, an environmental protection organization was held to have standing to litigate the environmental impact of railroad rates on recycled products. Standing was specifically found based on the organization's allegation that its members used the recycled products and used the environment that would be affected.

Quicknotes

INJUNCTION A remedy imposed by the court ordering a party to cease the conduct of a specific activity.

STANDING Whether a party possesses the right to commence suit against another party by having a personal stake in the resolution of the controversy.

Lujan v. Defenders of Wildlife

Government official (D) v. Environmental groups (P)

504 U.S. 555 (1992).

NATURE OF CASE: Appeal from affirmance of summary judgment on remand for plaintiffs in action challenging a regulation under the Endangered Species Act.

FACT SUMMARY: Defenders of Wildlife (Defenders) (P) and other environmental groups sought a declaration that the Endangered Species Act ("ESA" or "Act") applied to all actions of federal agencies outside of the United States, including those in other nations, and sought to have a regulation jointly issued by the Secretary of the Interior (D) and the Secretary of Commerce (D) revised in accord with such interpretation.

🏛 RULE OF LAW
Groups or individuals do not have standing to challenge agency regulations where the groups or individuals cannot show actual or imminent injury-in-fact to themselves.

FACTS: Defenders of Wildlife (Defenders) (P) and other environmental groups filed suit seeking a declaration that §7(a)(2) of the Endangered Species Act ("ESA" or "Act") applied to all actions of federal agencies outside of the United States, including those in other nations. The Act divides responsibility for protecting endangered species between the Secretary of the Interior and the Secretary of Commerce, and their respective agencies. These two secretaries initially promulgated a joint regulation that provided that §7(a)(2) applied to all actions occurring in foreign nations and that all federal agencies would have to consult with the Secretary of the Interior before taking actions abroad that might jeopardize the continued existence of any endangered or threatened species. However, the secretaries jointly revised the reach of the regulation, limiting it to actions taken in the U.S. and on the high seas. Defenders (P) contended that the Secretaries (D) had misinterpreted the ESA and sought to have them return to their original interpretation. Some of the theories—and evidence to support those theories—of standing presented by Defenders (P) included that its members would be deprived of seeing endangered species in foreign nations that were adversely affected by agency action; that any person who uses any part of a contiguous ecosystem adversely affected by a funded activity would have standing to challenge that activity even if the activity was located a great distance away ("ecosystem nexus"); that any person who has an interest in studying or seeing the endangered animals anywhere on the globe has standing ("animal nexus"); that any person who has a professional interest in such animals has standing ("vocational nexus"); and that the organizations had

suffered a "procedural injury" based on the Secretary's (D) failure to follow the consultation procedure required by §7(a)(2). The district court initially dismissed for lack of standing, but the court of appeals reversed and remanded. On remand, the district court denied the government (D) summary judgment on the standing issue and granted Defenders (P) summary judgment on the merits, ordering the Secretaries to reinstate their original interpretation. The court of appeals affirmed, and the United States Supreme Court granted certiorari.

ISSUE: Do groups or individuals have standing to challenge agency regulations where the groups or individuals cannot show actual or imminent injury-in-fact to themselves?

HOLDING AND DECISION: (Scalia, J.) No. Groups or individuals do not have standing to challenge agency regulations where the groups or individuals cannot show actual or imminent injury-in-fact to themselves. As the parties invoking federal jurisdiction, Defenders (P) bear the burden of showing standing by establishing, inter alia, that they have suffered an injury in fact, i.e., a concrete and particularized, actual or imminent invasion of a legally protected interest. To survive a summary judgment motion, they must set forth by affidavit or other evidence specific facts to support their claim. Standing is particularly difficult to show here, since third parties, rather than Defenders (P), are the object of the government action or inaction to which they object. Defenders (P) failed to demonstrate that they suffered an injury in fact. Assuming that they established that funded activities abroad threaten certain species, they failed to show that one or more of their members would thereby be directly affected apart from the members' special interest in the subject. Affidavits of members claiming an intent to revisit project sites at some indefinite future time, at which time they will presumably be denied the opportunity to observe endangered animals, do not suffice, for they do not demonstrate an "imminent" injury. Defenders (P) also mistakenly relied on a number of other novel standing theories. Their theory that any person using any part of a contiguous ecosystem adversely affected by a funded activity has standing even if the activity is located far away from the area of their use is inconsistent with this Court's precedent, and they state purely speculative, nonconcrete injuries when they argue that suit can be brought by anyone with an interest in studying or seeing endangered animals anywhere on the globe and anyone with a professional interest in such animals. Moreover, the court of appeals erred in holding

Continued on next page.

that Defenders (P) had standing on the ground that the statute's citizen-suit provision confers on all persons the right to file suit to challenge the Secretary's (D) failure to follow the proper consultative procedure, notwithstanding their inability to allege any separate concrete injury flowing from that failure. This Court has consistently held that a plaintiff claiming only a generally available grievance about government, unconnected with a threatened concrete interest of his own, does not state an Article III case or controversy. Vindicating the public interest is the function of the Congress and the Chief Executive. To allow that interest to be converted into an individual right by a statute denominating it as such and permitting all citizens to sue, regardless of whether they suffered any concrete injury, would authorize Congress to transfer from the President to the courts the Chief Executive's most important constitutional duty, i.e., to "take Care that the Laws be faithfully executed," Art. II, §3. Reversed and remanded.

CONCURRENCE: (Kennedy, J.) It is not reasonable to assume that the affiants relied on by Defenders (P) in this case will be using the sites on a regular basis, nor do they claim to have visited the sites since the project commenced. For this reason, standing is correctly denied in this case. This holding, however, does not necessarily preclude standing under different circumstances, on a nexus theory similar to the theories proffered by Defenders (P) in the case at hand. As government programs and policies become more complex and far-reaching, the courts must be sensitive to the articulation of new rights of action that do not have clear analogs in common-law tradition. The ESA in its citizen suit provisions confers a right on any person, but it does not of its own force establish that there is an injury in any person by virtue of any violation; Congress must do a better job of identifying the injury it seeks to vindicate and relating the injury to the class of persons entitled to bring suit.

CONCURRENCE: (Stevens, J.) The result obtained is correct because the Secretary (D) correctly interpreted the ESA. However, Defenders (P) did have standing.

DISSENT: (Blackmun, J.) First, Defenders (P) raised genuine issues of fact, both as to injury and as to redressability, that were sufficient to survive a motion for summary judgment on standing. Second, some classes of procedural duties are so enmeshed with the prevention of substantive, concrete harm that an individual plaintiff may be able to demonstrate a sufficient likelihood of injury solely through the breach of that procedural duty. Thus, there is no room for a per se rule or presumption excluding injuries labeled "procedural" in nature. In sum, the majority's ruling is a slash-and-burn expedition through the law of environmental standing.

ANALYSIS

Under the citizen suit provisions in the Endangered Species Act §11 (g), "any person" is authorized to bring suit in federal court to, among other matters, compel the Secretary to "perform any act or duty" under the Act "which is not discretionary." The alleged injury in this case arose from two members of the Defenders (P), who had been to Sri Lanka and Egypt and worried that public works projects in those countries, partially funded by the United States, would detrimentally alter the habitats of some endangered species in the area.

Quicknotes

JUDICIAL REVIEW The authority of the courts to review decisions, actions or omissions committed by another agency or branch of government.

REDRESSABILITY Requirement that in order for a court to hear a case there must be an injury that is redressable or capable of being remedied.

STANDING Whether a party possesses the right to commence suit against another party by having a personal stake in the resolution of the controversy.

Massachusetts v. EPA

State member of coalition (P) v. Government agency (D)

549 U.S. 497 (2007).

NATURE OF CASE: Appeal from affirmance of denial of rulemaking petition by agency.

FACT SUMMARY: A coalition of state and local governments and private organizations (collectively, "the coalition") (P) petitioned the Environmental Protection Agency (EPA) (D) to regulate greenhouse gas emissions pursuant to the Clean Air Act. In response, the EPA (D) contended, inter alia, that to reach the merits of the coalition's (P) petition, at least one of the petitioning coalition (P) members must have Article III standing to invoke federal court jurisdiction.

🏛 RULE OF LAW
A state is entitled to special treatment in asserting standing to challenge agency action in federal court, such that traditional standing requirements are relaxed.

FACTS: A coalition of state and local governments and private organizations (collectively, "the coalition") (P) petitioned the Environmental Protection Agency (EPA) (D) to regulate greenhouse gas emissions from new motor vehicles pursuant to the Clean Air Act (CAA). The EPA (D) denied the petition. In reaching its decision, the EPA (D) concluded that—contrary to the opinions of its former general counsels—the CAA did not authorize it to issue regulations to address global climate change, and, even if the EPA (D) did have the authority to set greenhouse gas emissions standards, it would decline to do so because such regulation would conflict with other administration priorities and would be unwise. The coalition (P) challenged the EPA's (D) order denying the petition in the court of appeals, which ruled against the coalition (P). The United States Supreme Court granted certiorari. In response to the coalition's (P) petition for certiorari, the EPA (D) argued that the Court could not address the merits of the case without determining whether at least one member of the coalition (P) had standing to invoke jurisdiction under Article III of the Constitution. Thereupon, the Court recognized that States are not normal litigants for the purposes of invoking federal jurisdiction, but determined that inasmuch as the parties' dispute turned on the proper construction of a congressional statute, the underlying matter was properly addressed before the federal court. To make applicable to the coalition (P) the federal statute authorizing challenge to EPA (D) action, the Court considered the special position and interest of Massachusetts (P).

ISSUE: Is a state entitled to special treatment in asserting standing to challenge agency action in federal court, such that traditional standing requirements are relaxed?

HOLDING AND DECISION: (Stevens, J.) Yes. A state is entitled to special treatment in asserting standing to challenge agency action in federal court, such that traditional standing requirements are relaxed. Congress authorized challenge of the EPA (D) action in 42 U.S.C. §7607(b)(1). To demonstrate standing, a litigant must show that it has suffered a concrete and particularized injury that is either actual or imminent, that the injury is fairly traceable to the defendant, and that a favorable decision will likely redress that injury. However, the law of *Lujan v. Defenders of Wildlife*, 504 U.S. 555 (1992), prescribes special status to the litigant with a vested procedural right—in particular, status to assert standing without meeting all the normal standing requirements. Only one petitioner needs to have standing to authorize review. Massachusetts (P) has a special position and interest here. It is a sovereign State and not, as in *Lujan*, a private individual, and it actually owns a great deal of the territory alleged to be affected. The sovereign prerogatives to force reductions in greenhouse gas emissions, to negotiate emissions treaties with developing countries, and (in some circumstances) to exercise the police power to reduce motor-vehicle emissions are now lodged in the federal government. Because Congress has ordered the EPA (D) to protect Massachusetts (P) (among others) by prescribing applicable standards, and has given Massachusetts (P) a concomitant procedural right to challenge the rejection of its rulemaking petition as arbitrary and capricious, the coalition's (P) submissions as they pertain to Massachusetts (P) have satisfied the most demanding standards of the adversarial process. The EPA's (D) steadfast refusal to regulate greenhouse gas emissions presents a risk of harm to Massachusetts that is both "actual" and "imminent," for purposes of satisfying *Lujan*, and there is a "substantial likelihood that the judicial relief requested" will prompt the EPA (D) to take steps to reduce that risk. The harms associated with climate change are serious and well recognized. The Government's (D) own objective assessment of the relevant science and a strong consensus among qualified experts indicate that global warming threatens, inter alia, a precipitate rise in sea levels, severe and irreversible changes to natural ecosystems, a significant reduction in winter snowpack with direct and important economic consequences, and increases in the spread of disease and the ferocity of weather events. As such, and because of the quasi-sovereign interests of Massachusetts (P) in preserving its coastal land, the sovereign prerogatives of Massachusetts (P) must be protected pursuant to federal statute. The fact that climate-change risks caused by global warming, to which the underlying emissions contribute, are widely shared does not diminish the

Continued on next page.

threat of harm to Massachusetts (P) in particular. The rising seas, as caused by global warming, have begun to swallow Massachusetts's (P) coastal land, thus creating a particularized injury to same. Over time, the rising sea levels will continue to harm Massachusetts (P) and, accordingly, despite the increasing emissions from developing nations such as China and India, the EPA (D) must take the incremental steps to slow or reduce the effects of global warming. And although the risk of catastrophic consequences associated with man-made global warming are remote, EPA (D) action here would redress injury to Massachusetts (P). Thus, it is manifest that the coalition (P) has standing to challenge the EPA's (D) denial of their rulemaking petition. Reversed and remanded.

DISSENT: (Roberts, C.J.) The problem of global climate change is properly addressed to the executive and legislative branches of government. The case and controversy requirement of Article III of the Constitution in fact precludes the Court from deciding the instant matter. Specifically, the party asserting standing to sue must allege concrete and particularized injury that is actual or imminent; the injury must be fairly traceable to the defendant's allegedly unlawful conduct; and the relief sought must likely redress the petitioner's injury. There is nothing in our jurisprudence that permits relaxation of Article III standing requirements for a State, and there is no distinction made by Congress as to whether a party is public or private. In fact, despite its assertion that States are to receive "special solicitude," the majority nonetheless applies the Article III standing test to Massachusetts (P) as a landowner. Here, by definition, the injury associated with global warming is not particularized to Massachusetts (P). But if the loss of coastal land may be considered particularized, the loss must be actual or imminent. Domestic greenhouse emissions are a small fraction of global emissions, and it is speculative that these emissions are linked to global warming and, ultimately, loss of land in Massachusetts (P). Moreover, it is wholly unclear how new EPA (D) regulations will likely prevent the loss of Massachusetts (P) coastal land. The coalition (P) cannot establish a causal connection between loss of coastal land in Massachusetts and the EPA's (D) lack of regulation of greenhouse gas emissions. Indeed, the majority uses "the dire nature of global warming itself as a bootstrap for finding causation and redressability." Moreover, redressability is even more problematic because 80 percent or so of global emissions originate outside the U.S. In this regard, the majority ignores precedent that holds that when the existence of an element of standing "depends on the unfettered choices made by independent actors not before the courts and whose exercise of broad and legitimate discretion the courts cannot presume either to control or to predict," a party must present facts supporting an assertion that the actor will proceed in such a manner. Here, there is no telling what other countries will do. Thus, the likelihood of redressing the (improbable) loss of Massachusetts's (P) land

through the reduction of domestic emissions is so slight as to be insufficient for the Article III standing test.

▶ ANALYSIS

In a speech following the decision in *Massachusetts v. Environmental Protection Agency*, EPA Administrator Lisa Jackson related that only a small percentage of greenhouse gas emitting facilities—the largest 10,000 of tens of millions of American businesses—will be required to report their emissions. Administrator Jackson observed that the EPA does not seek to place an undue burden on American business and does not seek to regulate everything from "cows to the local Dunkin' Donuts." See, Speech: Administrator Lisa P. Jackson, Remarks to the 2nd Annual Governors' Global Climate Summit at http://yosemite.epa.gov/opa/admpress.nsf/. However, it is the position of the Small Business Administration, Office of Advocacy, that numerous small business entities will be subject to the EPA permitting requirements for greenhouse gas emissions, thereby causing said small businesses significant additional expense. See, Small Business Administration: Letter dated 12/23/09 at http://www.sba.gov/advo/laws/comments/epa09_1223.html. As such, it may be that resulting litigation will affect both public and private sectors of the American economy for years to come.

Quicknotes

ARTICLE III, U.S. CONSTITUTION Limits federal judicial power to cases and controversies.

STANDING The right to commence suit against another party because of a personal stake in the resolution of the controversy.

Simon v. Eastern Kentucky Welfare Rights Organization

Federal agency (D) v. Community organization (P)

426 U.S. 26 (1976).

NATURE OF CASE: Appeal in action challenging an IRS Revenue Ruling. [The procedural posture of the case is not presented in the casebook excerpt.]

FACT SUMMARY: The Internal Revenue Service (IRS) (D) moved to dismiss indigents' (P) action challenging a Revenue Policy concerning the grant of charitable organization status to hospitals that failed to treat indigents, contending the indigents (P) lacked standing to sue.

> 🏛 **RULE OF LAW**
> Standing requires the plaintiff to have suffered an actual direct injury due to the conduct of the named defendant.

FACTS: The Internal Revenue Service (IRS) (D) issued a Revenue Ruling that allowed hospitals to be considered charitable organizations and receive tax deductible contributions even though they did not treat indigents to their full economic ability. Indigents (P), and organizations representing them, challenged the Ruling, contending it encouraged hospitals to deny treatment to indigents, who, they contended, were the intended beneficiaries of the pertinent tax code provisions relating to charities. The IRS (D) moved to dismiss the action for lack of standing to sue, claiming the administration of the tax laws was analogous to prosecutorial discretion, and a party may not challenge such administration as affects another party. The United States Supreme Court granted certiorari. [The procedural posture of the case is not presented in the casebook excerpt.]

ISSUE: Does standing require the plaintiff to have suffered an actual direct injury due to the conduct of the named defendant?

HOLDING AND DECISION: (Powell, J.) Yes. Standing requires the plaintiff to have suffered an actual direct injury due to the conduct of the named defendant. Standing to sue is established only when the plaintiff has suffered a direct injury due to the defendant's conduct rather than the conduct of a third party. In order for the federal judiciary to have the power to determine a dispute, the situation presented must be a case or controversy within the meaning of Article III of the Constitution. Central to this is that parties present a dispute wherein the plaintiff suffers actual injury at the hands of the defendant sued. Even if the indigents (P) did suffer a direct injury, it was at the hands of the hospitals, not the IRS (D)—and the hospitals were not named defendants here. It is mere speculation on the indigents' (P) part that the hospitals failed to treat indigents because of the Revenue Ruling. Therefore, the indigents (P) failed to establish standing to sue. Complaint dismissed. [The disposition of the case is not presented in the casebook excerpt.]

CONCURRENCE: (Stewart, J.) Outside of First Amendment cases challenging tax decisions, no one could conceivably have standing to litigate someone else's federal tax liability.

CONCURRENCE: (Brennan, J.) The Court rests its opinion on Article III. This deprives Congress of the ability to rectify the holding presented here if it so chose. This will result in the undesirable situation where no administrative action which allegedly frustrates the intent of legislation promulgated to give certain parties certain incentives will be subject to judicial review. This is so because of the almost impossible showing necessary to establish standing which this case presents. In this case, however, the indigents (P) failed to sufficiently establish any injury; therefore, they had no standing.

▌ **ANALYSIS**

Some commentators have argued that this case represents merely a special rule of standing for tax cases. The rationale for this argument is that the IRS would be placed in an untenable position if the beneficiaries of a tax law had standing to seek review of IRS administration of the law even where their own tax liability was completely unaffected by the law.

■━■

Quicknotes

ARTICLE III, U.S. CONSTITUTION Limits federal judicial power to cases and controversies.

INJURY-IN-FACT Harm that is sufficiently certain to give a plaintiff standing to sue and which is redressable by court-ordered relief.

STANDING Whether a party possesses the right to commence suit against another party by having a personal stake in the resolution of the controversy.

■━■

Steel Company v. Citizens for a Better Environment

Manufacturer (D) v. Environmentalists (P)

523 U.S. 83 (1998).

NATURE OF CASE: Appeal from denial of a Rule 12(b) motion to dismiss on the pleadings in a citizen's suit for past violations under the Emergency Planning and Community Right-To-Know Act. [The complete procedural posture of the case is not presented in the casebook excerpt.]

FACT SUMMARY: Citizens for a Better Environment (P) alleged that they had standing to sue Steel Company (D) for past violations of the Emergency Planning and Community Right-To-Know Act of 1986.

> ## 🏛 RULE OF LAW
> To have standing to sue, a party must request relief which would remedy the alleged harm that it has directly suffered.

FACTS: Citizens for a Better Environment (CBE) (P), a group of individuals interested in environmental protection, sued Steel Company (D) for past environmental violations under the citizen-suit provision of the Emergency Planning and Community Right-To-Know Act of 1986 (EPCRA). In particular, CBE (P) alleged that Steel Company's (D) failure to provide EPCRA information to the Environmental Protection Agency (EPA) was a direct injury to itself and its members. After the CBE (P) filed certain notices required under EPCRA before it could sue, Steel Company (D) provided to the EPA all the past reports required by EPCRA, thus coming into compliance. When EPA decided not to take legal action against Steel Company (D), CBE (P) brought suit. As relief, CBE (P) sought: a declaratory judgment that Steel Company (D) had violated EPCRA; authorization to periodically inspect Steel Company's (D) facility and records; copies of Steel Company's (D) submissions to the EPA; an order for civil penalties of $25,000 per day for each violation of EPCRA; its costs; and any other appropriate relief. The court of appeals ruled that the EPCRA authorized suit for past violations. The United States Supreme Court granted certiorari. [The complete procedural posture of the case is not presented in the casebook excerpt.]

ISSUE: To have standing to sue, must a party request relief which would remedy the alleged harm that it has directly suffered?

HOLDING AND DECISION: (Scalia, J.) Yes. To have standing to sue, a party must request relief which would remedy the alleged harm that it has directly suffered. Initial standing must be based on allegations of present or threatened injury. None of the relief sought by CBE (P) would remedy the alleged injury in fact it asserts. The complaint therefore fails the redressability test: None of the specific items of relief sought would serve to reimburse CBE (P) for losses caused by Steel Company's (D) late reporting, or to eliminate any effects of that late reporting upon CBE (P). Additionally, the government's argument, that injunctive relief does constitute remediation because "there is a presumption of [future] injury when the defendant has voluntarily ceased its illegal activity in response to litigation," even if that occurs before a complaint is filed, must be rejected. To accept the government's view would be to overrule clear precedent requiring that the allegations of future injury be particular and concrete. CBE (P) therefore lacks standing to maintain this suit. Reversed and remanded, with directions that the case be dismissed.

CONCURRENCE: (Stevens, J.) Today the Court has merely mechanistically applied the redressability prong of our standing analysis. The Court acknowledges that the plaintiff would have standing if Congress had created access to a compensatory payment, however minimal, for the injuries plaintiff allegedly sustained because of the company's actions. What the Court fails to acknowledge, however, is that a private party's enforcement of a statutory sanction against another private party does redress the enforcing party's injury. It commonly does so, in some form, when a punitive-damages award is paid to the sovereign; historically, private enforcement against other private parties has presumably redressed injury in England, the American colonies, and the United States. Today's decision is therefore a departure in our constitutional jurisprudence. Given the gravity of unnecessarily making sweeping new constitutional law, and given the ready availability of a statutory question in this case, prudence suggests that the Court should have answered the statutory question first.

CONCURRENCE: (Ginsburg, J.) Citizen-suits for wholly past violations are not authorized by the EPCRA.

▶ ANALYSIS

The court in this case applied the traditional tests for standing. The issue of injury in fact was never reached. The case was decided entirely on the basis of the requirement for redressability.

■▬■

Continued on next page.

Quicknotes

REDRESSABILITY Requirement that in order for a court to hear a case there must be an injury that is redressable or capable of being remedied.

STANDING Whether a party possesses the right to commence suit against another party by having a personal stake in the resolution of the controversy.

■═■

Friends of the Earth, Inc. v. Laidlaw Environmental Services, Inc.

Environment organization (P) v. Waste company (D)

528 U.S. 167 (2000).

NATURE OF CASE: Appeal of judgment in an action under the Clean Water Act. [The complete procedural posture of the case is not presented in the casebook excerpt.]

FACT SUMMARY: Laidlaw Environmental Services, Inc. (Laidlaw) (D) operated a hazardous waste incinerator that was discharging mercury into a river at a level high enough to violate its permit, which specified the amount of waste the company could put into the environment. Friends of the Earth, Inc. (P) sued Laidlaw (D) under the citizen-suit provision of the Clean Water Act.

🏛 **RULE OF LAW**
A plaintiff has standing to sue under the Clean Water Act for injunctive relief and civil penalties where the plaintiff proves, first, injury in fact, and, second, that penalties would be a deterrent to future violations.

FACTS: Laidlaw Environmental Services, Inc. (Laidlaw) (D) operated a hazardous waste incinerator and was granted a National Pollutant Discharge Elimination System (NPDES) permit by the South Carolina Department of Health and Environmental Control, authorizing it to discharge treated water into a river. The permit stated limits on the discharge of pollutants into the river and regulated the flow, temperature, toxicity, and pH of the effluent from the facility; it also imposed monitoring and reporting obligations. Repeatedly, Laidlaw's (D) discharges exceeded the limits set by the permit under the Clean Water Act (the Act). Friends of the Earth, Inc. (FOE) (P) filed an action against Laidlaw (D) under the Act alleging noncompliance with the permit and seeking injunctive relief and/or civil penalties. The citizen-suit provision of the Act allows people who have an interest and who may or may not be adversely affected in a matter to sue regarding that matter. The district court declined to order injunctive relief, finding that Laidlaw (D) had substantially complied with its permit requirements after the litigation was instituted, but the court assessed a civil penalty of $405,800 as a deterrent to future violations. The United States Supreme Court granted certiorari. [The complete procedural posture of the case is not presented in the casebook excerpt.]

ISSUE: Does a plaintiff have standing to sue under the Clean Water Act for injunctive relief and civil penalties where the plaintiff proves, first, injury in fact, and, second, that penalties would be a deterrent to future violations?

HOLDING AND DECISION: (Ginsburg, J.) Yes. A plaintiff has standing to sue under the Clean Water Act for injunctive relief and civil penalties where the plaintiff proves, first, injury in fact, and, second, that penalties would be a deterrent to future violations. FOE (P) had standing to seek injunctive relief because it showed injury in fact by stating that its members were unable to fish, wade, picnic, or participate in other recreational activities in and along the river because it looked and smelled polluted. These statements prove injury in fact because those making them aver that they use the affected area and that, for them, the aesthetic and recreational values of the area are lessened by the challenged activity. Furthermore, FOE (P) had standing to seek civil penalties because all civil penalties have some deterrent effect and, therefore, afforded redress to citizen plaintiffs who are injured or threatened with injury as a consequence of ongoing conduct. Moreover, a threat of civil penalties has no deterrent value unless it is credible that it will be carried out; it is reasonable for Congress to conclude that an actual award of penalties does bring deterrence above and beyond the mere prospect of penalties. [The disposition of the case is not presented in the casebook excerpt.]

DISSENT: (Scalia, J.) FOE (P) did not demonstrate injury in fact. Concern that water was polluted and a belief that the pollution had reduced the value of their homes does not show that they have suffered a concrete and particularized injury. In addition, in regard to redressability, the remedy FOE (P) seeks is inconsistent and doesn't satisfy their allegations of injury. Furthermore, it is unlikely that future polluters will be deterred. Finally, by permitting citizens to pursue civil penalties payable to the Federal Treasury, the Act does not provide a mechanism for individual relief in any traditional sense, but turns over to private citizens the function of enforcing the law. The undesirable and unconstitutional consequence of this aspect of the Act and of the majority's decision is to place the immense power of suing to enforce the public laws in private hands.

▶ **ANALYSIS**

In contrast to *Lujan v. National Wildlife Federation,* 504 U.S. 555 (1992), the affidavits in this case assert that Laidlaw's (D) discharges directly affected those affiants' recreational, aesthetic, and economic interests; in *Lujan,* the affidavits merely contained general averments and conclusory

Continued on next page.

allegations. Furthermore, unlike the Court in *Steel Company v. Citizens for a Better Environment,* 523 U.S. 83 (1998), which held that citizens lacked standing to seek civil penalties for violations that had abated by the time of the suit because the complaint did not allege any continuing or imminent violation and thus provided no basis for such an allegation, here the Court did not reach the issue of standing to seek penalties for violations that are ongoing at the time of the complaint and that could continue in the future.

■━━■

Quicknotes

AFFIDAVIT A declaration of facts written and affirmed before a witness.

INJUNCTIVE RELIEF A court order issued as a remedy, requiring a person to do, or prohibiting that person from doing, a specific act.

REDRESSABILITY Requirement that in order for a court to hear a case there must be an injury that is redressable or capable of being remedied.

■━━■

Federal Election Commission v. Akins

Regulatory agency (D) v. Voters (P)

524 U.S. 11 (1998).

NATURE OF CASE: Appeal in action challenging a Federal Election Commission determination. [The procedural posture of the case is not presented in the casebook excerpt.]

FACT SUMMARY: Voters (P) appealed a finding by the Federal Election Commission (FEC) (D) determining that the American Israeli Public Affairs Committee (AIPAC) is not a "political committee" for purposes of disclosure as required by the Federal Election Campaign Act.

> 🏛 **RULE OF LAW**
> Voters have standing to challenge a regulatory decision where Congress, through legislation, intended to protect voters from the kind of injury at issue, and harm in fact exists because the injury is sufficiently widespread and concrete.

FACTS: Certain voters (P) had views that were frequently in opposition to those of the American Israeli Public Affairs Committee (AIPAC). In order to compel disclosure of AIPAC membership, contributions, and campaign expenditures, the voters (P) petitioned the Federal Election Commission (FEC) (D) to regard APAIC as a "political committee," requiring it to disclose certain information pursuant to the Federal Election Campaign Act ("FECA" or "the Act"). The Act imposes penalties on an entity's spending in coordination with a political campaign that exceeds certain limits, as a means of stemming voting corruption. AIPAC asked the FEC (D) to dismiss the voters' (P) petition, and the FEC (D) found in favor of the APAIC on the grounds that the voters (P) had no standing to bring the matter to review, since the FEC (D) determined that the APAIC was primarily an issue-lobbying organization and not a campaign committee, and, therefore, not a "political committee." Accordingly, the FEC (D) declined to bring an enforcement action against APAIC. The voters (P) appealed the decision in federal court, and, eventually, the United States Supreme Court granted certiorari. [The procedural posture of the case is not presented in the casebook excerpt.]

ISSUE: Do voters have standing to challenge a regulatory decision where Congress, through legislation, intend to protect voters from the kind of injury at issue, and the injury is sufficiently widespread and concrete?

HOLDING AND DECISION: (Breyer, J.) Yes. Voters have standing to challenge a regulatory decision where Congress, through legislation, intended to protect voters from the kind of injury at issue, and harm in fact

exists because the injury is sufficiently widespread and concrete. "Prudential standing" exists where the injury asserted by the plaintiff falls within a range of interests protected by the applicable legislative statute. Here, the injury asserted by the voters (P)—the failure to obtain certain information—is the kind of injury that FECA seeks to address. Therefore, the voters (P) satisfy the "prudential" standing requirements. Furthermore, the federal courts can constitutionally adjudicate this matter because the voters have suffered a form of "injury in fact" by being denied information that must be publicly disclosed. Although general grievances, where the asserted harm is shared in equal measure by a large or widespread class of citizens, generally are not the kind of harms that confer standing and are better left to the political process, the harms in general grievance cases are usually abstract and indefinite. By contrast, in this case, the harm is concrete and widely shared. Therefore, the voters (P) have suffered the kind of injury in fact that does confer standing. Additionally, in this case, the injury suffered by the voters (P) as a group is directly traceable to the FEC's (D) decision, even though the agency (D) may have reached the same result lawfully through the exercise of its discretion, and a court can redress the voters' (P) injury. As a result, standing is conferred upon the voters (P) to have their case reviewed. Vacated and remanded for further proceedings.

DISSENT: (Scalia, J.) The voters' (P) allegations in the instant case are insufficient to render them "aggrieved" for the purpose of finding injury and standing. Their challenge asserts, in error, that the injury suffered is the result of the FEC's (D) refusal to place the needed information in the public domain. Instead, their challenge is to the FEC's (D) refusal to bring an enforcement action, which in turn might produce the information they seek. However, whether to bring enforcement actions is left to agency discretion, and it is doubtful that Congress intended to characterize as a "party aggrieved" any complainant whose petition for an enforcement action was rejected. Additionally, the majority's characterization of "general grievance" doctrine is wrong. The distinction is not between abstract and concrete, but, as precedent provides, between "particularized" and "undifferentiated." If the harm is particularized, it is personal in an individual way. If it is undifferentiated, it is common to all members of the public and must be redressed through the political process. In either case, the injury may be widely shared, but where the injury is particularized, each injured plaintiff suffers an individualized harm, and where the injury is undifferentiated, each

Continued on next page.

plaintiff suffers the same harm. Here, the harm suffered by the voters (P) was undifferentiated, and, therefore, was a general grievance that should not have been adjudicated. Further, the Court's hearing of this suit violates Article III. The requirement of a "case or controversy" is necessary to maintain a meaningful separation between the judicial branch and the executive branch, since if citizens are permitted to use the courts to force executive action, the power of the executive is severely diminished and the power of the judiciary is proportionately enhanced; therefore, Congress may not legislate to permit any person to manage the executive branch's enforcement of the law.

▶ ANALYSIS

The Court here interpreted the voters' challenge to the FEC's (D) initial ruling in two parts: (1) whether the voters (P) were specifically provided for as a group with regard to the legislation governing redress for the injury alleged; and (2) whether Congress actually had the power to authorize courts to adjudicate over these types of suits. In addition, the Court divided the standing analysis into "prudential" and "constitutional" forms of standing, requiring that both be satisfied before a suit could be successfully brought before it.

■═■

Quicknotes

REDRESSABILITY Requirement that in order for a court to hear a case there must be an injury that is redressable or capable of being remedied.

STANDING TO SUE Plaintiff must allege that he has a legally predictable interest at stake in the litigation.

■═■

Columbia Broadcasting System v. United States

Radio network (P) v. Federal government (D)

316 U.S. 407 (1942).

NATURE OF CASE: Appeal from a dismissal for lack of ripeness of an action challenging a Federal Communications Commission regulation.

FACT SUMMARY: Columbia Broadcasting System (P) brought suit challenging Federal Communications Commission (FCC) (D) regulations prescribing rules governing network contractual relations with affiliates, which suit was brought before any FCC (D) enforcement action was taken, and the district court dismissed the case for lack of ripeness.

🏛 RULE OF LAW
An administrative regulation that has the effect of an order and penalizes by its own force and effect is reviewable prior to any enforcement procedures being brought by the agency.

FACTS: The Columbia Broadcasting System (CBS) (P) radio network consisted of seven owned stations and 115 affiliates contractually bound to broadest CBS programming to the exclusion of all other networks. The Federal Communications Commission (FCC) (D) promulgated regulations that allowed it to deny licensees renewal of their licenses if they were parties to contracts such as those between CBS (P) and its affiliates. Because of these regulations, many affiliates threatened to disregard their CBS (P) contracts and not negotiate or renew any contract out of fear of losing their licenses. Prior to any enforcement action by the FCC (D), CBS (P) sought judicial review of the regulations. The district court dismissed, holding the controversy was not ripe for adjudication. CBS (P) appealed, and the United States Supreme Court granted review.

ISSUE: Is an administrative regulation that has the effect of an order and penalizes by its own force and effect reviewable prior to any enforcement procedures being brought by the agency?

HOLDING AND DECISION: (Stone, C.J.) Yes. An administrative regulation that has the effect of an order and penalizes by its own force and effect is reviewable prior to any enforcement procedures being brought by the agency. A regulation promulgated through the valid exercise of the agency's rulemaking power affects the behavior of all those who may be affected by it. It therefore differs from a court order which affects only the parties to the particular action. Therefore, such rules, if they are self-executing, operate to set standards of conduct in advance of any formal enforcement proceedings, and have the effect of an agency order. As a result, regulations such as those pre-sented in this case are reviewable prior to enforcement proceedings being brought by the agency. While it is true, as the FCC (D) argues, that its regulation announces its policy, the regulation does more than act as a press release; the regulation provides a legal basis for cancelling licenses that contravene it and acts to immediately harm parties to such licenses. Therefore, the action was improperly dismissed. Reversed.

DISSENT: (Frankfurter, J.) The regulations do not determine rights. They merely state what the FCC (D) will do with applications for new licenses or renewal of old licenses if the broadcaster engages in any conduct in violation of the regulations. They are merely an announcement of general policy, and, therefore, may not be reviewed until they are enforced.

▶ ANALYSIS

One of the elements that must be present in order for a dispute to be considered a justiciable case or controversy is that the dispute must be ripe for decision. This ripeness requirement demands that the issues be fully developed and not merely speculative in nature. If a delay in decision would serve to give greater clarity to the issues presented, the dispute is usually found to lack "ripeness" and will not be heard.

■==■

Quicknotes

JUDICIAL REVIEW The authority of the courts to review decisions, actions or omissions committed by another agency or branch of government.

LICENSE A right that is granted to a person allowing him or her to conduct an activity that without such permission he or she could not lawfully do, and which is unassignable and revocable at the will of the licensor.

RIPENESS A doctrine precluding a federal court from hearing or determining a matter, unless it constitutes an actual and present controversy warranting a determination by the court.

■==■

Abbott Laboratories v. Gardner

Drug manufacturer (P) v. Federal agency (D)

387 U.S. 136 (1967).

NATURE OF CASE: Appeal from the enjoining of a Food and Drug Administration order.

FACT SUMMARY: Abbott Laboratories (P) sought judicial review of a Food and Drug Administration (FDA) (D) order prior to its enforcement.

🏛 RULE OF LAW
Agency action is ripe for judicial review when the issues presented are fit for judicial decisions and the parties will suffer hardship if judicial consideration is not received.

FACTS: Under authority of the Food, Drug, and Cosmetic Act (the Act) the Commissioner of the Food and Drug Administration (FDA) (D) issued regulations requiring drug manufacturers to print the generic name of the drug on each product. Prior to any enforcement proceedings on these regulations, Abbott Laboratories (Abbott) (P) brought suit to enjoin enforcement, claiming the regulations exceeded the FDA's (D) statutory authority. The district court found for Abbott (P), but the court of appeals reversed, holding the case was not ripe for judicial review. Abbott (P) appealed, and the United States Supreme Court granted review.

ISSUE: Is agency action ripe for review when the issues presented are fit for judicial decision and where the parties will suffer hardship if they are denied reviews?

HOLDING AND DECISION: (Harlan, J.) Yes. Agency action is ripe for judicial review when the issues presented are fit for judicial decision and the parties will suffer hardship if judicial consideration is denied. In this case, the issues presented concern the interpretation of the Food, Drug, and Cosmetic Act. They are purely legal in nature. Consequently, further administrative proceedings would be meaningless. Therefore, the issues are fit for judicial review. Further, the regulations are final agency actions that are therefore ready for review. In addition, the regulations affect Abbott (P) in the conduct of its day-to-day business activities. Compliance would require great expense in changing labels, advertisements, and promotional strategies. Therefore, Abbott (P) would suffer great hardship if judicial review were denied. Moreover, contrary to the FDA's (D) argument, permitting judicial review will not impede effective enforcement of the Act, since if the FDA (D) prevails, a large part of the industry will be bound by the decree, and, if it loses, it will be able to revise the regulation more quickly. Therefore, this case is ripe for judicial review. Reversed and remanded.

▶ ANALYSIS

In *Toilet Goods Association, Inc. v. Gardner*, 387 U.S. 158 (1967), and *Gardner v. Toilet Goods Association, Inc.*, 387 U.S. 167 (1967), decided the same day as the present case, the Court held that the issues were purely legal in nature, yet held the case was not ripe for judicial review. The Court found no irremediable adverse consequences would result from denying review at that particular time. It has been argued that the holding in *Abbott* has made pre-enforcement review of agency regulations a common occurrence.

■══■

Quicknotes

JUDICIAL REVIEW The authority of the courts to review decisions, actions or omissions committed by another agency or branch of government.

RIPENESS A doctrine precluding a federal court from hearing or determining a matter, unless it constitutes an actual and present controversy warranting a determination by the court.

■══■

NLRB Union v. FLRA

Labor union (P) v. Government agency (D)

834 F.2d 191 (D.C. Cir. 1987).

NATURE OF CASE: Appeal from decision upholding validity of government regulations.

FACT SUMMARY: After the National Labor Relations Board Union (P) petitioned the Federal Labor Relations Authority (FLRA) (D) to amend rules it had adopted seven years earlier, the FLRA (D) contended that its negative response to the petitions was not an appealable final order under the statute, and that judicial review should be barred by the 60-day statute of limitations.

🏛 RULE OF LAW

An agency regulation may be appealed outside the appropriate statute of limitations period where a party who possesses standing asserts that the issuing agency acted in excess of its statutory authority in promulgating the regulation or the party petitions the agency for amendment or rescission of the regulations and then appeals the agency's decision where the petitioner's claim is that the regulation suffers from some substantive deficiency other than the agency's lack of statutory authority to issue that regulation, or the petitioner contends the regulation conflicts with the statute from which its authority derives.

FACTS: The National Labor Relations Board Union (Union) (P) sought to amend regulations which the Federal Labor Relations Authority (FLRA) (D) issued in final form on January 17, 1980, almost seven years before this appeal was filed in 1987. The FLRA (D) contended that while it was obliged to respond to the Union's (P) petition, its negative response to that petition was not an appealable final order under 5 U.S.C. §1723(a), and that judicial review should be barred by the regulation's 60-day statute of limitations. The court of appeals granted review.

ISSUE: May an agency regulation be appealed outside the appropriate statute of limitations period where a party who possesses standing asserts that the issuing agency acted in excess of its statutory authority in promulgating the regulation or the party petitions the agency for amendment or rescission of the regulations and then appeals the agency's decision where the petitioner's claim is that the regulation suffers from some substantive deficiency other than the agency's lack of statutory authority to issue that regulation, or the petitioner contends the regulation conflicts with the statute from which its authority derives?

HOLDING AND DECISION: (Edwards, J.) Yes. An agency regulation may be appealed outside the appropriate statute of limitations period where a party who possesses standing asserts that the issuing agency acted in excess of its statutory authority in promulgating the regu-

lation or the party petitions the agency for amendment or rescission of the regulations and then appeals the agency's decision where the petitioner's claim is that the regulation suffers from some substantive deficiency other than the agency's lack of statutory authority to issue that regulation, or the petitioner contends the regulation conflicts with the statute from which its authority derives. Here, the statute of limitations is 60 days. However, indirect attacks on the substantive validity of regulations initiated more than 60 days after their promulgation are distinguished from like attacks on their procedural lineage. Once the statutory limitations period has expired, there are two ways in which an agency's regulations still may be attacked. First, a party who possesses standing may challenge regulations directly on the ground that the issuing agency acted in excess of its statutory authority in promulgating them. Second, a party may obtain judicial review of agency regulations once the limitations period has run by petitioning the agency for amendment or rescission of the regulations and then appealing the agency's decision. However, a petitioner's contention that a regulation suffers from some procedural infirmity, such as an agency's unjustified refusal to allow affected parties to comment on a rule before issuing it in final form, will not be heard outside of the statutory limitations period. [The disposition of the case is not stated in the casebook excerpt.]

▶ ANALYSIS

The court stated in a prior case that the statutory time limit restricting judicial review of agency action was applicable only to cut off review directly from the order promulgating a rule. It did not foreclose subsequent examination of a rule where it was properly brought before the court for review of further agency action applying it. Since administrative rules and regulations are capable of continuing application, limiting the right of review of the underlying rule would effectively deny many parties ultimately affected by a rule an opportunity to question its validity.

■■■

Quicknotes

FINAL AGENCY ORDER The final disposition of a hearing before a public agency or the agency's interpretation or application of a statute.

JUDICIAL REVIEW The authority of the courts to review decisions, actions or omissions committed by another agency or branch of government.

■■■

National Automatic Laundry & Cleaning Council v. Shultz

Trade association (P) v. Government official (D)

443 F.2d 689 (D.C. Cir. 1971).

NATURE OF CASE: Action for declaratory and injunctive relief.

FACT SUMMARY: National Automatic Laundry & Cleaning Council (P) solicited and received a letter from a Wage-Hour Administration official on whether their employees were still subject to the 1966 Fair Labor Standards Act and then sought a declaratory judgment on the opinion expressed therein.

🏛 RULE OF LAW
Although as a general rule the courts should not interfere with the executive function by entertaining lawsuits challenging administrative action which is not yet final (i.e., not "ripe"), where an authoritative opinion is issued by the head of an administrative agency upon a concrete fact situation, the fact that the opinion is merely an informal one should not preclude judicial review on grounds of lack of finality or ripeness.

FACTS: National Automatic Laundry & Cleaning Council (NALCC) (P) is a national trade association for the cleaning industry. In order to clarify its legal status, NALCC (P) had its attorney write a letter to the administrator of the Federal Wage-Hour Administration to ask whether NALCC (P) employees were considered covered by the 1966 amendments to the Fair Labor Standards Act. The letter was detailed with facts concerning the subject employees. In response, the administrator sent NALCC (P) an opinion, supported by extensive legal analysis, expressing the administrator's position that the employees were, indeed, covered, whereupon NALCC (P) filed a declaratory judgment action as to whether the administrator was correct. The district court dismissed for lack of jurisdiction. On appeal, the court of appeals dealt with the question of whether informal action, such as the administrator's, could be considered "final" enough to be "ripe" for judicial review.

ISSUE: Although as a general rule the courts should not interfere with the executive function by entertaining lawsuits challenging administrative action which is not yet final (i.e., not "ripe"), where an authoritative opinion is issued by the head of an administrative agency upon a concrete fact situation, does the fact that the opinion is merely an informal one preclude judicial review on the grounds of lack of finality or ripeness?

HOLDING AND DECISION: (Leventhal, J.) No. Although as a general rule the courts should not interfere with the executive function by entertaining lawsuits challenging administrative action which is not yet final (i.e., not

"ripe"), where an authoritative opinion is issued by the head of an administrative agency upon a concrete fact situation, the fact that the opinion is merely an informal one should not preclude judicial review on the grounds of lack of finality or ripeness. No black-and-white rule exists for when informal action is final and ripe and appeal therefrom is possible. The facts of each case must be balanced to assure that preenforcement review will not impose excessive hardships or administrative confusion. Here, the balance tips in favor of review. The opinion here was supported by ample analysis given within the context of a concrete fact situation, and signed by the head of the federal agency who had ultimate responsibility for the opinion. The government's potential interest in avoiding multiple preenforcement litigations and in binding all members of a regulated industry to the outcome of a preenforcement challenge can be satisfied by insisting on maintenance of a preenforcement challenge as a class action, an alternative that likely is feasible where the challenge is brought by a trade association. There is no reason to deny review here. Reversed as to the jurisdictional issue. [Judgment for the government on the merits.]

▶ ANALYSIS

This case extends the basic *Abbott* test for administrative "ripeness" to cases of informal administrative action which otherwise meet the requirements for formality, *Abbott Laboratories v. Gardner,* 387 U.S. 136 (1967). Note that the balancing suggested by the court of appeals here is undertaken, not so much as an independent test, but as a test of whether the requirements of *Abbott* have been met. The *Abbott* decision itself, however, contained language which implies that the U.S. Supreme Court might not agree with *NALCC v. Schultz;* however, as the court specifically noted in *Abbott,* there was "no hint that this regulation is informal." In *NALCC,* the court of appeals suggests that the fact that the opinion is issued by the "head" of an agency makes it authoritative, but some writers point out that the president, not the wage-price administrator, is the real head of any executive agency. Indeed, the court of appeals can find precedent in looking beyond the mere form of administrative action to its substance in United States Supreme Court cases which have reviewed informal agency action. For example, in *Bantam Books v. Sullivan,* 372 U.S. 58 (1963), the Court reviewed the constitutionality of a state commission's informal censorship practices.

■=■

Continued on next page.

Quicknotes

DECLARATORY RELIEF A judgment of the court establishing the rights of the parties.

INJUNCTIVE RELIEF A court order issued as a remedy, requiring a person to do, or prohibiting that person from doing, a specific act.

JUDICIAL REVIEW The authority of the courts to review decisions, actions or omissions committed by another agency or branch of government.

RIPENESS A doctrine precluding a federal court from hearing or determining a matter, unless it constitutes an actual and present controversy warranting a determination by the court.

■■■

National Park Hospitality Association v. Department of the Interior

Trade association (P) v. Federal agency (D)

538 U.S. 803 (2003).

NATURE OF CASE: Appeal from affirmance of judgment for government in suit challenging, in part, the validity of a National Park Service (D) regulation regarding concession contracts.

FACT SUMMARY: National Park Service (NPS) (D) issued a regulation defining "concession contract" in a way that removed the term from the Contract Disputes Act (CDA) and also distinguished the term from service and procurement contracts under federal law. Without further action by the NPS (D) to implement that definition, the National Park Hospitality Association (D) sued, in part, to invalidate the regulation because of the definition.

🏛 RULE OF LAW

Challenges to administrative action must be fit for judicial review, and that review must be capable of alleviating hardship for the parties for such challenges to be ripe for suit.

FACTS: Acting on authority delegated by the Secretary of the Interior (D), the National Park Service (NPS) (D) adopted regulations that defined "concession contracts" in a way that removed such contracts from the protections of the Contract Disputes Act (CDA); the new regulations also distinguished such contracts from service and procurement contracts within the meaning of positive federal law. NPS (D) took no further action, however, by which this definition would have harmed the National Park Hospitality Association (NPHA) (P). NPHA (P) filed suit. The district court entered judgment for NPS (D) on the merits of NPHA's (P) complaint. The court of appeals affirmed the judgment for NPS (D), thus also reaching the merits of the dispute. NPHA (P) petitioned the United States Supreme Court for further review. [On its own motion, at oral argument the Supreme Court asked the parties to brief the issue of ripeness.]

ISSUE: Must challenges to administrative action be fit for judicial review, and must that review be capable of alleviating hardship for the parties for such challenges to be ripe for suit?

HOLDING AND DECISION: (Thomas, J.) Yes. Challenges to administrative action must be fit for judicial review, and that review must be capable of alleviating hardship for the parties for such challenges to be ripe for suit. In this case, the challenged regulation presents no actual hardship to NPHA (P) because the definition of "concession contracts" is only definitional, only a "general statement of policy," not in any sense, an immediately

adverse legal requirement. Nor does the definition limit NPHA's (P) primary conduct, and, indeed the regulation imposes no practical harm upon NPHA (P): NPS's (D) regulation permits NPHA (P) to follow CDA procedures in disputes if it wishes. Any anticipatory harm incurred from the uncertainty of entering concession contracts under the regulation would only lead courts to issue improper advisory opinions at the outset of business transactions. Moreover, this case is not fit for review because additional development of the facts underlying an actual, concrete dispute would greatly assist the Court's review of the issues. Vacated, with instructions to dismiss the count challenging the regulation's validity.

CONCURRENCE: (Stevens, J.) The case should be dismissed for a lack of the threshold necessity of standing; ripeness is not the issue. This case, requesting a judicial interpretation, will never be any more fit for judicial review than it is today. As for the less-important second prong of the ripeness analysis, the Court probably correctly finds that any hardship arising from the delay in a judicial decision will be minimal. What does matter is that NPHA (P) failed to allege any actual injury that is grounded in NPS's (D) definition of concession contracts. Without such an allegation, the complaint should be dismissed because the plaintiff does not have standing.

DISSENT: (Breyer, J.) NPHA (P) has standing, and this case is ripe for consideration. NPHA's (P) injury-in-fact is a future injury, but it is nevertheless concrete. NPS's (D) definition of concession contracts causes NPHA (P) injury by requiring its members to negotiate contracts with higher costs in mind. The injury-in-fact for standing also means that this case is ripe for review. Justice Stevens correctly notes that the only issue on the merits is purely legal, one that requires only a judicial interpretation, and, accordingly, the case is fit for the courts to decide. The ability to challenge the regulation later does weaken the case for ripeness, but such a concern is offset by the immediate injury sustained in the bidding process and by a federal statute that permits suits in response to just this kind of agency action. The challenge to the regulation is therefore ripe and should be heard now.

▶ ANALYSIS

As Justice Breyer assumes in his dissent, the same facts can serve double duty in judicial analysis, even on questions as abstract as those involving justiciability (standing,

Continued on next page.

ripeness, and mootness). Standing and ripeness can be, and often are, clearly separate considerations. *National Parks Hospitality Association* shows, however, that the injury-in-fact (standing) and hardship (ripeness) factors in the two analyses certainly can be seen to overlap.

■══■

Quicknotes

JUDICIAL REVIEW The authority of the courts to review decisions, actions or omissions committed by another agency or branch of government.

PROCUREMENT CONTRACT Government contract with a supplier of goods or services whereby a sale is made to the government, usually subject to regulations and standard forms.

RIPENESS A doctrine precluding a federal court from hearing or determining a matter unless it constitutes an actual and present controversy warranting a determination by the court.

STANDING The right to commence suit against another party because of a personal stake in the resolution of the controversy.

■══■

Myers v. Bethlehem Shipbuilding Corp.

Government board (D) v. Shipbuilder (P)

303 U.S. 41 (1938).

NATURE OF CASE: Appeal from affirmance of grant of injunction enjoining a National Labor Relations Board hearing.

FACT SUMMARY: Bethlehem Shipbuilding Corporation ("Bethlehem" or "the Corporation") (P) filed suit in the district court to enjoin the National Labor Relations Board (D) from holding hearings on its complaint against Bethlehem (P).

> ## RULE OF LAW
> A party is not entitled to judicial relief from injury resulting from administrative action until his prescribed administrative remedies have all been exhausted.

FACTS: Bethlehem Shipbuilding Corporation ("Bethlehem" or "the Corporation") (P) filed suit in the district court to enjoin the National Labor Relations Board (Board) (D) from holding hearings on a complaint filed against Bethlehem (P). Bethlehem (P) argued that the hearings were unwarranted since the plant concerning which the complaint had been brought was not engaged in the manufacture of goods involved in interstate commerce. It also claimed that the holding of hearings would result in irreparable damage in the form of costs, loss of time, and impairment of employee goodwill. The district court granted the injunction and the court of appeals affirmed, but the United States Supreme Court granted certiorari to consider the issue of the district court's jurisdiction to grant the injunction.

ISSUE: Is a party entitled to judicial relief from injury resulting from administrative action until his prescribed administrative remedies have all been exhausted?

HOLDING AND DECISION: (Brandeis, J.) No. A party is not entitled to judicial relief from injury resulting from administrative action until his prescribed administrative remedies have all been exhausted. In this case, Congress vested in the Board (D) the discretion to make an initial determination of whether or not hearings were appropriate, and the Corporation (P) does not claim that the statutory provisions and the procedures for hearings are illegal. Congress also provided that the Board's (D) conclusions could not be implemented prior to their affirmance by the circuit court of appeals. This grant of authority to the appellate court accords the Corporation (P) an adequate opportunity to secure judicial protection from the Board's (D) actions, and precludes the Corporation (P) from seeking judicial recourse through the district court until both the Board (D) and the circuit court of appeals have acted. [The disposition of the case is not presented in the casebook excerpt.]

▶ ANALYSIS

Myers v. Bethlehem Shipbuilding Company is the leading case in support of the rule that administrative remedies must be exhausted before judicial relief may be sought. Many reasons have been advanced for retaining this rule. Foremost among these observations is that the rule permits full factual development prior to judicial review, that it affords the agency full opportunity to exercise the discretion or expertise which Congress intended it to utilize, and that it preserves the autonomy of the agency. In addition, the rule recognizes the prospect that the appellant may prevail before the agency, thus obviating the need for judicial review. Nevertheless, despite these contentions, the exhaustion of remedies rule is fraught with exceptions and frequently is ignored.

■=■

Quicknotes

ADMINISTRATIVE HEARING A hearing conducted before an administrative agency.

ADMINISTRATIVE REMEDIES Relief that is sought before an administrative body as opposed to a court.

INJUNCTION A remedy imposed by the court ordering a party to cease the conduct of a specific activity.

JUDICIAL REVIEW The authority of the courts to review decisions, actions or omissions committed by another agency or branch of government.

■=■

FTC v. Standard Oil Co. of California

Federal agency (P) v. Petroleum company (D)

449 U.S. 232 (1980).

NATURE OF CASE: Appeal from decision finding averment in complaint not final agency action.

FACT SUMMARY: Standard Oil Co. of California (D) appealed from a decision finding that the issuance of a complaint was not final agency action of the Federal Trade Commission (P), and was thus not subject to judicial review before the conclusion of administrative adjudication.

> ## RULE OF LAW
> The issuance of a complaint by an agency merely averring "reason to believe" is not final agency action subject to judicial review before the conclusion of administration adjudication.

FACTS: The Federal Trade Commission (FTC) (P) averred in a complaint that it had "reason to believe" that Standard Oil Co. of California (Socal) (D) was violating the Administrative Procedure Act. Socal (D) immediately sought judicial review, claiming that the averment in the complaint was final agency action subject to judicial review. From a decision that the averment was not final agency action, Socal (D) appealed. The United States Supreme Court eventually granted certiorari. [The procedural posture of the case is not presented in the casebook excerpt.]

ISSUE: Is the issuance of a complaint by an agency merely averring "reason to believe" final agency action subject to judicial review before the conclusion of administrative adjudication?

HOLDING AND DECISION: (Powell, J.) No. The issuance of a complaint by an agency merely averring "reason to believe" is not final agency action subject to judicial review before the conclusion of administrative adjudication. The complaint of the FTC (P) in the present case merely serves to initiate the proceedings. Courts have interpreted this finality element in a pragmatic manner. Clearly, a complaint averring a "reason to believe" does not indicate a finality of position, it rather indicates the need for further investigation. The legal and practical effect of the complaint in the present case was the burden of requiring Socal (D) to respond to the complaint. Even though this is a substantial burden, it is different in kind and legal effect from any burdens attendant to what we have considered previously to be final agency action. This burden is one that is associated with living under government. The adverse effects of a contrary holding on the efficient operation of agencies would be substantial, and would turn the prosecutor into a defendant before

adjudication concludes. [The disposition of the case is not presented in the casebook excerpt.]

▶ ANALYSIS

Courts have developed a number of exceptions to the rule that administrative remedies must be exhausted before judicial review is granted. One of the most frequent exceptions that come into play is when the agency plainly exceeds its authority, immediate judicial review is available. Certainly, the pattern seems to be that the courts are taking a pragmatic view in deciding whether to grant judicial review.

■━■

Quicknotes

FINAL AGENCY ORDER The final disposition of a hearing before a public agency or the agency's interpretation or application of a statute.

JUDICIAL REVIEW The authority of the courts to review decisions, actions or omissions committed by another agency or branch of government.

■━■

McKart v. United States

Military draftee (D) v. Federal government (P)

395 U.S. 185 (1969).

NATURE OF CASE: Appeal from a conviction for failing to report for military service.

FACT SUMMARY: The Government (P) contended that McKart (D) was precluded from raising the defense of erroneous selective service classification in his criminal trial for failure to report for duty because he failed to exhaust his administrative remedies on the issue.

RULE OF LAW
Administrative remedies need not be exhausted prior to judicial review where the validity of the agency action is merely a function of statutory interpretation and the burden of denial of judicial review outweighs the interests underlying the exhaustion rule.

FACTS: McKart (D) was declared exempt from the military draft as a sole surviving son. Upon his mother's death, the Selective Service decided that since the family unit ceased to exist the statutory exemption ended. McKart (D) failed to pursue his administrative remedies to challenge the loss of military draft exemption. After he failed to appear for duty, McKart (D) was convicted of willful failure to report for service. On appeal, the Government (P) contended that McKart (D) could not raise the defense of erroneous selective service classification at his criminal trial because he failed to exhaust his administrative remedies.

ISSUE: Must administrative remedies be exhausted prior to judicial review where the validity of the agency action is merely a function of statutory interpretation and the burden of denial of judicial review outweighs the interests underlying the exhaustion rule?

HOLDING AND DECISION: (Marshall, J.) No. Administrative remedies need not be exhausted prior to judicial review where the validity of the agency action is merely a function of statutory interpretation and the burden of denial of judicial review outweighs the underlying interests of the exhaustion rule. If the question is one of statutory interpretation, the special expertise of an agency will be of no aid to a court, as the court is better able to interpret statutes than agencies, and no fact-finding is necessary. Further, where a defendant is facing criminal charges, he may be denied the right to assert a defense resulting in imprisonment if he is forced to pursue his administrative remedies first. In this case, by allowing judicial review of Selective Service decisions such as in this case, others with administrative remedies will not be induced to seek initial judicial review. They would risk imprisonment by denying the Selective Service a chance to correct its

errors. As a result the underlying interests of the exhaustion rule are not seriously compromised while McKart's (D) potential imprisonment, if he is denied judicial review, is a large threat to his interests. Therefore, the exhaustion rule does not apply. Because on the basis of statutory interpretation the exemption was incorrectly rescinded, McKart's (D) conviction is overturned. Reversed and remanded for judgment of acquittal.

CONCURRENCE: (White, J.) Courts frequently defer to agencies' interpretations of statutes, and reviewing courts should have the benefit of such interpretations. In this case, however, the essentials of exhaustion have been met because the claim had been presented to a local board and the board had consulted with higher authorities prior to rejecting it.

ANALYSIS

This case illustrates the underlying rationale of the exhaustion rule. By requiring agencies to be the initial step, the exhaustion rule allows the facts of the case to be fully developed prior to judicial review, it allows agencies to act on their own expertise and it creates a possibility that judicial review will be unnecessary. Further, it is felt that an agency is weakened if judicial review of its actions is too readily available.

Quicknotes

ADMINISTRATIVE REMEDIES Relief that is sought before an administrative body as opposed to a court.

EXHAUSTION RULE Requirement that a party exhaust all administrative remedies available before a court will intervene in the controversy.

JUDICIAL REVIEW The authority of the courts to review decisions, actions or omissions committed by another agency or branch of government.

Woodford v. Ngo

State prison official (D) v. State prisoner (P)

548 U.S. 81 (2006).

NATURE OF CASE: Appeal in §1983 action challenging rejection of a grievance filed by a state prisoner. [The procedural posture of the case is not presented in the casebook extract.]

FACT SUMMARY: Ngo (P), a state prisoner, filed a grievance later than required by state law, and after the grievance was rejected as untimely, he filed a §1983 action in federal district court challenging the rejection of his grievance.

RULE OF LAW

The Prison Litigation Reform Act's exhaustion requirement requires proper exhaustion of administrative remedies, rather than the unavailability of further administrative remedies.

FACTS: Ngo (P), a state prisoner, filed a grievance six months after the incident on which his grievance was based. State law required filing of the grievance 15 days after the incident, and also provided for several administrative appeals. After his grievance was rejected as untimely, Ngo (P) filed a §1983 civil rights action in federal district court. Although The Prison Litigation Reform Act of 1995 (PLRA) requires a prisoner to exhaust any available administrative remedies before challenging prison conditions in federal court, Ngo (P) contended that this meant that he could bring suit after administrative remedies were no longer available to him, whereas the State (D) contended this required proper exhaustion, i.e., which means using all steps that the agency holds out, and doing so properly. The United States Supreme Court eventually granted certiorari. [The procedural posture of the case is not presented in the casebook excerpt.]

ISSUE: Does the Prison Litigation Reform Act's exhaustion requirement require proper exhaustion of administrative remedies, rather than the unavailability of further administrative remedies?

HOLDING AND DECISION: (Alito, J.) Yes. The Prison Litigation Reform Act's exhaustion requirement requires proper exhaustion of administrative remedies, rather than the unavailability of further administrative remedies. The key issue is what is meant in the statute by "exhaust." By referring to "such administrative remedies as are available," the PLRA text strongly suggests "exhausted" means what it means in administrative law. Construing the text to require proper exhaustion also serves the PLRA's goals. It gives prisoners an effective incentive to make full use of the prison grievance process, thus providing prisons with a fair opportunity to correct their own errors. It

reduces the quantity of prisoner suits, and it improves the quality of those suits that are filed because proper exhaustion often results in creation of an administrative record helpful to the court. In contrast, Ngo's (P) interpretation would make the PLRA's exhaustion scheme totally ineffective, since exhaustion's benefits can be realized only if the prison grievance system is given a fair opportunity to consider the grievance. That cannot happen unless the grievant complies with the system's critical procedural rules. Under Ngo's (P) interpretation, the prisoner has no incentive to comply with procedural rules and he can simply bypass administrative remedies by purposely filing his grievance late. Ngo (P) also relies, without persuasiveness, on a distinction between a tolling provision of the AEDPA [Antiterrorism and Effective Death Penalty Act of 1996], which specifies the need for "proper exhaustion," and the PLRA's exhaustion requirement, which does not use the word "proper." Although the AEDPA and the PLRA were enacted at roughly the same time, they are separate and detailed pieces of legislation. Moreover, the AEDPA and PLRA provisions deal with separate issues: tolling in the case of the AEDPA and exhaustion in the case of the PLRA. Moreover, the similarity between the wording of the PLRA exhaustion provision and the AEDPA exhaustion provision does not indicate that the PLRA provision was meant to incorporate the narrow technical definition of exhaustion that applies in habeas. However, this interpretation would not duplicate the habeas scheme, for it would permit a prisoner to bypass deliberately administrative review with no risk of sanction, whereas the habeas scheme does not. Finally, Ngo (P) contends that requiring proper exhaustion will lead prison administrators to devise procedural requirements that are designed to trap unwary prisoners and thus to defeat their claims. However, there is no contention that anything like this occurred in his case, and it is speculative that this will occur in the future. [The disposition of the case is not presented in the casebook excerpt.]

DISSENT: (Stevens, J.) Because the PLRA does not impose a procedural waiver, i.e., does not impose a sanction of waiver or procedural default upon those prisoners who make procedural errors, a prisoner who procedurally defaults his federal claims in a state prison grievance proceeding meets the technical requirements for exhaustion, as there are no state remedies any longer available to the prisoner. The majority ignores the PLRA's plain text, and instead reads into the statute a procedural waiver provision. However, precedent makes clear that such

Continued on next page.

extratextual waiver sanctions are only appropriate if a statute directs a federal court to act as an appellate tribunal directly reviewing the decision of a federal agency, and ordinary principles of administrative law do not justify engrafting procedural waiver onto the statute, especially since it is a statutory scheme in which laymen (the prisoners), unassisted by trained lawyers, initiate the process. Finally, the PLRA's purposes would be served even without the Court's engrafting a procedural default sanction into it. First, prison officials already have the opportunity to address claims that were filed in some procedurally defective manner, and, second, the PLRA has already had the effect of reducing the quantity of prison litigation, without the need for an extrastatutory procedural default sanction.

▌ *ANALYSIS*

The Court emphasized in this case that requirements for proper exhaustion are set by the administrative proceedings themselves, rather than by the PLRA or by federal law. Following this principle, the Court subsequently held in *Jones v. Bock,* 549 U.S. 199 (2007), that a prisoner who failed to name a prison official had exhausted administrative remedies where prisoners were required to be "as specific as possible" but were not expressly required to identify all defendants. In *Jones,* the Court, while not holding that the prisoner had properly exhausted all his remedies, held that a failure to name all defendants was not a per se failure to exhaust—based on the state's administrative requirements.

■═■

Quicknotes

ADMINISTRATIVE REMEDIES Relief that is sought before an administrative body as opposed to a court.

EXHAUSTION RULE Requirement that a party exhaust all administrative remedies available before a court will intervene in the controversy.

■═■

United States v. Western Pacific R.R.

Federal government (D) v. Railroad (P)

352 U.S. 59 (1956).

NATURE OF CASE: Appeal from judgment in action to enforce a railroad freight rate.

FACT SUMMARY: The Government (D) contended that the issue of which railroad rate applied to its shipment of napalm bombs should have been determined by the Interstate Commerce Commission instead of being presented in court.

🏛 RULE OF LAW
The doctrine of primary jurisdiction requires that, where issues are presented in court that under a regulatory scheme must be determined within the special competence of an agency, the judicial proceeding be suspended and the issues be referred to the agency.

FACTS: Western Pacific R.R. (P) charged a tariff on napalm bombs shipped by the Government (D). The tariff charged applied to "incendiary" bombs. The Government (D) claimed the bombs lacked a fuse and therefore the lower rate applicable to gasoline in steel drums should be charged. Western Pacific (P) sued after the Government (D) refused to pay the higher tariff. The Court of Claims rejected the Government's (D) claim that the issue over which tariff applied was within the primary jurisdiction of the Interstate Commerce Commission (ICC), and determined for itself that the higher tariff applied. The Government (D) appealed. The United States Supreme Court granted certiorari.

ISSUE: Does the doctrine of primary jurisdiction require that, where issues are presented in court that under a regulatory scheme must be determined within the special competence of an agency, the judicial proceeding be suspended and the issues referred to the agency?

HOLDING AND DECISION: (Harlan, J.) Yes. The doctrine of primary jurisdiction requires that, where issues are presented in court that under a regulatory scheme must be determined within the special competence of an agency, the judicial proceeding be suspended and the issues referred to the agency. The doctrine seeks to promote proper relationships between the courts and administrative agencies. There is no set formula for when primary jurisdiction inheres, and the question as to when the doctrine applies usually revolves around the need for uniformity and the necessity for expertise in deciding the issues. Further, the doctrine allows agencies, who are prescribed by Congress as having special expertise, to have a degree of lawmaking power over commercial relationships. In this case, the classification of these weapons requires considerable expertise more efficiently found in the ICC than in the courts. Therefore the ICC has primary jurisdiction over the issue, and the Court of Claims action should have been suspended. [Reversed and remanded.]

▶ ANALYSIS

The doctrine of primary jurisdiction may be applied in cases where the administrative agency's determination will dispose of the entire case. It can also apply where the issues are not fully dispositive. In the latter case, the court will simply carry the case on its docket pending the agency determination.

■■■

Quicknotes

JURISDICTION The authority of a court to hear and declare judgment in respect to a particular matter.

■■■

Nader v. Allegheny Airlines

Consumer advocate (P) v. Airline (D)

426 U.S. 290 (1976).

NATURE OF CASE: Appeal from an order staying a tort action pending administrative agency determination of specific issues.

FACT SUMMARY: The court of appeals stayed Nader's (P) suit against Allegheny Airlines (Allegheny) (D) for fraudulent misrepresentation, holding that the issue of whether Allegheny's (D) flight booking policy was fraudulent was within the primary jurisdiction of the Civil Aeronautics Board.

> ## 🏛 RULE OF LAW
> The doctrine of primary jurisdiction does not apply to suspend judicial proceedings on a common-law cause of action where the issues to be decided by the court and those to be decided by an agency are not absolutely inconsistent.

FACTS: Nader (P) sued Allegheny Airlines (Allegheny) (D) in federal district court after they intentionally over-booked a flight resulting in Nader (P) being bumped to a later flight. Nader (P) refused to accept denied-boarding compensation, and sued for fraudulent misrepresentation. The court of appeals held that the Civil Aeronautics Act provided that the Civil Aeronautics Board (the Board) must determine whether a particular airline practice is unfair or deceptive, and therefore Nader's (P) suit should be suspended pending a determination of this issue by the Board. Nader (P) appealed, and the United States Supreme Court granted certiorari.

ISSUE: Does the doctrine of primary jurisdiction apply to suspend judicial proceedings on a common-law cause of action where the issues to be decided by the court and those to be decided by the agency are not absolutely inconsistent?

HOLDING AND DECISION: (Powell, J.) No. The doctrine of primary jurisdiction does not apply to suspend judicial proceedings on a common-law cause of action where the issues to be decided by the court and those to be decided by the agency are not absolutely inconsistent. If the court were to decide this case on the merits of the negligent misrepresentation claim, it would in no way infringe upon the Board's determination whether under the Civil Aeronautics Act overbooking was an unfair or deceptive practice. A conflict would exist only if there was a Board requirement that an airline engage in overbooking. Absent this, the Court's disposition of the common-law action on its merits is not absolutely inconsistent with a Board determination, and the doctrine of primary jurisdiction will not suspend the suit. Therefore, Nader's (P) tort action is not stayed pending reference to the Board; the court of appeals decision on this issue is reversed. Remanded.

CONCURRENCE: (White, J.) Whatever determination the Board makes concerning whether overbooking is or is not an unfair or deceptive practice, such determination would not affect the state law claim here presented.

▶ ANALYSIS

This case illustrates one of the limits of the applicability of the doctrine of primary jurisdiction. If the issues at hand necessarily conflict in that a court's determination will encroach upon a determination meant to be made by an agency, the court should, under the doctrine of primary jurisdiction, suspend the court action and refer the issue to the agency. This was the case in *Texas & Pacific R. Co. v. Abilene Cotton Oil Co.*, 204 U.S. 426 (1907).

Quicknotes

JURISDICTION The authority of a court to hear and declare judgment in respect to a particular matter.

Glossary

Common Latin Words and Phrases Encountered in the Law

A FORTIORI: Because one fact exists or has been proven, therefore a second fact that is related to the first fact must also exist.

A PRIORI: From the cause to the effect. A term of logic used to denote that when one generally accepted truth is shown to be a cause, another particular effect must necessarily follow.

AB INITIO: From the beginning; a condition which has existed throughout, as in a marriage which was void ab initio.

ACTUS REUS: The wrongful act; in criminal law, such action sufficient to trigger criminal liability.

AD VALOREM: According to value; an ad valorem tax is imposed upon an item located within the taxing jurisdiction calculated by the value of such item.

AMICUS CURIAE: Friend of the court. Its most common usage takes the form of an amicus curiae brief, filed by a person who is not a party to an action but is nonetheless allowed to offer an argument supporting his legal interests.

ARGUENDO: In arguing. A statement, possibly hypothetical, made for the purpose of argument, is one made arguendo.

BILL QUIA TIMET: A bill to quiet title (establish ownership) to real property.

BONA FIDE: True, honest, or genuine. May refer to a person's legal position based on good faith or lacking notice of fraud (such as a bona fide purchaser for value) or to the authenticity of a particular document (such as a bona fide last will and testament).

CAUSA MORTIS: With approaching death in mind. A gift causa mortis is a gift given by a party who feels certain that death is imminent.

CAVEAT EMPTOR: Let the buyer beware. This maxim is reflected in the rule of law that a buyer purchases at his own risk because it is his responsibility to examine, judge, test, and otherwise inspect what he is buying.

CERTIORARI: A writ of review. Petitions for review of a case by the United States Supreme Court are most often done by means of a writ of certiorari.

CONTRA: On the other hand. Opposite. Contrary to.

CORAM NOBIS: Before us; writs of error directed to the court that originally rendered the judgment.

CORAM VOBIS: Before you; writs of error directed by an appellate court to a lower court to correct a factual error.

CORPUS DELICTI: The body of the crime; the requisite elements of a crime amounting to objective proof that a crime has been committed.

CUM TESTAMENTO ANNEXO, ADMINISTRATOR (ADMINISTRATOR C.T.A.): With will annexed; an administrator c.t.a. settles an estate pursuant to a will in which he is not appointed.

DE BONIS NON, ADMINISTRATOR (ADMINISTRATOR D.B.N.): Of goods not administered; an administrator d.b.n. settles a partially settled estate.

DE FACTO: In fact; in reality; actually. Existing in fact but not officially approved or engendered.

DE JURE: By right; lawful. Describes a condition that is legitimate "as a matter of law," in contrast to the term "de facto," which connotes something existing in fact but not legally sanctioned or authorized. For example, de facto segregation refers to segregation brought about by housing patterns, etc., whereas de jure segregation refers to segregation created by law.

DE MINIMIS: Of minimal importance; insignificant; a trifle; not worth bothering about.

DE NOVO: Anew; a second time; afresh. A trial de novo is a new trial held at the appellate level as if the case originated there and the trial at a lower level had not taken place.

DICTA: Generally used as an abbreviated form of obiter dicta, a term describing those portions of a judicial opinion incidental or not necessary to resolution of the specific question before the court. Such nonessential statements and remarks are not considered to be binding precedent.

DUCES TECUM: Refers to a particular type of writ or subpoena requesting a party or organization to produce certain documents in their possession.

EN BANC: Full bench. Where a court sits with all justices present rather than the usual quorum.

EX PARTE: For one side or one party only. An ex parte proceeding is one undertaken for the benefit of only one party, without notice to, or an appearance by, an adverse party.

EX POST FACTO: After the fact. An ex post facto law is a law that retroactively changes the consequences of a prior act.

EX REL.: Abbreviated form of the term "ex relatione," meaning upon relation or information. When the state brings an action in which it has no interest against an individual at the instigation of one who has a private interest in the matter.

FORUM NON CONVENIENS: Inconvenient forum. Although a court may have jurisdiction over the case, the action should be tried in a more conveniently located court, one to which parties and witnesses may more easily travel, for example.

GUARDIAN AD LITEM: A guardian of an infant as to litigation, appointed to represent the infant and pursue his/her rights.

HABEAS CORPUS: You have the body. The modern writ of habeas corpus is a writ directing that a person (body) being detained (such as a prisoner) be brought before the court so that the legality of his detention can be judicially ascertained.

IN CAMERA: In private, in chambers. When a hearing is held before a judge in his chambers or when all spectators are excluded from the courtroom.

IN FORMA PAUPERIS: In the manner of a pauper. A party who proceeds in forma pauperis because of his poverty is one who is allowed to bring suit without liability for costs.

INFRA: Below, under. A word referring the reader to a later part of a book. (The opposite of supra.)

IN LOCO PARENTIS: In the place of a parent.

IN PARI DELICTO: Equally wrong; a court of equity will not grant requested relief to an applicant who is in pari delicto, or as much at fault in the transactions giving rise to the controversy as is the opponent of the applicant.

IN PARI MATERIA: On like subject matter or upon the same matter. Statutes relating to the same person or things are said to be in pari materia. It is a general rule of statutory construction that such statutes should be construed together, i.e., looked at as if they together constituted one law.

IN PERSONAM: Against the person. Jurisdiction over the person of an individual.

IN RE: In the matter of. Used to designate a proceeding involving an estate or other property.

IN REM: A term that signifies an action against the res, or thing. An action in rem is basically one that is taken directly against property, as distinguished from an action in personam, i.e., against the person.

INTER ALIA: Among other things. Used to show that the whole of a statement, pleading, list, statute, etc., has not been set forth in its entirety.

INTER PARTES: Between the parties. May refer to contracts, conveyances or other transactions having legal significance.

INTER VIVOS: Between the living. An inter vivos gift is a gift made by a living grantor, as distinguished from bequests contained in a will, which pass upon the death of the testator.

IPSO FACTO: By the mere fact itself.

JUS: Law or the entire body of law.

LEX LOCI: The law of the place; the notion that the rights of parties to a legal proceeding are governed by the law of the place where those rights arose.

MALUM IN SE: Evil or wrong in and of itself; inherently wrong. This term describes an act that is wrong by its very nature, as opposed to one which would not be wrong but for the fact that there is a specific legal prohibition against it (malum prohibitum).

MALUM PROHIBITUM: Wrong because prohibited, but not inherently evil. Used to describe something that is wrong because it is expressly forbidden by law but that is not in and of itself evil, e.g., speeding.

MANDAMUS: We command. A writ directing an official to take a certain action.

MENS REA: A guilty mind; a criminal intent. A term used to signify the mental state that accompanies a crime or other prohibited act. Some crimes require only a general mens rea (general intent to do the prohibited act), but others, like assault with intent to murder, require the existence of a specific mens rea.

MODUS OPERANDI: Method of operating; generally refers to the manner or style of a criminal in committing crimes, admissible in appropriate cases as evidence of the identity of a defendant.

NEXUS: A connection to.

NISI PRIUS: A court of first impression. A nisi prius court is one where issues of fact are tried before a judge or jury.

N.O.V. (NON OBSTANTE VEREDICTO): Notwithstanding the verdict. A judgment n.o.v. is a judgment given in favor of one party despite the fact that a verdict was returned in favor of the other party, the justification being that the verdict either had no reasonable support in fact or was contrary to law.

NUNC PRO TUNC: Now for then. This phrase refers to actions that may be taken and will then have full retroactive effect.

PENDENTE LITE: Pending the suit; pending litigation under way.

PER CAPITA: By head; beneficiaries of an estate, if they take in equal shares, take per capita.

PER CURIAM: By the court; signifies an opinion ostensibly written "by the whole court" and with no identified author.

PER SE: By itself, in itself; inherently.

PER STIRPES: By representation. Used primarily in the law of wills to describe the method of distribution where a person, generally because of death, is unable to take that which is left to him by the will of another, and therefore his heirs divide such property between them rather than take under the will individually.

PRIMA FACIE: On its face, at first sight. A prima facie case is one that is sufficient on its face, meaning that the evidence supporting it is adequate to establish the case until contradicted or overcome by other evidence.

PRO TANTO: For so much; as far as it goes. Often used in eminent domain cases when a property owner receives partial payment for his land without prejudice to his right to bring suit for the full amount he claims his land to be worth.

QUANTUM MERUIT: As much as he deserves. Refers to recovery based on the doctrine of unjust enrichment in those cases in which a party has rendered valuable services or furnished materials that were accepted and enjoyed by another under circumstances that would reasonably notify the recipient that the rendering party expected to be paid. In essence, the law implies a contract to pay the reasonable value of the services or materials furnished.

QUASI: Almost like; as if; nearly. This term is essentially used to signify that one subject or thing is almost analogous to another but that material differences between them do exist. For example, a quasi-criminal proceeding is one that is not strictly criminal but shares enough of the same characteristics to require some of the same safeguards (e.g., procedural due process must be followed in a parole hearing).

QUID PRO QUO: Something for something. In contract law, the consideration, something of value, passed between the parties to render the contract binding.

RES GESTAE: Things done; in evidence law, this principle justifies the admission of a statement that would otherwise be hearsay when it is made so closely to the event in question as to be said to be a part of it, or with such spontaneity as not to have the possibility of falsehood.

RES IPSA LOQUITUR: The thing speaks for itself. This doctrine gives rise to a rebuttable presumption of negligence when the instrumentality causing the injury was within the exclusive control of the defendant, and the injury was one that does not normally occur unless a person has been negligent.

RES JUDICATA: A matter adjudged. Doctrine which provides that once a court of competent jurisdiction has rendered a final judgment or decree on the merits, that judgment or decree is conclusive upon the parties to the case and prevents them from engaging in any other litigation on the points and issues determined therein.

RESPONDEAT SUPERIOR: Let the master reply. This doctrine holds the master liable for the wrongful acts of his servant (or the principal for his agent) in those cases in which the servant (or agent) was acting within the scope of his authority at the time of the injury.

STARE DECISIS: To stand by or adhere to that which has been decided. The common law doctrine of stare decisis attempts to give security and certainty to the law by following the policy that once a principle of law as applicable to a certain set of facts has been set forth in a decision, it forms a precedent which will subsequently be followed, even though a different decision might be made were it the first time the question had arisen. Of course, stare decisis is not an inviolable principle and is departed from in instances where there is good cause (e.g., considerations of public policy led the Supreme Court to disregard prior decisions sanctioning segregation).

SUPRA: Above. A word referring a reader to an earlier part of a book.

ULTRA VIRES: Beyond the power. This phrase is most commonly used to refer to actions taken by a corporation that are beyond the power or legal authority of the corporation.

Addendum of French Derivatives

IN PAIS: Not pursuant to legal proceedings.

CHATTEL: Tangible personal property.

CY PRES: Doctrine permitting courts to apply trust funds to purposes not expressed in the trust but necessary to carry out the settlor's intent.

PER AUTRE VIE: For another's life; during another's life. In property law, an estate may be granted that will terminate upon the death of someone other than the grantee.

PROFIT A PRENDRE: A license to remove minerals or other produce from land.

VOIR DIRE: Process of questioning jurors as to their predispositions about the case or parties to a proceeding in order to identify those jurors displaying bias or prejudice.

Casenote® Legal Briefs